T0375053

Mere Bagatelles

Liverpool Studies in Irish Literature

Liverpool Studies in Irish Literature

Series Editors:
Eve Patten, Trinity College Dublin
Frank Shovlin, University of Liverpool
Tom Walker, Trinity College Dublin

This monograph series offers insights into a diverse range of texts, themes, moments, figures and networks in Irish literature from c.1800 through to the present. Presenting rigorous scholarship on Irish literary production in the English language, the series seeks to expand and challenge current understandings of the Irish literary field. Titles will reflect the wealth of innovative and exciting critical, historical and biographical research currently being conducted into Irish literature, drawing on new methodologies and perspectives, as well as the best traditions of literary scholarship. The series editors welcome proposals from both early-career and established scholars for monographs on under-examined writers, works, genres, issues and ideas in Irish literary history, but will also consider fresh approaches to more well-established movements and figures.

Mere Bagatelles

Women's Diaries from Ireland, 1760–1810

Amy Prendergast

LIVERPOOL UNIVERSITY PRESS

First published 2024 by
Liverpool University Press
4 Cambridge Street
Liverpool
L69 7ZU

British Library Cataloguing-in-Publication data
A British Library CIP record is available

ISBN 978-1-83553-726-8 (paperback)
eISBN 978-1-83553-780-0 (epdf)
eISBN 978-1-83553-727-5 (epub)

Typeset by Carnegie Book Production, Lancaster

This evening enter'd into my head the notion of making a journal. I am a great journalist & have made several, but none I expect will be so clever as this, they are mere <u>bagatelles</u> – & pray what is this but a <u>bagatelle</u> too! But I hope to divert myself & two or three of my female friends with it, if I have constancy to finish.

Mary Shackleton, later Leadbeater, 27/6/1774.

For Elise and Esmé

Contents

Acknowledgements

The acknowledgements for this book must begin with thanks to Professors Aileen Douglas, Moyra Haslett, and Ian Campbell Ross, my triumvirate of mentors. The project began in earnest during a particularly rainy afternoon in Dublin where Ian and Aileen offered extensive advice and feedback on my ideas for a book on diaries. Moyra steered the project through its composition and sustained the work over our wonderful fortnightly talks during the pandemic, championing the work and encouraging its author. Their support for the project has been unwavering, and I am thankful to all three for their meticulous feedback on individual chapters, for tirelessly attending talks on the project, and indeed for supporting me in every aspect of academic life.

I have been so fortunate in the support I have received from the academic community across Ireland, particularly from colleagues at both Trinity College Dublin (TCD) and Queen's University Belfast (QUB). This project has received funding from the European Union's Horizon 2020 research and innovation programme under the Marie Skłodowska-Curie grant agreement, no. 101029901. During my time as Marie Curie Fellow at QUB, I was assisted in my research by colleagues from across the Faculty of Arts, Humanities and Social Sciences, receiving particular support from Peter Gray, Crawford Gribben, Leonie Hannan, Edel Lamb, Daniel Roberts, and Mary O'Dowd. For assistance in securing the award itself, I must mention the generosity of Alison Garden, who will be thanked across monographs for many years to come.

At TCD, Jarlath Killeen has been a remarkably supportive Head of School. I am grateful to him at a personal level and for his commitment to championing research within the School more generally. The School of English truly represents the most collegiate of environments, and I want to thank all colleagues, though I must sneak in specific thanks to Rosie Lavan, who has been a great friend to the project and to me. In TCD History, I would like to thank my eighteenth-century counterpart Patrick Walsh for offering feedback on the introduction and Jane Ohlmeyer for her interest and support.

This book draws on the expertise of many eighteenth-centuryists, and the work is so much stronger for their generosity. With thanks due to Jürgen Barkhoff, Andrew Holmes, Susan Manly, Ivar McGrath, Lesa Ní Mhunghaile, Ruth Thorpe, and Diane Urquhart for answering my calls for information. For their advice, support, and encouragement more broadly, I must thank Andrew Carpenter, Niall Gillespie, Harriet Kramer Linkin, Anne Markey, Jason McElligott, Clare O'Halloran, David O'Shaughnessy, Eve Patten, and Julie Anne Young.

I would like to thank the members of the Eighteenth-Century Ireland Society who offered feedback on various papers on diaries over the years and also the members of Centre for Eighteenth-Century Studies, University of York, particularly Jane Rendall and Catriona Kennedy, who offered the last bit of motivation as the book was being completed.

All the archivists and librarians who enabled access to the wonderful diaries across Ireland, the UK, and the USA are due acknowledgement also, with particular thanks to the volunteers at the Religious Society of Friends in Ireland Historical Library, E. C. Schroeder at the Beinecke Rare Book and Manuscript Library, and the staff of the Manuscripts and Archives Research Library, TCD, particularly Jane Maxwell. At Liverpool University Press, thanks must go to Christabel Scaife, who has been a pleasure to work with. I would also like to thank the series editors for accepting the title, anonymous Readers 1 and 2 for the most generous and detailed of responses, and Marian Olney, copyeditor, for her exceptional attention to detail. This book is derived in part from an article published in *Life Writing*, 2022, copyright Taylor & Francis (available online: http://www.tandfonline.com/10.1080/14484528.2020.1803537) as well as from an article published in the *European Journal of Life Writing*, 2021.

This book was written over the course of four pregnancies and the arrival of our two beloved children. It could not have been written without the support of my husband, Alan Smyth, who shares the care and welfare of the girls equally with me. It also exists thanks to the labour of Naomi Fagan and Renata Farrelly, two brilliant childminders, who allowed me the space to write in the knowledge that the girls were happy and safe. My family members – my parents James and Deirdre; my parents-in-law James and Majella; my brother Evan; and an unrivalled cast of cousins, aunts, and uncles, who enquired about the diarists over wedding wine or birthday cake – have all encouraged my research pursuits. Finally, I must acknowledge the help of an extraordinarily supportive neighbourhood in Donnycarney, which sustained my writing throughout lockdowns and losses. Thank you one and all.

List of Figures

Abbreviations

BSECS	British Society for Eighteenth-Century Studies
CECS	Centre for Eighteenth-Century Studies
DIB	Dictionary of Irish Biography
HMC	Historical Manuscripts Commission
HRO	Hampshire Record Office
IMC	Irish Manuscripts Commission
KCL	King's College, London
NLI	National Library of Ireland
NLW	National Library of Wales
ODNB	Oxford Dictionary of National Biography
OED	Oxford English Dictionary
PROI	Public Record Office of Ireland
PRONI	Public Record Office of Northern Ireland
QUB	Queen's University Belfast
RSFIHL	Religious Society of Friends in Ireland Historical Library
TCD	Trinity College Dublin
UCSB	University of California, Santa Barbara

List of Diarists

Below are the names of the key diarists featured in this study, followed by their dates of birth and death, where known, and the dates of their diaries. Lastly, there is a brief indication regarding the location of each woman's manuscript diary, where extant. For full location details of those diaries that have not been destroyed or lost, see the Bibliography.

Adlercron, Meliora Bermingham (d. 1797). Diary (1782–1794). MS in NLI.

Balfour, Letitia Townley (1746–1838). Diary destroyed.

Bayly, Katherine Morley (d. 1775). Diary (1721–1774). Lost from PROI.

Bennis, Elizabeth Patten (1725–1802). Diary (1749–1779). MSS in St. George's Methodist Church, Philadelphia.

Blachford, Theodosia Tighe (1744–1817). Diary (1773–1774). MSS in NLI.

Butler, Eleanor (1739–1829). Diary (1784–1821). MSS in NLW.

Clibborn, Elizabeth Grubb (1780–1861). Diary (1807–1818). MS in RSFIHL.

Dawson, later Quin, Mary Anne (1763–1831). Diary (1782–1784). MSS in TCD.

Edgeworth, Elizabeth (1781–1800). Diary (1797–1800). MS in NLI.

Edgeworth, 'Maria' [queried attribution to Maria Edgeworth (1768–1849)] Diary (1803). MS in NLI.

ffolliott, Frances Homan (1769–1855). Diary (1808). MS in PRONI.

ffolliott, later Young, Marianne (1794–1876). Diary (1809–1827). MS in PRONI.

Fortescue, Mary Anne McClintock (1767–1849). Diary (1797–1800). MSS in family possession.

Galloway, Letitia (dates unknown). Diary (1809–1810). MS in NLI.

Goddard, Elinor Shuldham (d. 1802). Diary (1774–1782). MSS in NLW.

Grubb, Sarah Tuke (1756–1790). Diary (1782). MS location unknown.

Guild, Elizabeth Quincy (1757–1825). Diary (1790–1791). MS in Harvard University.

Hamilton, Eliza (1807–1851). Diary largely destroyed.

Hancock, later Hogg, Mary (1773–1828). Diary (1788). MS in PRONI.

Harvey, Margaret Boyle (1786–1832). Diary (1809–1812). MS copy in RSFIHL.

Herbert, Dorothea (1770–1829). Diary (1806–1807). MSS in TCD.

Jocelyn, Anne (c. 1797–1822). Diary (1818–1822). Transcript in NLI.

Jocelyn, Anne Hamilton (1730–1802). Diary (1797–1802). MS location unknown.

Jocelyn, later Wingfield, Frances Theodosia (1795–1820). Diary (1810–1812). Transcript in NLI.

Johnson, later King, Dorothea Garrat (1732–1817). Diary (1771–1817). MS location unknown.

Kiernan, 'Harriet' (dates unknown). Diary (1799–1808). MS transcript in PRONI.

Leadbeater, Mary Shackleton (1758–1826). Diary (1769–1826). MSS in NLI.

Lecky, Charity (1782–?). Diary (1796–1797). MS in Beinecke Library, Yale.

Mathew, Mary (1724–1777). Diary (1772–1773). MS in NLI.

Ponsonby, Sarah (1755–1831). Diary (1778). MS in NLW.

Shackleton, Elizabeth Carleton (1726–1804). Diary (1753–1763). MSS in Beinecke Library, Yale University.

Shackleton, Sarah (1760–1847). Diary (1787–1821). MSS in UCSB.

Skeffington, Harriet Jocelyn (1755–1831). Diary (1798). MS in QUB.

Slack, Angel Anna (1748–1796?). Diary (1785–1796). Typescript in Ballinamore Library, Co. Leitrim.

Stirum, Elizabeth Richards (1778–1863). Diary (1798–1825). MS transcript in Municipal Archives Rotterdam. Archive Huis ten Donck.

Strangman, Maria (dates unknown). Diary (1788). MS in PRONI.

Tighe, Mary Blachford (1772–1810). Diary (1787–1802). MS transcript by cousin, Caroline Hamilton, in NLI.

Trench, Melesina Chenevix St. George (1768–1827). Diary (1791–1827). MSS in HRO.

Walker, Anna (1763–1816). Diary (1802–1805). Typescript in PRONI.

Ward, Arabella Crosbie (1757–1813). Diary (1804). MS in PRONI.

Weldon, Anne Cooke (1726–1809). Diary (1761–1773). MSS in family possession.

Manuscript Transcription Policy

The intention has been to preserve the diarists' original punctuation and spellings.

Interlineations and additions by the diarists have been indicated by using the symbol '^' at the beginning and end of the word or phrase inserted by the diarist into the text.

Editorial interventions, including ellipses, have been set in square brackets. The ellipses within square brackets are used authorially to show an incomplete quotation.

Where an unsure reading is proffered a question mark has been inserted into square brackets.

Where a word has been crossed out and/or is indecipherable, this has been indicated as '[illegible]'.

Content Warning

The following chapters focus on many difficult issues, including, but not limited to, multiple aspects of gender and sexual violence in Chapter 3 and miscarriage, stillbirth, infant and child mortality, and bereavement in Chapter 4.

Introduction

1. Textuality, Place, and the Self

1.1 Textuality: The Diary Form

Diaries were embraced by women of all ages in Ireland in the late eighteenth and early nineteenth centuries and composed from childhood to old age. The diaries acted as a repository for these women's memories, a chronicle of their days, a record of events, an account of their expenditure, and a charting of their growing or shrinking families. They are mundane, humdrum quotidian exercises, the writer plodding along with a sense of obligation. They are the epitome of sparkling prose, showcasing their author's extensive literary capabilities and rhetorical prowess. The texture of these works shifts and evolves, not simply across the different diaries and diary volumes, but across the daily entries, as the diarists experiment with prose, either luxuriating in reflection and the mental space permitted for composition or finding themselves prohibited from expounding by the material slightness of the diary itself, by family obligations, by an absence of leisure time, by indolence or melancholia. The diary form forces a dismantling of any neat binaries of public and private, of imaginative and non-imaginative prose writing, complicating our understandings of each, with almost all the surviving Irish diaries exhibiting an explicit awareness of audience, whether contemporary or posthumous.

What then, exactly, are diaries? Those under discussion here meant different things to individual diarists and another thing entirely to those who dismissed them outright.[1] Writing in her early 50s, the Bluestocking Hester Lynch Thrale Piozzi, née Salusbury, champions her diary as 'my

---

1 Irina Paperno, 'What Can Be Done with Diaries?' *The Russian Review* 63.4 (October 2004): 561–73.

Confident, my solitary Comfort, and Depository of every Thought as it arose' (3/1/1791), elevating the form and bestowing it with human qualities.[2] Anne Jocelyn, Countess Dowager of Roden (1730–1802), of Dundalk, Co. Louth, alludes flippantly to her diary as the 'foolish little notes of the occurrences of each day' (30/10/1799), downplaying its import in the manner of many contemporary poets and playwrights whose prefaces underplay the author's worth, often in deference to expectations of female propriety.[3] Mary Shackleton, later Leadbeater (1758–1826), similarly references her various diaries as 'mere bagatelles', understating their significance in an entry that simultaneously celebrates and champions the form. Early in a diary writing career that spanned a full lifetime, 16-year-old Mary signals her intention of 'being minute in relating the transactions of evry day' (30/6/1774).[4] This daily or 'at least fairly regular periodic account of one's life' is at the core of definitions of the diary form, with entries that have been both created and arranged chronologically.[5] Magdalena Ożarska expands on this to itemise the major characteristics of diaries as being 'serial yet autonomous entries; dating; a relatively loose and formless structure …; metadiscursive reflection; the presence of the narrator …; and lacunae … all set against a spatial and temporal backdrop'.[6] Beyond this broad listing, the diary's essential features can be isolated as precise dating and serial quality.[7] In the eighteenth and nineteenth centuries, diaries were embraced for a multitude of different purposes and employments, and they possess an emphatically heterogeneous nature. The multifunctionality of the form is immediately apparent from a quick survey of the surviving diaries that make up this study. These reveal the full spectrum of possibilities the diary form afforded their authors, whether for better mental health, negotiation of national identity, assistance in the

2 Hester Lynch Thrale, *Thraliana, The Diary of Hester Lynch Thrale (Later Mrs Piozzi) 1776–1809*. Ed. Katherine C. Balderston. Oxford: Clarendon Press, 1951. 2nd ed. 2014.

3 Anne Jocelyn, *The Diary of Anne, Countess Dowager of Roden, 1797–1802*. Dublin, 1870.

4 Mary Leadbeater, Diaries covering the years 1769–1826 in 54 volumes. NLI MSS 9292–9346. NLI MS 9297.

5 'All are daily or at least fairly regular periodic accounts of a life created and arranged chronologically.' Heather Beattie, 'Where Narratives Meet: Archival Description, Provenance, and Women's Diaries'. *Libraries & the Cultural Record* 44.1 (2009): 83.

6 Magdalena Ożarska, *Lacework or Mirror? Diary Poetics of Frances Burney, Dorothy Wordsworth and Mary Shelley*. Cambridge: Cambridge Scholars Publishing, 2014, 5. For similar definitions see also Christina Sjöblad, 'From Family Notes to Diary: The Development of a Genre'. *Eighteenth-Century Studies* 31.4 (1998): 517–21.

7 Ożarska 5.

transition to adulthood, coping with bereavement, dealing with assault, or establishing a literary voice.[8]

While the famous seventeenth-century diaries by John Evelyn and Samuel Pepys were not published until the nineteenth century (1818 and 1825 respectively), eighteenth-century diarists did in fact have access to multiple examples of earlier diaries by both men and women. There is evidence for this awareness of the long tradition of women's diary writing within the diaries themselves. Mary Anne Dawson (1763–1831) notes her own perusal of 'Lady Louisa Clayton's Journal' in her diary entry for 8/8/1782, for instance.[9] Perhaps one of the most salient models for the diarists, and certainly an indication of the appropriateness of the undertaking for younger women, was the existence of diaries written by previous generations of one's own family. Diaries were frequently written by several generations across the same family, either sequentially, or with overlapping periods recorded by different family members. In addition to the period's most prolific diarist, the Shackleton family diarists also included Mary Leadbeater's sister Sarah [Sally] Shackleton (1760–1847) and her mother Elizabeth Shackleton, née Carleton (1726–1804). We also have the example of the diarist Marianne ffolliott (1794–1876) and her mother Frances ffolliott, née Homan (1769–1855).[10] The family of Anne Jocelyn, née Hamilton, is a particularly good example of a multi-generational dynasty of diary writers, encompassing at least Anne's own grandmother Elizabeth Mordaunt, née Carey (1632–1679), whose diary was published by her descendant as *The Private Diarie of Elizabeth, Viscountess Mordaunt* (1856); her daughter Harriet (1755–1831), who married Chichester Skeffington; and her granddaughters, the children of her son Robert, 2nd Earl of Roden: Anne (*c.* 1797–1822), and Anne's sister, Frances Theodosia, later Lady Powerscourt (1795–1820). While the author Maria Edgeworth did not keep a diary, her siblings included many diary writers.[11] Her sister Elizabeth (1781–1800) wrote a short diary that ceased with her untimely death; while her younger

---

8 Multifunctionality of diary form continues into later centuries, and across differing places and circumstances. See, for example, Alexis Peri, *The War Within: Diaries from the Siege of Leningrad*. Cambridge, MA: Harvard UP, 2017, in which Peri describes the diaries functioning as 'a repository of thought, a confessional space, a site of self-examination, a medium for communicating with far-flung relatives, a historical chronicle, and a coping mechanism', 12.

9 Mary Anne Dawson, Diary of Mary Anne Dawson, 1782–84. Clements Papers, TCD MSS 7270–7270a.

10 Marianne is named in catalogues and elsewhere as Mary Anne. Marianne is preferred here as this is the name she herself signs within her diary.

11 Maria Edgeworth did keep a record of conversations and meetings in small books and note-books, such as NLI POS 9028 366A, but did not record her impressions as

sisters, Frances Maria (1799–1848) and Sophia (1803–1837), daughters of her stepmother Frances Beaufort, wrote travel journals between 1819 and 1823, relating tours of England and Scotland respectively.[12] A second Edgeworth diary in the National Library of Ireland, focused primarily on the political events of 1803, has been attributed to Maria Edgeworth herself.[13] However, the evidence points strongly to its having been composed by a male member of the Edgeworth family, most probably Elizabeth's close contemporary, her brother Henry.[14]

As we will see, the eighteenth-century diary owed much to earlier spiritual journals, which explored an individual's religious journey, documenting a conversion, an awakening, or a strengthened relationship with God. The diarists were able to draw on these previous traditions and examples of secular and spiritual diaries, while their writing was also in constant dialogue with a range of different literary genres. They interacted with travel diaries, account books, almanacs, and chronicles, as well as many emerging literary forms.[15] There are exceptionally numerous intersections apparent between the corpus of diaries and contemporary prose fiction, notable across the modes of realism, sentimentalism, and the Gothic in particular. Eighteenth-century novels quickly became a source of inspiration for diarists who borrowed their narrative techniques, as well as echoing their phraseology and content, traits especially notable in those adolescent diaries from Ireland. What is immediately evident too is the symbiotic nature of the exchanges, with diary writing also informing the emerging literary form – novels made use of diaries and epistolary writing to establish the effects of authenticity, while diaries borrowed from and were informed by the narrative voices featured in the new genre.[16]

such or keep a diary. With sincere thanks to Susan Manly for sharing her thoughts on Edgeworth's lack of engagement with the diary form and directing me to these details.

12 Frances Edgeworth, Fanny's journal of a tour of England, 1819–20. Bodleian Library, University of Oxford, MS Eng. Lett. c744, fols. 129–72; Sophia Edgeworth, Sophy's journal of a tour of Scotland, 1823. Bodleian Library, University of Oxford, MS Eng. Lett. c746, fols. 166–92.

13 Diary of Maria Edgeworth, with references to political affairs; June–December 1803. NLI MS 18,752. POS 9038. [Attribution queried].

14 Supporting evidence for the interpretation that the diary was not written by Maria Edgeworth includes the diarist writing constantly to men, and, notably, asking one man, a Mr Wickham, to resign. There are also such pointed signals as the diarist referring to a letter received being addressed to Maria from Lady Granard.

15 Alec Ryrie, 'Writing'. *Being Protestant in Reformation Britain*. Oxford: OUP, 2013, 298–314; 301. This echoes the way the earlier spiritual diary drew on a variety of secular forms.

16 In an English context, see Lorna J. Clark, 'The Diarist as Novelist: Narrative

The distinction between fictional and non-fictional narratives during this period is in fact often tenuous.[17] It is clear that the diarists drew from these intertwined traditions and further complicate our own sense of the often dubious distinction between imaginative and non-imaginative works, with the diary representing 'a liminal form that disturbs our sense of what is "real" and what is "fiction"'.[18] The corpus of diaries reveals many instances of generic intersections, experimentation, and innovation, showcasing the literary and cultural cross-fertilisation that was so widespread in the eighteenth century. We can note multiple overlaps between imaginative and non-imaginative prose – relating to style, content, and approach. One need only think of the fictional travelogues and autobiographies that proliferated from early in the century that purported to be authentic histories, most famously those penned by Daniel Defoe, such as *The Fortunes and Misfortunes of the Famous Moll Flanders... Written from her own Memorandums* (1721). In general, writing from eighteenth-century Ireland is notable for being particularly rich in textual diversity, with a remarkable formal fluidity across genres, as writers drew from different generic forms, narrative structures, and rhetorical tropes, epitomised by Laurence Sterne's *The Life and Opinions of Tristram Shandy, Gentleman* (1759–1767), itself, of course, a fictional autobiography.[19] Diaries from Ireland reflect this diversity and are a celebration of the possibilities of the form. Indeed, the diary entries themselves shift seamlessly from prose reflection to verse, to the recitation of remembered dialogue, to the insertion of original poetry.

The foregrounding of these diaries as literary works – whether through their own rich literary texture or their influence on more established genres – makes us change the way we think about eighteenth-century writing and about Irish literature more broadly. The diarists' grasp of rhetorical strategies, their use of narrative voice, and their employment of a suite of

Strategies in the Journals and Letters of Frances Burney'. *English Studies in Canada* 27.3 (2001): 283–302.

17 See Paul Longley Arthur, 'Eighteenth-Century Imaginary Voyages to the Antipodes'. *The Eighteenth Century* 49.3 (2008): 197–210; and Katrina O'Loughlin, *Women, Writing, and Travel in the Eighteenth Century*. Cambridge: CUP, 2018.

18 Dan Doll and Jessica Munns, *Recording and Reordering: Essays on the Seventeenth- and Eighteenth-Century Diary and Journal*. Lewisburg: Bucknell UP, 2006, 20.

19 Moyra Haslett, 'Experimentalism in the Irish Novel, 1750–1770'. *Irish University Review* 41.1 (2011): 63–79. Laurence Sterne, *The Life and Opinions of Tristram Shandy, Gentleman*. Ed. Ian Campbell Ross. Oxford: OUP, 2009. Sterne's *Journal to Eliza* also showcases this literary fluidity as Sterne, as Yorick or the Brahmin, repeats material in different letters and in different imaginings, as well as suggesting his own experience as suitable for incorporation into *Tristram Shandy*. See Ian Campbell Ross, *Laurence Sterne: A Life*. Oxford: OUP, 2001.

different literary techniques are frequently apparent, and the expressive skills, creativity, and literary prowess of many of these women deserve to be more widely known. The chapters that follow celebrate the diary form, highlighting the advantages of its fragmentary, sequential nature, which is more commonly dismissed. It promotes a reappreciation of the diaries and of those figures who composed them, celebrating the form as a creative outlet for many women. Several of the diarists in this study also successfully engaged with other genres, particularly poetry and memoirs: key examples of the first are offered by Mary Tighe, née Blachford (1772–1810) and Melesina St. George Trench, née Chenevix (1768–1827); while Dorothea Herbert (1770–1829) and Mary Leadbeater offer notable examples of the latter.[20] The different genres are frequently shaped by each other, with the diary form serving alternately as source material or as a platform for literary experimentation, as well as providing a space for women and girls to explore new ideas and to ponder the emotional resonances of their experiences.

Despite the significant progress made to overturn longstanding ideas about privacy in this period, there is still a real need to argue against the impression that diaries were exclusively private texts. The following comment from 2018 offers an indication of the assumptions frequently made regarding diaries and audience: 'Some of the writers explored in this chapter kept diaries and were therefore not consciously writing their life story or expecting anyone else to read their work.'[21] Though almost exclusively unpublished in their lifetimes, the Irish diaries considered here were in fact frequently read and indeed circulated in manuscript form, and the vast majority of the diaries were explicitly written with an audience firmly in mind. These audiences varied from trusted family members to wider networks of friends to intended posthumous readers. Regardless of whether these audiences represent one trusted sister, the writer's children or grandchildren, or unmet future generations, those diaries that have survived almost all anticipate an eventual readership, which disrupts any understanding of the diary as an inherently private document. This of course

20 Mary Tighe, *The Collected Poems and Journals of Mary Tighe*. Ed. Harriet Kramer Linkin. Lexington: University Press of Kentucky, 2005; Diaries of Melesina St. George, later Trench, from 1791 to 1802. HRO, 23M93/1, and *The Remains of the Late Mrs. Richard Trench. Being Selections from her Journals, Letters, & Other Papers*. Ed. Dean of Westminster. London, 1862; Dorothea Herbert, Retrospections, and Dorothea Herbert, 1806–1807 Diary, both on deposit at TCD. Dorothea Herbert, *Retrospections of Dorothea Herbert*. Dublin: Town House, 1988.

21 Maria Luddy, 'Irish Women's Spiritual and Religious Life Writing in the Late Eighteenth and Nineteenth Centuries'. *A History of Irish Autobiography*. Ed. Liam Harte. Cambridge: CUP, 2018, 70. This chapter offers an excellent overview of 'first person accounts of religious experience' by women in Ireland at this time.

influences how these diarists engaged with the form and how we in turn interpret their writings. Women whose diaries serve to record significant events were keenly aware that their musings might inform others of these events, and their entries were guided by this factor. For others, their literary aspirations are to the fore, and the diary is very much a showcase of their talent, whether for a contemporary audience or posterity.

1.2 Diaries and Protestantism: Religious Affiliation, Context, and Ireland

Diaries were, however, certainly originally written primarily to improve the self rather than engage an audience. From its earliest origins in the early modern period, the diary held a fundamental connection with ideas of Protestant self-examination. Concepts of self-accounting and improvement, wherein the writer seeks to explain their failings and achievements without the confessional sacrament available to Roman Catholics, were intrinsic to the development of numerous Protestant faiths.[22] Manuals for self-examination abounded, supplementing sermons encouraging the practice, and, although much of this self-reflection was *not* intended to be written down, spiritual diaries became increasingly popular as men and women sought to keep a physical account of their days.[23] The diary of English Puritan Richard Rogers, dating from 1587, has been identified as the oldest surviving British diary, with John Beadle in 1656 cited as the 'first British cleric to advocate such journals at any length'.[24] The account book itself was undoubtedly an influence, and the primary purpose of such diaries was to justify one's daily actions and *account* for one's behaviour before God, rather than recording public events, emotional responses, leisure pursuits enjoyed, or observations on the internal self.[25] The spiritual diary (1656–1678) of the Anglican Elizabeth Mordaunt offers an example of such a practice, with the diarist tallying up her accomplishments and her failings. At one point in 1657, Mordaunt explicitly divides a portion of her diary into two columns, entitled 'to returne thanks' and 'to repent of'. She offers thanks, for example, 'for my helthe and safety', while asking forgiveness for having 'sayd one or to things that wer not exactly true'.[26] This tradition of diary writing continued into

22 Effie Botonaki, 'Seventeenth-Century Englishwomen's Spiritual Diaries: Self-Examination, Covenanting, and Account Keeping'. *The Sixteenth Century Journal* 30.1 (1999): 3–21.

23 Ryrie 298–314.

24 Ryrie 298–99.

25 For the tradition of historical writing on Protestantism and capitalism going back to Max Weber, see Jere Cohen, *Protestantism and Capitalism: The Mechanisms of Influence*. London: Routledge, 2002.

26 Elizabeth Mordaunt, *The Private Diarie of Elizabeth, Viscountess Mordaunt*. [d. 1678]. Ed. Robert Jocelyn Roden. Duncairn, 1856, 226.

the eighteenth century with the connection between religious background and the form firmly maintained. Conversely, the argument has been made that those from a Roman Catholic tradition in Ireland 'seem to have favoured poetry, ballads and anecdotes – more collective forms of memorial' over other forms of life writing, with the memoir in particular signalled as 'in some ways a quintessentially Protestant form'.[27]

Such formal connections between Protestantism and diary writing are reflected in the material that survives. The diaries that represent the core sources for this book are almost exclusively composed by those subscribing to a Protestant faith, across a spectrum of denominations. In an Irish context, this means that the diaries are drawn from the minority of the population. The 1831 census, released in 1834, on religious numbers and religious observance, showed that Catholics made up approximately 80.9% of the population in Ireland, while 10.7% adhered to the Church of Ireland and 8.1% to Presbyterianism, with Quakers and Methodists accounting for less than 0.3%.[28] Until recently, it was difficult to propose a reliable figure for the period under study here, falling as it does between that later report and the previous poll tax survey of 1660. However, a 2022 analysis of the ecclesiastical census of 1766, which brought together parish-level returns from repositories across Ireland, enabled the researchers to propose a conjectured figure of approximately 25% for the shared Protestant population in Ireland at a national level, at that date.[29]

There was a significant, deliberate, correlation between social standing and denomination at this time in Ireland, so that Catholics tended to be mostly at the bottom of the social scale, though increasingly represented among the merchant classes, while the landowning class was primarily composed of those from a Church of Ireland background, whose adherents also 'took control of parliament, the army and the offices of the crown'.[30] Mostly descended from English settlers from a variety of plantations,

27 Siobhán Kilfeather, 'Dinah Goff'. *The Field Day Anthology of Irish Writing, Volumes 4 and 5, Irish Women's Writing and Traditions*. Eds. Angela Bourke et al. Cork: Cork UP, 2002, IV 856.

28 Sarah Roddy, 'Introduction'. *Population, Providence and Empire*. Manchester: MUP, 2014, 3.

29 Brian Gurrin, Kerby A. Miller, and Liam Kennedy, *The Irish Religious Censuses of the 1760s: Catholics and Protestants in Eighteenth-Century Ireland*. Dublin: IMC, 2022, 121.

30 Toby Barnard has stated, 'put crudely: repeated confiscations and prohibitions left a large majority of the Catholics – at least 75% of Ireland's population – poor'. Toby Barnard, *Making the Grand Figure, Lives and Possessions in Ireland, 1641–1770*. New Haven and London: Yale UP, 2004, xix. See also Toby Barnard, *A New Anatomy of Ireland: The Irish Protestants, 1649–1770*. New Haven and London: Yale UP, 2004; Crawford Gribben, *The Rise and Fall of Christian Ireland*. Oxford: OUP, 2021, 122.

beginning with those of counties Laois and Offaly in the mid-sixteenth century, many of the diarists in this book were privileged Anglican women with titles, wealthy women with extensive land still in their family's possession following multiple waves of confiscation of land from the majority Catholic population.[31] These confiscations were upheld and strengthened by a raft of legislation referred to as the Penal Laws, including the 1704 Act to Prevent the Further Growth of Popery, in which Catholics were barred from acquiring land by purchase, confined to leases of 31 years or less, and prevented from inheriting land from Protestants, while Catholic properties were to descend by gavelkind rather than primogeniture.[32] By the late eighteenth century, over 95% of Ireland's land was in the possession of *c.* 5,000 Protestant landowners.[33] Many diaries were composed in expensive Dublin town houses or were set down in large country demesnes, and there is a significant silence throughout the majority of the diaries regarding the lived realities of the impoverished population beyond these walls.

Despite making up three quarters of the population at this time, very few Irish Catholic diaries survive, or, perhaps, even existed.[34] There are no

31 The Cromwellian era 'witnessed the single largest transfer of land (raising the percentage in Protestant possession from 30 per cent in 1641 to 67 percent in c. 1675'. James Kelly and Ciarán Mac Murchaidh, eds. *Essays on the Irish Linguistic Cultural Frontier, 1600–1900.* Dublin: Four Courts, 2012, 24. For further insight into the mentalities of this group, through considerations of their correspondence, see Arabella Denny, '"My dear Lady C": Letters of Lady Arabella Denny to Lady Caldwell, 1754–1777'. Ed. Rosemary Raughter. *Analecta Hibernica* 41 (2009): 133–200, which explores and reproduces the letters between these two women, the latter of whom, Elizabeth Hort, married Sir James Caldwell, 'fourth baronet and owner of an estate of over 2,000 acres on the border of counties Fermanagh and Donegal', bringing with her a dowry of £10,000, 138.

32 Thomas O'Connor, 'The Catholic Church and Catholics in an Era of Sanctions'. *The Cambridge History of Ireland, Volume 3, 1730–1880.* Ed. James Kelly. Cambridge: CUP, 2018, 261. Michael Brown has identified the aims of the penal laws as 'to humiliate the Catholic community, to effect their social degradation, and to humble their leadership in the eyes of their confreres'. Michael Brown, *The Irish Enlightenment.* Cambridge, MA: Harvard UP, 2016, 113.

33 'More than 95 per cent of the island's land resources were held by around 5,000 landowning gentry in the 1770s, much of which incorporated comparatively large extents of territory over which one owner exercised considerable power and control.' Patrick Duffy, 'Landed Estates in 19th Century Ireland'. *Dis(Placing) Empire.* Eds. L. J. Proudfoot and M. M. Roche. Aldershot: Ashgate, 2005, 15–40.

34 Examples of surviving English-language diaries by Catholic men include the diary (1773–1814) of Tipperary farmer James Scully, preserved by the NLI, and described as 'an invaluable source for agricultural matters' (C. J. Woods, 'James Scully'. *Dictionary of Irish Biography (DIB)*), and that of his son Denys (1773–1830), a leader in the cause

diaries written by Catholic women across the corpus, with the one exception of the aristocratic Eleanor Butler (1739–1829), daughter of the 16th Earl of Ormond. Reasons for the lack of Catholic diaries from Ireland during this time are twofold. In addition to the formal interconnectedness of Protestantism and the diary tradition in this period, one must remember that for much of the Catholic population of eighteenth-century Ireland, literacy remained relatively low.[35] In addition, many of these men and women communicated in Irish, a language with a rich oral literary tradition, which had been actively maintained and promoted in preference to a written one; consequently, there was only a very minor Irish-language tradition of diary writing.[36]   English became the mass vernacular in the early seventeenth century in Ireland, but Lesa Ní Mhunghaile estimates 'in excess of 40% of the population may still have been Irish speaking by the turn of the nineteenth century'.[37] The well-known nineteenth-century diary (1827–1835) kept in Co. Kilkenny by the Kerry-born schoolteacher, *seanchaí*, antiquarian, and draper Amhlaoibh Ó Súilleabháin (1780–1838) is generally presented as anomalous, described by Proinsias Ó Drisceoil as a 'highly unusual document generically within the corpus of Irish-language writing at the time' and as a 'form of writing for which no real precedent existed in Irish'.[38] Vincent Morley's work has been able to identify earlier, seventeenth-century diaries, namely by Tadhg Ó Cianáin and Toirdhealbhach Ó Mealláin, which he praises for their value in chronicling the 1607 Flight of the Earls and the War of the 1640s, respectively.[39] Morley also notes a variation of the tradition in the eighteenth-century writings of the schoolmaster, scribe, and scholar Tadhg Ó Neachtain (*c.* 1671–1752) and the Enlightenment scholar

---

of Catholic Emancipation, Denys Scully, *The Irish Catholic Petition of 1805: The Diary of Denys Scully*. Dublin: Irish Academic Press, 1992.

35 Figures from the 1861 census record 46% of Catholics *unable* to read and write 'compared with 16% of Anglicans and 11% of Presbyterians'. Luddy 71.

36 Additionally, the number of Irish-language titles *published* in Ireland between 1700 and 1750 has been described as 'statistically insignificant' with only four during that period. Kelly and Mac Murchaidh 29.

37 Kelly and Mac Murchaidh 24; Lesa Ní Mhunghaile, 'Gaelic Literature in Transition, 1780–1830'. *Irish Literature in Transition, 1780–1830*. Ed. Claire Connolly. Cambridge: CUP, 2020, 38.

38 Proinsias Ó Drisceoil, 'Cín Lae Amhlaoibh: Modernization and the Irish Language'. *Ireland and Romanticism: Publics, Nations and Scenes of Cultural Production*. Ed. Jim Kelly. Basingstoke: Palgrave, 2011, 13. See also Liam P. Ó Murchu, *Cinnlae Amhlaoibh Uí Shúileabháin: Reassessments*. London: Irish Texts Society, 2004. Desmond McCabe, 'Amhlaoibh Ó Súilleabháin (Humphrey Sullivan)'. *DIB*.

39 Vincent Morley, 'The Irish Language'. *The Princeton History of Modern Ireland*. Eds. Richard Bourke and Ian McBride. Princeton and Oxford: Princeton UP, 2016, 325; 330.

and Catholic activist Cathal Ó Conchúir (1710–1791), known in English as Charles O'Conor of Ballinagare.[40]

These few surviving examples point also to a gender distinction in the eighteenth century, not reflected in the English-language diaries from Ireland. Lesa Ní Mhunghaile's work makes clear that writing in Irish during the long eighteenth century was the exclusive pursuit of men, and that, even with them, literacy was achieved through English, as a result of the national school system.[41] There are no examples of manuscripts written by women in Irish from the long eighteenth century, and private correspondence in Irish is non-existent. The same is true of women poets: there are only two known examples of Irish-speaking women who composed poetry during the long eighteenth century – Máire Ní Chrualaoich and the author of *Caoineadh Airt Uí Laoghaire*, Eibhlín Dubh Ní Chonaill – both of whom composed orally.[42]

As with Catholic examples, this survey includes no diaries from a Presbyterian tradition. Indeed, with the exceptions of the diary of Coleraine apprentice John Tennent (1772–1813) and that of celebrated artist and Founder Member of the British Royal Academy, Nathaniel Hone (1718–1784), it is difficult to identify surviving Presbyterian diaries from this period.[43] This absence correlates with a lack of personal papers for any Presbyterian, male or female, during these years.[44] The situation with regards to female Presbyterian

40 Vincent Morley, 'Cíona lae na Gaeilge agus an stair,' *Cúnraí Staire* https://cstair. blogspot.com/search?q=dialann. It should be pointed out that between 1750 and 1850, Ireland was always 'an intensely bilingual and diglossic society'. Niall Ó Ciosáin, *Print and Popular Culture in Ireland, 1750–1850*. Basingstoke: Palgrave, 1997, 6. See also Vincent Morley, *The Popular Mind in Eighteenth-Century Ireland*. Cork: Cork UP, 2017.

41 I am greatly indebted to Lesa Ní Mhunghaile for her expertise in this area and for being so generous in sharing this knowledge with me and informing this section.

42 Tríona Ní Shíocháin, 'The Oral Tradition'. *A History of Irish Women's Poetry*. Eds. Ailbhe Darcy and David Wheatley. Cambridge: CUP, 2021. *Caoineadh Airt Uí Laoghaire (The Lament for Art O'Leary)* is one of the most famous Irish-language texts of the period, though it was not transcribed until later in the nineteenth century, and its attribution is still contested. Doireann Ní Ghríofa's resplendent *A Ghost in the Throat*. Dublin: Tramp Press, 2020, includes a translation into English of the *Caoineadh*, as well as a reimagining of Eibhlín Dubh's life embedded in the narration of Ní Ghríofa's own.

43 John Tennent, 'The Journal of John Tennent, 1786–90'. Ed. Leanne Calvert. *Analecta Hibernica* 43 (2012): 69–128; Nathaniel Hone, Diaries and Memoranda, 1752–1753. British Library MS 44024–25. Nineteenth-century examples include Rev. Robert Magill, who kept a diary from 1827 to 1828.

44 With thanks to Andrew Holmes for his generous assistance on this section. Holmes notes that the situation hardly improves for the nineteenth and twentieth centuries when even the most significant male figures within the denomination failed to leave any personal archives of note.

experience in general is even worse.[45] As ever, it is difficult to determine whether this lack of material is evidence of an absence of concern among individuals with their own experience, religious or otherwise, or simply an absence of evidence.[46] Andrew Holmes's research has shown that Presbyterians in Ireland were indeed concerned about personal piety and spiritual introspection, as expressed through personal covenants, their reading materials, and personal devotions, but so far no diaries by women have been discovered.[47]

In contrast to the lack of Presbyterian sources, the Methodist community produced numerous diaries, and indeed many of these were published during the lifetimes of the diarists themselves. Rosemary Raughter has noted that 'The keeping of a diary of conscience, or spiritual "acccount book", was a puritan tradition, which was followed by Wesley himself and by many of his fellow evangelicals.'[48] Methodist diaries can generally be categorised as spiritual diaries, and many take the form of conversion narratives. All of the Methodist diaries address the diarist's relationship with God and serve primarily (though not exclusively) as a record of spiritual developments and to act as an example for others. Women often played a central role in the development of Methodism both in Ireland and abroad.[49] Examples of spiritual diaries composed by Methodist women in Ireland include those written by Angel Anna Slack (1748–1796?) and Dorothea Johnson, née Garrat, later King (1731–1817).[50] The diarist Theodosia Blachford, née Tighe (1744–1817) famously shaped Methodism's developments in Ireland, but

45 Leanne Calvert's work makes use of records of church disciplinary cases in the eighteenth century to delve into the lives of ordinary Presbyterians, with a specific focus on gender relations. See Leanne Calvert, "'From a woman's point of view': The Presbyterian Archive as a Source for Women's and Gender History in Eighteenth and Nineteenth-Century Ireland'. *Irish Historical Studies. Special Issue: A New Agenda for Women's and Gender History in Ireland* 46 (2022): 301–18.

46 Martha McTier and William Drennan, *The Drennan-McTier Letters 1776–1819.* Eds. Jean Agnew and Maria Luddy. 3 vols. Dublin: IMC, 1998–2000, give a glimpse into the inner life of an exceptional Presbyterian individual, via McTier's letters to her brother. See also Olivia Elder, *The Poems of Olivia Elder.* Ed. Andrew Carpenter. Dublin: IMC, 2020.

47 Andrew Holmes, *The Shaping of Ulster Presbyterian Belief and Practice, 1770–1840.* Oxford: OUP, 2006.

48 Elizabeth Bennis, *The Journal of Elizabeth Bennis 1749–1779.* Ed. Rosemary Raughter. Dublin: Columba Press, Blackrock, 2007, 31.

49 For more on women and the expansion of evangelical Protestantism, see C. H. Crookshank, *Memorable women of Irish Methodism in the last century.* London, 1882.

50 Dorothea Johnson, *The memoirs of Mrs. Dorothea Johnson, late of Lisburn: extracted from her journals and other papers.* Ed. Adam Averell. Cavan, 1818. There is a typescript of the diary of Angel Anna Slack in Ballinamore Library, Co. Leitrim, File 275.

Blachford converted the year *after* her surviving diary concludes in 1774, and so could not be said to belong to a Methodist diary tradition.[51]

The best-known Methodist woman from Ireland is the Limerick diarist Elizabeth Bennis, née Patten (1725–1802), whose diary ran from 1749 to 1779. Both her life and her diary were shaped and informed primarily by her devotion to Methodism, to which she converted from Presbyterianism at age 24. The following extract from a letter from Bennis to the lay-preacher John Stretton reveals the diarist's own thoughts on both diary writing and diary reading:

> I wish you to pursue the diary that I formerly recommended; you will find it a great help. I have often experienced much comfort in reading over past experience, and have often felt happiness and support in comparing past with present … Only do not write much at a time, that it be not burthensome, except when your heart is particularly engaged; then it may not be well to cramp yourself, but let your heart and pen flow together, to the glory of God. (24/7/1777)[52]

Bennis's motivations for engaging with the diary form are made explicitly clear here, and her understanding of the form's relationship with serving God is underscored.

Those from Church of Ireland and Quaker backgrounds represent the two largest groups in this study. Their diaries are significantly less religous in character than the surviving Methodist diaries. Indeed, we can see that the mid-eighteenth century witnessed a general shift away from the spiritual diaries that had predominated in the seventeenth century to those of a much more secular emphasis. Such diaries were still composed by those subscribing to and adhering to the tenets of their faith, but without the core emphasis being on justification for their actions within an exclusively religious context. Many of the diaries from the period still retain the earlier focus on spiritual accounting. However, the diaries that represent the core of this study focus primarily on secular pursuits, with religious devotion a secondary consideration. From about 1760, core emphasis came to be placed on the diary as a space to record one's life, thoughts, and activities as a souvenir or memory, rather than focusing on life as a spiritual journey with one's spiritual development at its core. The adolescent Frances Jocelyn's comment that: 'This day was so very pleasant that I need hardly write it down to remember it' (21/1/1811), indicates her own understanding of the

51 Theodosia Blachford, Journal of Theodosia Blachford (née Tighe), covering the years 1773–1774. NLI MS 38,639/1/7.
52 XCVII, Christian Correspondence, cited in Bennis 58.

purpose of her diary in recording her quotidian pursuits.[53] In addition to the multiple diarists from Frances Jocelyn's extended family (who became associated with Evangelicalism in the early nineteenth century), and the ffolliott and Edgeworth families discussed above, diarists from Church of Ireland backgrounds included Mary Anne Fortescue, née McClintock (1767–1849) from Co. Louth; the young Mary Anne Dawson; and the widowed Elinor Goddard, née Shuldham (d. 1802), best known for her connections with Sarah Ponsonby (1755–1831), one of the so-called Ladies of Llangollen, who also wrote a diary.[54] The level of piety evident in the diaries of these women varies greatly. This is reflected in the degrees of intertextual allusion to religious sources in their diaries, for example, as well as the frequency of their references to God, and their propensity for church attendance or avoidance.

The most prolific of all the diarists in this study is Mary Shackleton Leadbeater, a Quaker who composed 54 volumes over the course of her lifetime.[55] While grounded in her experiences of being a Quaker girl and woman, Leadbeater departs from an emphasis on the spiritual to encompass all facets of life in Ballitore, Co. Kildare, 'the only planned and permanent quaker settlement in eighteenth-century Ireland', charting her time there from the age of 11 until her death in 1826.[56] Members of the Quaker community were frequently supported in their production of life writing, encouraged 'by the emphasis on individual experience and social equality within the society of friends'.[57] A survey of surviving manuscript diaries preserved by the Religious Society of Friends in Ireland, undertaken in the mid-twentieth century, indicates the breadth of writing produced by this

53 Frances Jocelyn, Diary of Frances Theodosia Jocelyn. 1810–1812. NLI MS 18430.

54 Examples of Anglican men's diaries from Ireland include that of Church of Ireland clergyman, Thomas Campbell, *Dr Campbell's Diary of a Visit to England in 1775*. Ed. James L. Clifford. Cambridge: CUP, 1947; that of Tipperary-born antiquary Austin Cooper (1759–1830), extracts in *An Eighteenth-Century Antiquary*. Ed. Liam Price. Dublin: Falconer, 1942; the diary of Kerry politician and judge, Robert Day, *Mr. Justice Robert Day (1746–1841): The Diaries and the Addresses to Grand Juries 1793–1829*. Ed. Gerald O'Carroll. Tralee, Co. Kerry: Polymath Press, 2004; and that of United Irishman, Theobald Wolfe Tone, *Life of Theobald Wolfe Tone… Written by himself, and continued by his Son; with his Political writings, and Fragments of his Diary…* Ed. William Theobald Wolfe Tone. Washington, 1826.

55 The most substantial diary (1758–1807) to survive from eighteenth-century America was also written by a Quaker, Elizabeth Drinker (1735–1807). *The Diary of Elizabeth Drinker, the Life Cycle of an Eighteenth-Century Woman*. Ed. Elaine Forman Crane. Pennsylvania: University of Pennsylvania Press, 2010.

56 Maureen E. Mulvihill, 'Mary Leadbeater (née Shackleton)'. *DIB*.

57 Harte 63.

community between 1697 and 1864.[58] In addition to the diaries by Mary Shackleton Leadbeater, her mother Elizabeth, and her sister Sarah, the relatively small Quaker community in Ireland during the long eighteenth century produced the diarists Sarah Grubb, née Tuke (1756–1790), Elizabeth Clibborn, née Grubb (1780–1861), and Mary Hancock, later Hogg (1773–1828).[59] Amongst these men and women, there was a strong tradition of reading and promoting the spiritual diaries of their co-religionists. The memoirs of Richard and Elizabeth Shackleton, compiled by their daughter Mary Leadbeater, includes mention of how,

> Of a winter's evening, Elizabeth Shackleton frequently brought those scholars who belonged to her own religious society, into the parlour, to read her the journals of Friends, as she sat at work.[60]

Diaries were frequently read aloud within this family environment, as Mary's own diary entries make clear: 'Brother read some of John Woolman's journal + adding instructive remarks of his own' (23/1/1790).[61] Mary's own reading is noted at the end of most of her diary volumes in list form, and frequently includes mention of the diaries of other Quakers. On the back flyleaf of her diary for 1781, for example, she reports 'Books which I read this year', and these include the journal of James Gough, a schoolmaster of Dublin.[62] Later diary volumes note a variety of diaries by other members of the Religious Society of Friends, such as those of Samuel Bownas, John Woolman, and William Edmundson, as well as extracts from Dr John Rutty's spiritual diary. Leadbeater's diary for 1793 records her reading of *Some account of the life and religious labours of Sarah Grubb...* (Dublin, 1792). Grubb, who ran a girls' school in Clonmel, Co. Tipperary, died aged 34, and her *Life*, published just two years following her death, includes extracts from her diary.[63]

There is a 'formidable tradition of life writing' amongst the seventeenth- and eighteenth-century Quaker communites across both Europe and America that produced such spiritual diaries, which primarily served to record 'their

58 Olive C. Goodbody, 'Irish Quaker Diaries'. *Guide to Irish Quaker Records, 1654–1860*. Dublin: IMC, 1967, 1–14.

59 Sarah Grubb, *Some account of the life and religious labours of Sarah Grubb...* Dublin, 1792; Elizabeth Clibborn, Journal of Elizabeth (Grubb) Clibborn (1780–1861). RSFIHL P9; Mary Hancock, Diary of Mary Hancock, Sister of Isabella Steele-Nicholson, 1788. PRONI D3513/3/1.

60 Mary Leadbeater, *Memoirs and Letters of Richard and Elizabeth Shackleton, Late of Ballitore, Ireland; Compiled by their Daughter, Mary Leadbeater...* London, 1822, 28.

61 NLI MS 9315.

62 NLI MS 9307.

63 NLI MS 9318.

antagonistic relationship with a particular community and their relationship with the divine'.[64] However, many of the Quaker diaries from this period in Ireland are not overtly spiritual, and instead encompass and even foreground the quotidian. Elizabeth Clibborn's diary, for example, includes extensive entries on childbirth in Co. Tipperary, including the traumatic labour that preceded the birth of her fifth child, her daughter Elizabeth: 'Eliza Clibborn was born after fifty two hours of dreadful Suffering. My flesh seemed like mummy for a considerablde time' (23/2/1808)[65]. Her multiple diary entries fully recount the physical and mental toll of birth, and employ the diary as a means of recording and processing the experience. In this regard, Clibborn's diary might be connected with the diary of aforementioned Philadelphia Quaker Elizabeth Drinker, which also emphasises a shift from the spiritual to the physical by a Quaker diarist, and provides readers with advice on birth control and pain relief.[66] Diaries such as Clibborn's frequently combine the individual's own experience with their impression of belonging to a wider community, both of which inform the diarist's sense of self.

1.3 The Self

Working at the intersection of genre and personal identity, the textuality of the diary can be examined alongside the production and performance of selves and identities, with fresh insights on issues of identity and signifiers of belonging possible. A cast of selves is presented to the reader within and across the range of diaries, encompassing a wide spectrum of figures.[67] All the diaries exhibit an intersectional representation of the self, inflected by age, gender, religion, place, and class, and reveal attempts to create a coherent narrative voice that combines these different elements. The Irish diaries showcase the existence of various unique and autonomous communities of Quakers, Methodists, and those from the Church of Ireland, and religious affiliation is to the fore in terms of shaping and strengthening a communal identity in particular. The sense of a communal identity *within* these Protestant groups is one that immediately becomes evident in a survey of Irish diaries from the long eighteenth century. The reading aloud of diaries

64 Jennifer Desiderio, 'The Life Itself: Quaker Women's Diaries and the Secular Impulse'. *Early American Literature* 49.1 (2014): 188.

65 RSFIHL P9.

66 Desiderio 194.

67 For foundational ideas on the self as 'ideological construct', see Felicity Nussbaum, *The Autobiographical Subject: Gender and Ideology in Eighteenth-Century England*. Baltimore: Johns Hopkins UP, 1989, which reflects on 'the writing of multiple versions of the self – in diaries, journals, lives, and letters – under the guise of a self that is always the same', 101.

amongst members of the same religion, such as was done by the Shackleton family, serves to further reinforce this shared identity. Writing their own diary entries also offered an opportunity for individual diarists to reflect upon how they belonged to their own particular religious community. It allowed them to signal and then negotiate their sense of belonging to Methodism or the Religious Society of Friends, for instance, with their social practices and cultural orientation being informed by their denominational affiliation as well as their Protestant formation.

In addition to their reinforcement of specific denominational identities within Ireland, the diaries also trace relationships with a larger Protestant community. Many religious networks transcended national boundaries to inform an individual's sense of self. The Huguenot diaspora is a community that had a particularly rich tradition of diary writing. Expelled from France due to their religious identity following the Revocation of the Edict of Nantes in 1685, these French Protestants were frequently drawn to diary writing as a means of preserving their history, identity, and traditions.[68] Though of a Calvinist background, the Huguenots were often supported by and or absorbed into the Established Church, both physically and ideologically.[69] The Huguenot community in Ireland included the diarists Melesina Trench and Meliora Adlercron, née Bermingham (d. 1797) of Dawson Street, Dublin. Trench was granddaughter of Richard Chenevix, the Anglican Bishop of Waterford, whose own grandfather had been pastor in Lismay, near Nantes in France, but had relocated to England following the Revocation and the religiously motivated murder of his brother.[70] Trench's diary is informed by her belonging to this diasporic community and her sense of self is shaped by this and by her travels in France and elsewhere in Europe, particularly with her second husband, fellow Huguenot Richard Trench.

In a well-known study, Linda Colley highlighted a subscription to Protestantism, alongside war and trade, as being central to British identity.[71] This emergent British identity is defined by many as being moulded in

68 Ruth Whelan, 'Marsh's Library and the French Calvinist Tradition: The Manuscript Diary of Élie Bouhéreau (1643–1719)'. *The Making of Marsh's Library: Learning, Politics and Religion in Ireland, 1650–1750*. Eds. Muriel McCarthy and Ann Simmons. Dublin: Four Courts Press, 2004. Élie Bouhéreau, *The Diary and Accounts of Élie Bouhéreau*. Eds. Marie Léoutre et al. Dublin: IMC, 2019.
69 The Lady Chapel of St. Patrick's Cathedral, Dublin was given to the Huguenots in the seventeenth century; it remained theirs until 1816 and was known as the French Church of St. Patrick.
70 Henry Morse Stephens, 'Chenevix, Richard (1698–1779)'. *DIB*.
71 Linda Colley, *Britons: Forging the Nation, 1707–1837*. New Haven: Yale UP, 1992.

opposition to the Catholic French or Spanish.[72] As the survey of Irish diaries immediately makes clear, such an oppositional definition of identity is untenable for eighteenth-century Ireland. The division of Catholic and Protestant had long been taken as the defining binary of Ireland (both historically and in twentieth-century scholarship), but more recent approaches have challenged this, giving way to 'a new history of a changing, heterogeneous nation'.[73] The full corpus of Irish diaries testifies to this complexity. While the attendance of 14-year-old Charity Lecky (1782–?) at a variety of churches during her time in Bath with her mother in the winter of 1796 does gesture towards the possibility of a pan-Protestantism, in general the diaries present us with a panoply of quite distinct, autonomous communities.[74] Although the writers are all from 'Protestant' backgrounds, there are substantial differences between their beliefs, their lives, and their diary writing traditions. It is worth recalling that there was a significant fracture line between the Established Church of Ireland and the Presbyterian community, for example, with the Penal Laws – described by Edmund Burke as a machine 'well fitted for the oppression, impoverishment and degradation of a people' – explicitly excluding both Catholics and Dissenters from participation in the state's framework.[75] Quakers, Methodists, and even ostensibly Anglican Huguenots also occupied a liminal space, adjacent but not quite part of the Anglican confessional state.

The degree to which Irishness was embraced by those outside of a Roman Catholic tradition shifts throughout the century and is informed by a wide spectrum of considerations, from the person's own family circumstances to

72 '[T]he Continent, especially its Catholic states, and still more particularly powerful and proximate France, plays the role of the defining counterpoint, the menacing "Other" that gives Englishness and Britishness meaning.' Stephen Conway, *Britain, Ireland, and Continental Europe in the Eighteenth Century: Similarities, Connections, Identities.* Oxford: OUP, 2011, 2.

73 Moyra Haslett, 'Introduction'. *Irish Literature in Transition, 1700–1780.* Cambridge: CUP, 2020, 4. In the same work, see particularly, Ian Campbell Ross, '"We Irish": Writing and National Identity', 49–67.

74 Lecky mentions an Anabaptist service with hymns, long extempore prayer, songs, and sermons; 'a decenting Chapel' where the sermon had but one flaw, 'that it was an hour & ten minutes long'; and elsewhere 'the first strange Church I received the Sacrament in'. Anon. [Charity Lecky]. Diary of a Winter in Bath, 1796–97. James Marshall and Marie-Louise Osborn Collection, Beinecke Rare Book and Manuscript Library, Yale University, Osborn c446.

75 Edmund Burke's 1792 letter to Hercules Lamgrishe, cited in Michael Brown and Lesa Ní Mhunghaile, 'Enlightenment and Antiquarianism in the Eighteenth Century'. *Cambridge History of Ireland, Volume 3.* Cambridge: CUP, 2018, 381. John Bergin et al., *New Perspectives on the Penal Laws, Eighteenth-Century Ireland* Special Issue 1 (2011): 1–290.

their political beliefs to economic policy or warfare.[76] Irishness was and is an evolving term that is embraced by people from differing religious and ethnic backgrounds. While individual circumstances are paramount, trends are also apparent, and shifts in attitude are particularly noticeable in the final two decades of the eighteenth century. The 1780s and 1790s were marked by outbreaks of unrest and malaise, agrarian riots and outright rebellion, but also by the patriot movement, by significant antiquarian discovery, translation from the Irish language, and a general interest in the history and culture of the Irish past.[77] Many more men and women explicitly identified as Irish, celebrating this aspect of their identity, while others drew upon their family's links to Britain to define their identity and subscribed to an Anglo-Irish Protestant identity.[78] Conversely, not all elite women of this period in Ireland felt their choice was between two such national identities (Irish and English), or even an amalgam of both, as some drew upon a more cosmopolitan or European sense of self. Where an identification exists, what one finds across the diaries is a spectrum of national affiliation, reflecting the fluidity of identity felt amongst the wider society in Ireland and elsewhere. Most common of all, however, is for no mention to be made of national identity in the diaries, with the focus instead being on the denominational, familial, regional, or local, as the source of communal identity, as demonstrated in Chapter 5.

Leinster is overwhelmingly the province with which the diarists are primarily connected across the full corpus of diaries. Co. Louth is particularly well represented, with multiple generations of Jocelyn diarists, but there are also numerous examples extant associated with counties Kildare (the Shackleton family); Kilkenny (Goddard, Ponsonby, and Butler); Longford (the Edgeworth family); and Wicklow (the Tighe family), while most of the diaries include entries written while the diarist was in Dublin and several while they were visiting Wicklow. The remaining provinces have

76 Joep Leerssen's work remains one of the most helpful studies of Irish identity during the long eighteenth century. *Mere Irish and Fíor-Ghael: Studies in the Idea of Irish Nationality, Its Development, and Literary Expression Prior to the Nineteenth Century.* Amsterdam: John Benjamins, 1986.

77 Joel Herman argues for a more inclusive public sphere in 1779 also. Joel Herman, 'Imagined Nations: Newspapers, Identity, and the Free Trade crisis of 1779'. *Eighteenth-Century Ireland* 35 (2020): 51–69. See also Clare O'Halloran, *Golden Ages and Barbarous Nations: Antiquarian Debate and Cultural Politics in Ireland, c.1750–1800.* Cork: Cork UP, 2004; Padhraig Higgins, *A Nation of Politicians: Gender, Patriotism, and Political Culture in Late Eighteenth-Century Ireland.* Wisconsin: University of Wisconsin Press, 2010.

78 Amy Prendergast, *Literary Salons Across Britain and Ireland in the Long Eighteenth Century.* Basingstoke: Palgrave, 2015, 78–131.

seen significantly fewer surviving diaries composed therein, though Co. Tipperary is particularly popular in Munster as the site of composition for the diaries of Mary Mathew (1724–1777), Elizabeth Clibborn, and Dorothea Herbert. The female members of the ffolliott family of Hollybrook House in Co. Sligo are the only Connacht-based diarists in the study, while the short extract from the diary of Arabella Crosbie Ward (1757–1813), of Castle Ward, Co. Down, is one of the few surviving examples of the form that was written in Ulster, though Charity Lecky travelled to England from Co. Derry and Anne Jocelyn frequently writes from the family's Tollymore Estate in Co. Down.[79] The diverse networks that existed within and across these different counties, inevitably reflect the social standing of the diarists. The diarists during this period in Ireland were either from the upper echelons of society, from the aristocracy, or the gentry and middling classes.[80] Writing by women from the lower classes is wholly absent from the surviving corpus of diaries.[81] Literacy was an essential requirement, and all the diarists bar Anne Weldon, née Cooke (1726–1809), display an excellent command of the written word, with modern orthography.[82]

Diary writing was perceived by many from these upper classes as a leisure activity. For others, writing was a crucial element of life and represented a religious duty. Irrespective of this, the diarists were aware of the practical

79 Arabella Ward, Extract from the diary of Lady Arabella Ward, 1804. PRONI D2092/1/10. Castle Ward is now a National Trust property, where Neil Watt is the House and Collections Manager. Tollymore House was demolished in 1952, following a period of dereliction, and the estate became Northern Ireland's first national forest park in 1955. Eileen Battersby, 'The Forest of Nobility'. *The Irish Times*, 11 February 2006.

80 Barnard, *Making the Grand Figure*. See also Rachel Wilson, *Elite Women in Ascendancy Ireland, 1690–1745: Imitation and Innovation*. Woodbridge: Boydell & Brewer, 2015.

81 Tim Murtagh, *Irish Artisans and Radical Politics, 1776–1820*. Liverpool: LUP, 2022, examines Ireland's eighteenth-century [male] workers. Interaction between the diarists and those of a lower class is generally confined to intermittent references to servants, which feature in many of the diaries, with comments such as Mary Anne Dawson's 'Sat with my Mother while Henrietta & the Maid were at Church' and 'my Bro. Richard's Servant arrived', TCD MS 7270 (27/9/1783). For analysis of surviving letters by two Irish domestic servants, see Marie-Louise Coolahan, '"It is with pleasure I lay hold of evry occasion of wrightin": Female Domestic Servants, *The Bordeaux-Dublin Letters*, and the Epistolary Novel'. *Ireland, France and the Atlantic in a Time of War: Reflections on the Bordeaux-Dublin Letters, 1757*. Ed. Thomas M. Truxes. London: Routledge, 2017, 180–93.

82 Anne Weldon's grasp of the English language is considerably poorer than the other diarists surveyed throughout this work, despite her status as daughter of a baronet, Sir Samuel Cooke, and wife of an MP. Anne Cooke Weldon, 'Anne Cooke Diary'. *Journal of the County Kildare Archaeological Society* VIII (1915–1917): 104–32; 205–19; 447–63.

limitations upon the composition of each entry and the possibilities for exposition. When did women write their diaries? Where did they do so?[83] These are questions that present themselves to contemporary readers eager to appreciate the mechanics of the process of diary writing and its implications for understandings of the quotidian. The adolescent Mary Shackleton wryly observes, 'When I am ^in a^ hurry (as I have been since I begun this till now) I just write down what happens, but when I have some leisure as I have now I make remarks – very pertinent to be sure' (22/12/1774). Frequently, the diaries provide information regarding the structure of the individual diarist's usual routine, recording when precisely the diarists wrote and how this activity fitted with their other occupations and activities. In addition to available leisure time, many of the diaries frequently allude to the lack of available space for composition, the latter of which is almost always informed by questions of gender.[84] Anticipating the perennially cited 'room of one's own' desired by Virginia Woolf, herself an avid diarist from the age of 14 onwards, Elizabeth Clibborn is explicit in her regret at not having access to a separate physical space within the home: 'I feel very much the want of a sitting room or quiet apartment to retire from the nursery the continual disturbance at night & noise of the day is too much for my present suffering state...' (12/1/1808).[85] What is evident across the Irish diaries is that privacy and individual determination of location and space were not an automatic entitlement for these diary writers, regardless of elite status or seniority within the family.

The surviving diaries unite the perspectives of both younger and older women, as well as those of middle age, allowing access to cross-generational voices. Though we do not have information on all the diarists' ages, and certainly not their exact dates of birth, by using the data that does exist, we know that the most common age for women to begin a diary in Ireland was 15 years old, with the youngest diarist commencing at 11 and the oldest at 67. Most of the women and girls in the corpus began writing a diary between the ages of 14 and 30. Commencing a diary in one's 30s and 40s was less common, though still took place with some frequency.

---

83 Questions such as these are engagingly explored in the following two works: Dena Goodman, *Becoming a Woman in the Age of Letters*. Ithaca: Cornell UP, 2009; and Amanda Vickery, *Behind Closed Doors in Georgian England*. New Haven: Yale UP, 2009. See also Leonie Hannan, *Women of Letters: Gender, Writing and the Life of the Mind in Early Modern England*. Manchester: MUP, 2016.

84 For example, Mary Leadbeater's diary, NLI MS 9298 (18/12/1774).

85 Elizabeth Clibborn, RSFIHL P9. Virginia Woolf, *A Writer's Diary, Being Extracts from the Diary of Virginia Woolf*. Ed. Leonard Woolf. New York: Harcourt, 1954. The Woolf manuscript diaries are held by New York Public Library. Berg Coll MSS Woolf.

Anne Jocelyn is the only woman over 50 to commence a diary in the survey, for whom dates have survived. Certain preoccupations or themes are discernible when the diarists are considered by the grouping of age. One encounters adolescents preparing for the marriage market; younger wives struggling with pregnancies or nervously anticipating childbirth; mothers concerned with their children's health, inoculations, and sicknesses; and widows lamenting lost husbands and worrying about adult children. One can also recognise patterns regarding form, in terms of the narrative links, tone, and voice embraced by adolescent diarists in particular, whose diaries frequently sparkle with hyperbole and jocularity, and convey a breathless quality.[86] Conversely, Elizabeth Clibborn laments, 'I am thirty years of age, it is an awful consideration, even if it should be a long life the prime is over' (29/12/1810). The state of middle age is explicitly defined by Elinor Goddard as: 'my time of life, when past the prime of it, and not yet enter'd into the infirmities of age' (6/12/1778).[87] Goddard was very interested in medicine and used the diary form to record her state of mental health, noting feeling dull and dissatisfied with herself at times, or fretful and despondent at others. Indeed, the form is used as a platform for better mental health across all age groups, representing a particularly notable unifying factor. The various diaries offer us women's accounts of their emotional states, including their recorded experiences of anxiety and bereavement, for example.

Perennially defined by eighteenth-century society in terms of their relationship with other family members – whether parents, husbands, or children – the diarists represent women navigating available familial definitions. Married women composed the majority of those diaries written by adults. Indeed, the diaries of Mary Mathew and Dorothea Herbert are the only ones composed by unmarried women of middle age, apart from those maintained by the couple Sarah Ponsonby and Eleanor Butler, who moved to Wales to secure their lifelong relationship.[88] Adolecent diarists

86 See Chapter 2.
87 Elinor Goddard, Mrs Elinor Goddard: Journal (1774–1778). NLW 22993A. Consulted on microfilm, NLI POS 9617.
88 Butler and Ponsonby are the only example of a same-sex couple among the diarists. Their relationship prompted great speculation both during and after their lifetime, including from Anne Lister, whose own diaries (1806–1840) chart her lesbian relationships in nineteenth-century England, concealed through difficult handwriting and the use of an esoteric code: 'my peculiar handwrit[in]g and wh[a]t I call crypthand – I ment[ione]d the alm[o]st imposs[ibilit]y of its being decypher[e]d' (16/8/1819). Diary of Anne Lister of Shibden Hall, 11 April 1819 to 22 November 1819. West Yorkshire Archive Service, Calderdale, SH:7/ML/E/3. I have not observed a comparable code in any of the Irish diaries. The diaries of Butler and Ponsonby, as is the case with their heterosexual peers in Ireland, focus on the couple's love and friendship for one another

anticipate an eventual marriage, with descriptions of weddings featuring alongside disparaging references to old maids. Some diarists married during the course of their diary writing, as was the case for Tighe, Leadbeater, and Elizabeth Stirum, née Richards (1778–1863), while Frances Jocelyn ceased her entries immediately prior to her marriage to Lord Powerscourt. The age of marriage ranges over some 20 years, with Frances Jocelyn and Melesina Trench married at 18, while Marianne ffolliott is the oldest bride at 38. The average age for the diarists to marry was 25. Unhappy Irish marriages have been recorded in other sources, but the surviving diaries do not disparage husbands and present either a portrait of happy married life or do not overtly allude to the state.[89] For many, such as Anne Jocelyn, their identity was happily bound up with their status as wife. Anne struggled intensely with grief following the passing of her husband, and her discomfort with her new identity is etched upon almost every entry. Her widowhood prompted the composition of the diary itself, as was the case for Theodosia Blachford, with both women embracing the form to manage their grief and navigate their new identity as widows.

The diaries showcase the intertwined nature of marriage and childbearing, with the latter seen as the logical culmination of the former. Disapproval was meted out to those who did not comply. Elinor Goddard's diary records an acquaintance belittling her, 'saying that a man could not love, nay must be disgusted by, a wife that he had no children by' (29/10/1777).[90] The diary does not make clear the circumstances which led to the absence of children in this marriage, but the impact on Goddard of this denigrating comment is deeply felt, with the diarist noting in the same entry that, 'his indelicacy to me a few hours before stuck in my stomach'. The association between women as wives and as bearers of children was universally held and motherhood is an aspect of identity navigated with difficulty by many. Often silenced from polite conversation, issues of fertility, miscarriage, and infant mortality find a space for discussion in the diaries, and the women's written responses to such difficult events are scattered throughout many of the surviving diaries and considered at length in Chapter 4. In addition to their classification as mothers or wives by both male and female peers, there is a clear sense of *self*-identification as mother being embraced positively by several diarists. The espousal of 'mother' as predominant descriptor is evident in several diaries, with diarists such as Mary Anne Fortescue embracing the

rather than on sex and sexuality. See 'The Ladies of Llangollen'. *The British Museum*. https://www.britishmuseum.org/collection/desire-love-and-identity/ladies-llangollen.

89 See Mary O'Dowd and Maria Luddy, *Marriage in Ireland, 1660–1925*. Cambridge: CUP, 2020.

90 Goddard NLW 22993A/NLI POS 9617.

appelation and foregrounding that aspect of their lives. Almost every entry in Mary Anne's diary serves to record the good health or otherwise of her husband and children, with repeated instances of the phrase, 'Fortescue & the children well thank God'.[91]

As with all aspects of identity, nuance is key, and maternal or spousal identity should be understood as fluid. Often an individual entry is far from representative of a diary as a whole, though it can be a true representation of the diarist's sense of self on the day in question. The diary of Elizabeth Stirum, née Richards, represents a case in point. Her exclamation that there is 'only true happiness when with children and their father' must be examined and considered in relation to coexisting expressions regarding the difficulties in existing solely or even primarily as a wife and mother.[92] Childcare is appreciated by Stirum in enabling a positive spousal relationship as well as allowing the possibility of personal autonomy: 'My mother took Eliza, Frederick and Thomas. When Theodora and Menno were Asleep, Stirum read French aloud whilst I worked. This reminded me of "halcyon days"' (4/7/1808).[93] Such examples remind us of the dangers of analysing diary entries in isolation.

The myriad references to positive marital relationships showcased in the diaries exist alongside a more sinister external male presence, one which is often only hinted at. All the diarists are affected by the realities of a patriarchal society, and several diaries also contain instances of abuse, female vulnerability, assault, non-consensual touch, and male pursuit. Diaries were embraced by both men and women for a multitude of purposes, but the ways in which the diary form served as a platform for the recording of such instances of abuse, as testimony of challenges faced and injustices suffered due to gender, set the women's diaries apart. In her study of English women's diaries, Harriet Blodgett argued that diaries allowed a woman to 'compensate for societal devaluation' and 'enable[d] her to sustain her sense of selfhood', and this applies to the diaries from Ireland too.[94] Men from Ireland frequently composed diaries too, and this was certainly not

91 Mary Anne Fortescue, 'The Diary of Marianne Fortescue, 1797–1800'. Ed. Noel Ross. *Journal of the County Louth Archaeological Society* 24.2–3 (1998): 222–48; (1999): 357–79. As the first entry of the latter is signed, 'I began this Journal on Wednesday the 18th of October 1797 M. A. Fortescue', my preference throughout has been for the use of Mary Anne rather than Marianne.

92 Elizabeth Richards, *The Diary of Elizabeth Richards (1798– 1825): From the Wexford Rebellion to Family Life in the Netherlands*. Ed. Marie de Jong-Ijsselstein. Intro. Kevin Whelan. Hilversum: Verloren, 1999, 68.

93 Richards 63.

94 Harriet Blodgett, *Centuries of Female Days: Englishwomen's Private Diaries*. New Brunswick: Rutgers UP, 1988, 89.

an entirely different phenomenon, though their entries generally present less of a focus on the intricacies of life within the home and instead chart their fuller participation in the associational life available to those of their gender.[95] However, for eighteenth-century women, who did not have access to a variety of public platforms and other forms of expression, the diaries often afforded them an *exclusive* way of communicating with posterity, as well as providing them with a means of processing emotions and offering testimony.

2. '[B]urn unread everything which I leave behind in the form of a diary': Diary Survival and Transmission

Although diverse and wide-ranging, the many diaries that comprise the focus of this study are representative only of those that have managed to survive into the twenty-first century. The transmission of such documents was one fraught with neglect and derision, and diaries were always among the most vulnerable in a family's papers. The artist Caroline Hamilton's reflections on her cousin, the poet and author Mary Tighe's propensity for journal-keeping offer an indication of the diary form's textual vulnerability:

> She was always in the habit of writing a journal, which was a practise recommended by her mother but tho' it gave a fluency to her style, it only gave her survivors the painful trouble of burning it as it contained only the trifling adventures of a gay life.[96]

One can only speculate on the nature, tone, contents, and indeed number of diaries that were lost in this way, but it seems likely that Tighe's journal was one of many that was destroyed by family members who judged the documents either too inflammatory, too immodest, or too insignificant to be preserved.[97] Despite the above implication that all her diary be consigned to

---

95 In addition to those diaries already cited in 1.2 see, for example, the diaries (composed intermittently in 1768–1791) of William Stacpoole (1743–1796) of Eden Vale, Co. Clare, which chart Stacpoole's adventures on the Continent, as well as his presence at the Ennis assizes, Dublin Castle, the theatre, coffee houses, and a variety of taverns. William Stacpoole, 'The Diary of an Eighteenth-Century Clare Gentleman'. Ed. Leo F. McNamara. *North Munster Antiquarian Journal* 23 (1981): 25–65. The diary does also record details of domestic staff hired and fired, his wedding day, his children's christenings, and the death of his first wife Dorothea Burton, 'the most loving & affectionate wife' (2/11/1775).

96 Caroline Hamilton on 'Mary Tighe'. Mary Tighe, *The Collected Poems and Journals of Mary Tighe*, 258.

97 Notes by Margaret Anne Harvey on the diary of her mother, Margaret Boyle

the flames, those portions that reflected a religious character and dedication to her faith were deemed acceptable for preservation by Tighe's mother, the devout Theodosia Blachford, by then a committed Methodist, and were for a long time thought to be the only sections of Tighe's diaries that did survive.[98] Such selections and decisions offer an indication of what different family members deemed worthy of preservation at a particular moment and reflect the family's own priorities, values, and interests, rather than necessarily those of the individual diarist.

The vast majority of the diary of a second Irish Romantic poet, Eliza Hamilton (1807–1851), was also destroyed by an immediate family member. The poet's brother, the scientist William Hamilton, mutilated her writing, destroying all but the section that mentioned the poet William Wordsworth's visit to their observatory, thus ensuring the account of that affiliation was preserved.[99] Certain wills provide evidence that occasionally it was the diarists themselves who instructed that their diaries be eradicated upon their demise, ensuring their private writings did not circulate freely. The codicil to the will of Letitia Townley Balfour (1746–1838), for example, instructed executors to 'burn unread everything which I leave behind in the form of a diary especially four or five volumes of such, which are in my bedroom'.[100] Such actions echo the earlier destruction of spiritual diaries and sin lists by men and women who did not wish their catalogue of misdemeanours to be discovered and read by others.[101]

It is difficult to determine how many Irish manuscript diaries were removed from the records. Those that have survived are scattered across a variety of repositories. Most Irish manuscript diaries have been preserved in two of the national repositories in Ireland, namely the National Library of Ireland and the Public Record Office of Northern Ireland. Following

Harvey, transcribed in the early twentieth century by the next generation, state, 'She kept a journal on her way home at sea, but it was burnt with some other loose papers, some years ago, by a family who was ignorant of its value'. Margaret Boyle Harvey, Journal 1809–1812, RSFIHL P10.

98 Harriet Kramer Linkin has since unearthed additional diary material preserved amongst the Hamilton family papers at the NLI, including NLI MS 38,639/1/14–20. See Harriet Kramer Linkin, 'Mary Tighe's Newly Discovered Letters and Journals to Caroline Hamilton'. *Romanticism* 21.3 (2015): 207–27.

99 Adriana Craciun, 'Eliza Mary Hamilton.' *Irish Women Poets of the Romantic Period*. Alexandria, VA: Alexander Street Press, 2008.

100 Codicil to will of Letitia Townley Balfour, 23 May 1837, Townley Hall Papers, NLI D15,133–D15,178. With thanks to Ruth Thorpe for this reference. See Ruth Thorpe, 'Elite Women and Material Culture in Ireland, 1760–1830'. PhD Thesis, QUB, 2017.

101 Ryrie 299.

her decades-long residence in Llangollen, Eleanor Butler's diaries have been preserved in the National Library of Wales. Several of the diaries also found their way into university collections in Ireland, with examples in the collections at Trinity College Dublin and Queen's University Belfast. The Beinecke Rare Book and Manuscript Library at Yale University and the Houghton Library at Harvard University also hold diaries in their Irish collections.[102] Local libraries and record offices in Ireland and the UK also have examples, with the Hampshire Record Office in possession of Melesina Trench's multiple diaries. The Religious Society of Friends in Ireland Historical Library in South County Dublin has preserved the writings of the various Quaker diarists, with the exception of the 54 volumes of Mary Shackleton Leadbeater, held by the NLI. Finally, some of the manuscript diaries are still in family possession, while others exist only as manuscript or typescript copies within the repository. There is evidence of at least one woman's diary having been lost in the destruction of the Irish Public Record Office during the Civil War in 1922. This was the diary (1721–1774) of Katherine Bayly, née Morley, whose writing was initially preserved due to her having been married to an official in the Treasury.[103] Issues of provenance and custodial history are always important in dealing with such archival material, and there is still much that is unknown regarding the diaries' immediate post-history, such as how did they arrive in the individual repository? And, particularly pertinent to the above discussions, who valued the manuscript diaries and preserved them?

Cataloguing itself plays a role in aiding and abetting a project such as this. Far from being a neutral activity, archival descriptions often gesture towards the values of the archivist themselves. We should bear in mind that 'many records are consciously created for audiences which may not be immediately apparent'.[104] Until more recent decades, women's life writing did not represent a priority for researchers, librarians, or family archivists generally. One consequence of this is that diaries often existed unknown and uncatalogued amidst a family's papers. They were sometimes included alongside writing classified as 'verse and worse', or a female family member's 'personal writings', which could be an un-itemised bundle of letters, accounts,

102 I would like to acknowledge the support of the A. C. Elias, Jr. Irish-American Research Travel Fellowship in facilitating research in these libraries in the USA.
103 Ciarán Wallace, 'Katherine Bayly and her Daughters: Dublin 1753–1772'. *Beyond 2022 | Ireland's Virtual Record Treasury*. https://shorturl.at/U8Q0B. H. F. Berry, 'Notes from the Diary of a Dublin Lady [Katharine Bayly] in the Reign of George II'. *The Journal of the Royal Society of Antiquaries of Ireland* 8.2 (1898): 141–54.
104 Adrian Cunningham, 'The Mysterious Outside Reader,' *Archives and Manuscripts* 24.1 (1996), 133–34, cited in Beattie 91.

scrapbooks, poetry, and inventories, for instance, requiring much time to unravel. Worse still is the indicator 'other', which can encompass centuries of women's undated writings and may or may not include diaries. Conversely, where women's diaries were catalogued, they were frequently attributed to the wrong person. New methods and sensitivities have transformed the possibilities for research in the field of life writing, with attention now widely paid to issues of gender, inclusivity, and accessibility. The implications of the global pandemic of 2020, and the need to work remotely and in new ways, have also increased certain repositories' cataloguing capabilities and priorities, and additional sources have been coming to the fore, with helpful descriptors added to collection guides and databases since this project began.

The chances of a diary's physical survival are also impacted by the material reality of the text. Many of the manuscript diaries from Ireland epitomise fragility and ephemerality. Unlike the six-volume, calf-bound, gold-embossed *Thraliana* – the diary and observations of Hester Lynch Thrale Piozzi – or the diary of Elizabeth Mordaunt, 'originally bound in vellum and closed with a silver lock', many of the diaries considered here are made up simply of an amalgam of loose sheets, as is the case with Theodosia Blachford's diary.[105] Mary Shackleton Leadbeater's comments on one of her diaries for the year 1774 offer an indication of this fragility: 'I have not cover for my journal & if I do not get one soon it will be worn out I am afraid, *& oh what a sad thing that would be* [diarist's own emphasis].'[106] Many of Mary's later diaries were instead proudly begun in pocket books gifted to her for that purpose. Similarly, pre-bound blank paper books were popular for use as diaries, as well as serving as the material for commonplace books, compilations, and albums.[107] Harriet Skeffington's diary was written in a small notebook, whose frontispiece features a blank printed account for Robert Douglas, Douglas Inn, Castle Douglas.[108] Mary Mathew's diary appears half-way through a large folio containing other forms of life writing by her, including recipes and accounts.[109] Other diarists had to make do with documents that had been repurposed from other texts, such as the incomplete account books of family members: the inverse of the diary of the young Letitia Galloway (dates unknown) for example, shows it was

---

105 Hester Lynch Piozzi, Thraliana, 1776–1809. Huntington Library, California, HM 12183. Mordaunt 1.
106 NLI MS 9297.
107 Michelle Levy and Betty A. Schellenberg, *How and Why to Do Things with Eighteenth-Century Manuscripts*. Cambridge: CUP, 2021, 9.
108 Harriet Skeffington, Diary, 5–25 June 1798. QUB MS1/206.
109 Mary Mathew, Cookery recipes, household accounts and diary by Mary Mathew, 1741–1777. NLI MS 5102.

originally intended as an account of her brother, John Galloway's expenses.[110] These factors impact upon the space for diary composition and can guide or frame the diarist's individual entries, allowing them room to reflect, or causing the compression of entries. Such considerations can be unintentionally overlooked when the diaries are only accessed in published form.

The reasons certain diaries were initially chosen for publication are wide-ranging and again reflect the evolving attitudes of both families and scholars over the intervening decades and centuries. Inevitably, as with those manuscript diaries that were preserved – either within private collections and muniment rooms or in public repositories – early publication decisions overlapped substantially with the recognition, or not, of a diary's public value by family members. Subsequent generations frequently privileged the preservation and publication of those diaries that recorded details about events over those reflecting upon the self and private activities. This was true in the case of many 1798 diaries, for example.[111] The survival of so many diaries describing the Rebellion of that year is almost certainly owing to these diaries' being awarded value due to their role in recording an event of both historical and socio-cultural importance. It seems a diary was much more likely to survive – and possibly then make its way into print – if it privileged the public over the private, or the social world over the interior world of the self. Beyond the eighteenth-century tradition of publication of spiritual diaries by Methodists and Quakers, a rough trajectory of the publication history of Irish diaries sees an initial selection of ostensibly appropriate material set down by the diarist's descendants in the nineteenth century, celebrating the family's earlier activities and achievements; the printing in journals and small editions of diaries reflecting on local history by historical or archaeological societies, such as those in Co. Louth and Co. Kildare in the twentieth century; and a late twentieth and early twenty-first century recuperation of diaries by women in particular, encouraged by a feminist drive for recovery.[112]

Publication increased the reach of these diaries, making them accessible to swathes of new audiences. However, it should be borne in mind that

110 Letitia Galloway, Diary of Letitia Galloway, NLI MS 32,517.

111 See, for example, the anthology edited by John D. Beatty, which includes extracts from several diaries, *Protestant Women's Narratives of the Irish Rebellion of 1798*. Dublin: Four Courts Press, 2001.

112 For example, Melesina Chenevix St. George Trench, *Journal Kept During a Visit to Germany in 1799, 1800*. Ed. Dean of Westminster. 1861. N.p.; Mary Anne Fortescue, 'The Diary of Marianne Fortescue, 1797–1800'; Dorothea Herbert, *Introspections: The Poetry & Private World of Dorothea Herbert*. Ed. Frances Finnegan. Kilkenny: Congrave Press, 2011; Mary Mathew, *The Diary of Mary Mathew*. Ed. Maria Luddy. Thurles: Co. Tipperary Historical Society, 1991.

comparisons between manuscript diaries and nineteenth- and earlier twenti-eth-century printed editions frequently reveal a difference in content, both domestic and public, with editorial jettisoning of many topics deemed overly sensitive or personal, echoing the destruction or mutilation of manuscript diaries, discussed above. My own research methods place a large emphasis on text and paratext through the prioritisation of manuscript diaries, promoting a focus on the original handwritten diary where it still survives. In addition to ensuring greater representation of original content, my emphasis on manuscript sources draws attention to the innovation and experimentation inherent in the form, as well as offering internal evidence regarding questions of audience, readership, diary writing, and editorial practices, all key for understanding authorship at this time, through inclusion of paratexts.[113]

The terms 'diary' and 'journal' themselves are both employed in the twenty-first century to describe and analyse these multipurpose works. They tend to be used interchangeably and are understood to imply the same form.[114] Indeed, Kathryn Carter has argued that distinctions between the terms are 'spurious and arbitrary', concluding that 'attempts at categorisation prove fruitless'.[115] The majority of the eighteenth-century diarists from Ireland do in fact use the term 'journal' when referencing their own writing. However, 'diary' is a more practical choice when alluding to such works now. It immediately communicates its meaning to an audience and allows one to distinguish the form from periodicals. So, while the terms can and will be used interchangeably, preference will be for 'diary' throughout.

Diaries are of course just one instance of life writing – that is, non-fiction writing that recounts the life or memories of one person or a small group of people – alongside many other forms, from the more established letters and memoirs to recipe books, accounts, confessions, and testimonies.[116] Indeed, Angela Byrne has recently argued persuasively for the inclusion of poetry in

---

113 See Chapter 1.

114 For an opposing view see, Yáñez-Bouza who separates journals and diaries by register. Nuria Yáñez-Bouza, "'Have you ever written a diary or a journal?' Diurnal Prose and Register Variation'. *Neuphilologische Mitteilungen* 116.2 (2015): 449–74. The *OED* offers the first example of 'diary' being used as 'a daily record of events or transactions, a journal' in 1581, and of 'journal' as 'a daily record of events or occurrences kept for private or official use' in 1610, with a distinction being made with the latter 'now usually implying something more elaborate than a diary'.

115 Kathryn Carter, *The Small Details of Life: 20 Diaries by Women in Canada, 1830–1996*. Toronto: University of Toronto Press, 2002, 7–8.

116 Chris Baldick, 'Life Writing'. *Oxford Dictionary of Literary Terms*, 4th ed. Oxford: OUP, 2015. See Amy Culley, *British Women's Life Writing, 1760–1840, Friendship, Community and Collaboration*. Basingstoke: Palgrave, 2014. For a helpful overview of women's letters from Ireland, see Jane Maxwell, 'The Personal Letter as a Source for

our understanding of life writing.[117] Diaries can be relatively easily isolated from all these as a focus of study. However, there are several instances of works that have been categorised and continue to be referred to as diaries that will only feature tenuously in this study. Exclusions include what I term *pseudo-diaries*, that is, memoirs presented as diaries, with individual entry descriptions of days written retrospectively after a significant or prolonged period of time. This is an especially common approach when pertaining to traumatic events, such as the 1798 Rebellion or the Napoleonic Wars.[118] The life writing of Barbara Lett and Dinah Goff, which both recall the 1798 Rebellion are good examples of this.[119] Both texts represent recollections of the 1790s during the 1850s, and yet both are sometimes referred to as diaries.[120] *Letter-journals*, by which I mean serial entries describing each day, intended for a named recipient to whom they are sent at intervals, have also been excluded. They are in fact frequently based on an actual, separate diary, as the following example from author Elizabeth Sheridan to her older sister Alicia Le Fanu makes clear: 'I sent you a few lines tuesday [23rd May] meerly that you might not think us lost. At present I am more myself and so devote my first hour to you, as to my little bit of journal I have put up so carefully that I can not find it but I will give the best account of myself I can' (1/6/1786).[121] *Subject-specific diaries* have also been largely omitted. These include, but are not limited to, travel diaries, nature diaries, and weather diaries.[122] These have set limitations rather than encompassing all aspects of

the History of Women in Ireland, 1750–1830'. PhD Thesis, TCD, 2016, which assesses marital letters and letters by children, among other categories.

117 Angela Byrne, 'Life Lines: Agency and Autobiography in Sarah Curran's Poetry'. *Women's History Review* 32.1 (2023): 126–41.

118 See Frances Burney's 'Waterloo journal', for example, written in 1823.

119 Barbara Newton Lett, 'A '98 Diary by Mrs. Barbara Newton Lett, Killaligan, Enniscorthy'. *The Past: The Organ of the Uí Cinsealaigh Historical Society* 5 (1949): 117–78; Dinah Goff, *Divine Protection Through Extraordinary Dangers During the Irish Rebellion in 1798*. Philadelphia, 1890.

120 See, for example, Helen Elizabeth Hatton, *Largest Amount of Good: Quaker Relief in Ireland, 1654-1921*. Montreal: McGill-Queen's Press, 1993, 39–40; and Kevin Whelan, 'Introduction'. Richards 12.

121 Elizabeth Sheridan, *Betsy Sheridan's Journal*. Ed. William Le Fanu. Oxford: OUP, 1986, 84.

122 Important travel journals were kept by various members of the Beaufort family, including Louisa Beaufort (1781–1863), her mother Mary Beaufort, née Waller (1739–1831), and her father Daniel Augustus (1739–1821), an Anglican clergyman of Huguenot descent. These are held by TCD. For travel diaries by the Wilmot sisters, held by the Royal Irish Academy, see Angela Byrne, 'Supplementing the Autobiography of Princess Ekaterina Romanovna Dashkova: The Russian Diaries of Martha and Katherine Wilmot'. *Irish Slavonic Studies* 23 (2011): 25–34. For insightful work on

daily life. However, spiritual journals are addressed in Chapter 4 and will feature intermittently throughout this study, although the primary focus is explicitly on secular diaries.

The study begins by emphasising the materiality of the diary, showcasing the innovation and experimentation inherent in women's diaries and foregrounding questions of audience. Paratextual apparatus is examined, from title pages to corrections, additions, and marginalia, alongside authorial attention to presentation, historical contextualisation, and the employment of various textual strategies to communicate with different readers. Chapter 1 teases out the literary aspirations of those diarists who sought a large audience, but did not achieve fame, such as Elizabeth Edgeworth. It also examines recognised diarist-authors, reflecting upon the diaries of Mary Leadbeater, for example, as well as those of the poet Melesina Trench. Authority and agency are integrated as points of emphasis throughout. The role of diaries in shaping a family's narrative and legacy is considered, highlighting connections between diaries, the writing of history – whether family or public – and female authority.

Focusing on the diaries of several young women and girls, including Mary Anne Dawson, Charity Lecky, and Frances Jocelyn, Chapter 2 offers a better understanding of the individual's perception of the lived experience of youth in the eighteenth century. The chapter engages with young women's anxieties and preoccupations, offering arguments for continuities with today's ideas of adolescence. It focuses on how these young women and girls constructed a narrative voice for themselves, often emulating those found in novels. An examination of the parallels and continuities with sentimental, picaresque, and epistolary novels is undertaken. Key parallels in expression and style are identified across the diaries – for example hyperbole, sensibility, and the use of superlatives – offering a sense of the style preferred by young people. Adolescence is the overarching emphasis, and the chapter considers the diarists' portrayal of such instances and events as conflict with parental figures; intense friendship; courtship and flirting; and the young diarists' navigation and preparation for marriage and/or the marriage market. It demonstrates how young women and girls use diaries to navigate this transitional period from childhood to adulthood.

Chapter 3 takes as its point of departure marital, familial, and gender violence. All the diaries relate instances of women's limited options, curtailed movements, general vulnerability, and frequent lack of agency, while several also note women being violently pursued or receiving unwanted sexual

officers' diaries and campaign journals, see Catriona Kennedy, *Narratives of the Revolutionary and Napoleonic Wars. Military and Civilian Experience in Britain and Ireland.* Basingstoke: Palgrave, 2013.

attention, as in the case of Sarah Ponsonby. Many of these writers did not have an available vocabulary with which to vocalise experiences of non-consensual touch, and diarists often turned to imaginative literature to make sense of their experiences and to communicate them. This chapter examines how diarists drew upon both the Gothic tradition and amatory fiction or so-called seduction narratives in order to vocalise their experiences of a patriarchal world in which assault, abduction, incarceration, and rape were frequent events, drawing particular attention to the diaries of Dorothea Herbert and Marianne ffolliott. It investigates how women frame their experiences and present their diaries in response to different challenges, as well as recognising their own occasional internalisation of various misogynistic tropes.

Exploring how we might consider diaries as an unfamiliar aspect of the widespread eighteenth-century ethic of improvement, Chapter 4 demonstrates how various female diarists drew upon but challenged the discourse of improvement and contributed to a larger tradition of improvement writing. Actively inserting themselves into a greater cultural conversation, the entries reveal diarists striving for autonomous self-improvement to achieve both better public and private outcomes, and the diaries of women such as Anne Jocelyn and Mary Mathew show the intersections that existed across spiritual, emotional, moral, and intellectual dimensions of improvement of the self. The chapter also allows us to reimagine the landscape of mental health and wellbeing in the long eighteenth century, which is intertwined with the ethos of self-improvement espoused within the diary form. The manner in which these eighteenth-century women employed their diaries to manage anxiety and reduce stress reveals a centuries-old tradition of using diaries in a bid to achieve better mental health.

Chapter 5, the final chapter, explores and dissects aspects of the physical landscapes the different women inhabited, as well as the curated landscapes and abstract homelands they created within their diaries, reflecting on questions of place, community, and identity, and considering how the diarists both responded to and shaped their environments. It highlights how the diarists drew on the language and traditions of the sublime, the classical pastoral, and topographical poetry to convey the landscape unfolding before them and to conceal certain elements and people from view, with almost no allusion in the diaries to the sufferings and hardships experienced by the rural poor, for instance. Focusing on the diaries of Frances Jocelyn and Letitia Galloway in particular, the chapter explores the paradoxes inherent in the diarists' simultaneous celebration of the ecological majesty of waterfalls and rivers alongside the steadfast commitment to an ethos of improvement that sought to tame and civilise evidence of wildness, ultimately in order to lessen Irish difference. Incorporating different voices, opinions, and evocations of place, the chapter reflects on how we can better understand the self, informed by ideas of community and communal identity.

In addition to the Irish perspective, the diaries are also considered within a broader European Enlightenment context, one that encouraged self-reflection and introspection. We see the Irish diaries providing examples of how these writers participated in larger intellectual debates and discourses, and how their musings allowed them to constitute themselves not only in relation to Ireland, but to the wider world. Many of the diarists writing within homes in Ireland viewed themselves as distinctly cosmopolitan. Their actions and writings echo and inform developments taking place across Europe, particularly with regards to sensibility and philanthropy, as the mid-eighteenth century witnessed an increased emphasis on emotional responses to events and situations. These Irish diaries also contributed to and shaped Enlightenment discourse, and the project offers a strong challenge to the exclusion of Irish women from modern scholarship around the Enlightenment. By reinserting life writing into considerations of Enlightenment discourse, we get a more encompassing sense of women's involvement and of their intellectual capacity. Exclusion of manuscript material, including diaries, alters our understanding of Enlightenment output and participants.[123] The diarists frequently committed many of their reflections on current debates, literary musings, and recordings of encounters with recognised Enlightenment figures to their diaries, while individual entries showcase instances of engagement with discourse surrounding Enlightenment strands of thought, such as improvement.

Diaries written by women were neglected for much of the twentieth century and, until fairly recently, had been almost wholly absent from literary analysis.[124] However, projects of literary recovery and a vibrant interest in women's writing means that this is no longer the case. Indeed, given the contemporary world's fascination with ideas of self-presentation and curation, there has been an upsurge of scholarly research devoted to life writing in recent years. Both Europe and North America have witnessed a rejuvenation of the field, with the production of articles, editions, and anthologies on the subject, as well as the receipt of funding for large-scale research projects.[125] With the notable exception of Harriet Blodgett's

---

123 The source material for Michael Brown's influential *The Irish Enlightenment* (2016) is explicitly printed primary, with support from an extensive catalogue of secondary material. The exclusion of archival material, and life writing in particular, has a larger impact on the monograph's engagement with both gender and network theory, and is perhaps one reason why so few women feature in the study.
124 Doll and Munns 9–22.
125 For example, *European Journal of Life Writing*, established 2012; 'RECIRC, The

sweeping transhistorical work, which showed continuities in British diaries from the seventeenth to the twentieth century, the majority of studies on diaries have taken the form of edited collections and individual articles rather than monographs, perhaps owing to the scale of sources, which can appear overwhelming.[126] In contrast to the multi-contributor works, there have also been numerous single diary studies, published by smaller presses. These tend to be local case studies that are aimed at heritage groups rather than an academic market.[127] Strong comparative work has also been done by Magdalena Ożarska and Barbara Hughes, who offer case studies focusing on the diaries of three British and two Irish diarists respectively.[128] The core research on diaries remains that body of work undertaken by Philippe Lejeune, focusing on French diary writing.[129] Seminal work, representing a full career's commitment to life writing, its arguments now appear in need of some revision, particularly in terms of sexuality and gender. In addition to integrating methodologies and approaches from literary criticism and social

Reception and Circulation of Early Modern Women's Writing, 1550–1700', ERC project led by Marie-Louise Coolahan at University of Galway; 'Ego-Media: The Impact of New Media on Forms and Practices of Self-Presentation', ERC project at King's College London (KCL); Lucia Boldrini and Julia Novak, eds. *Experiments in Life Writing*. Basingstoke: Palgrave, 2017; Francoise Simonet-Tenant, 'À la recherche des prémices d'une culture de l'intime'. *Itinéraires* (2009): 39–62; Desirée Henderson, 'Reading Digitized Diaries: Privacy and the Digital Life-Writing Archive'. *Auto/Biography Studies* 33.1 (2018): 157–74. See also the second edition of the landmark Sidonie Smith and Julia Watson, *Reading Autobiography: A Guide for Interpreting Life Narratives*. Minneapolis: University of Minnesota Press, 2001. 2nd ed. 2010.

126 Particularly influential editions on life writing in Britain and Ireland include Julie A. Eckerle and Naomi McAreavey, *Women's Life Writing & Early Modern Ireland*. Lincoln: University of Nebraska Press, 2019; Liam Harte, ed. *A History of Irish Autobiography*. Cambridge: CUP, 2018; Amy Culley and Daniel Cook, eds. *Women's Life Writing, 1700–1850: Gender, Genre and Authorship*. Basingstoke: Palgrave, 2012; Michelle M. Dowd and Julie A. Eckerle, *Genre and Women's Life Writing in Early Modern England*. London: Routledge, 2007.

127 Mary Hardy, *The Diary of Mary Hardy 1773–1809*. Ed. Margaret Bird. Kingston upon Thames: Burnham Press, 2013; Sarah Hurst, *The Diaries of Sarah Hurst, 1759–1762: Life and Love in Eighteenth-Century Horsham*. Ed. Susan C. Djabri. Stroud: Amberley Publishing, 2009.

128 Ożarska. Barbara Hughes, *Between Literature and History: The Diaries and Memoirs of Dorothea Herbert and Mary Leadbeater*. Bern: Peter Lang, 2010.

129 See for instance, Philippe Lejeune, *On Diary*. Ed. Jeremy D. Popkin and Julie Rak. Honolulu: University of Hawaii, 2009 and *Aux Origines du Journal Personnel: France, 1750–1815*. Paris: Honoré Champion, 2016. Lejeune has been described as 'arguably the preeminent life writing theorist in the world'. Jelena Lakūs and Anita Bajić, 'Interpreting Diaries: History of Reading and the Diary of the Nineteenth-Century Croatian Female Writer Dragojla Jarnević'. *Information & Culture* 52.2 (2017): 177.

and cultural history, this monograph aims to shed new light on the diary form by also incorporating emerging ideas and theoretical frameworks from across gender studies, ecocriticism, and mental health studies.

The surviving diaries showcase women in Ireland's engagement with a developing form that allowed them to explore their subjectivity and to experiment with their presentation of self. This corpus of Irish diaries permits the emergence of new perspectives on the self during the period, providing us with fresh insights and provoking a range of questions – what patterns or distinctions can be identified within and across generations in the construction of the female self, for instance, or what is the significance and impact of an overriding sense of communal, collective identity? The diaries demonstrate the creativity and literary capabilities of a host of women from Ireland. These 'bagatelles' should be treated as literary works that influenced and were influenced by the wider cultures of reading and writing, underlining the generic fluidity at play. They contain many carefully crafted entries, written in a style that is often remarkable and frequently striking. The content of these diaries prompts a re-evaluation of the very contours of Irish writing and what we consider as literature, while allowing us to rediscover the importance of manuscripts to our explorations of literary culture.

CHAPTER ONE

The Diarist as Author

Literary Aspirations, Audiences, and Legacies

Initially connected with spiritual reflections and the confessional mode, the eighteenth-century diary was generally deemed a permissible literary form for young women. Indeed, when presented as an explicitly private interest, as a project of introspection and self-improvement, the diary was frequently depicted as a positive domestic pursuit for the elite or a spiritual tool for the devout.[1] Unconnected with publication or the public sphere, a young woman could scribble thoughts in her leisure time without attracting more than idle mockery for her supposed frivolity. However, the presence of a glossary or prefatory material in a diary makes it clear that a public was sometimes anticipated, an audience clearly envisaged, and the text conceived of as potentially a public document. A survey of the surviving Irish diaries demonstrates that an audience was frequently intended, particularly a future or posthumous one. None of the Irish diaries were published in the lifetime of the diarists, though various ones have since appeared in print, from the nineteenth century onwards. While several of the diarists explicitly name and address a reader, whether a specific family member or unknown descendant, other diarists were more subtle in their quest for posterity, and all the diaries require close analysis and interpretation to fully understand both the literary aspirations of the individual diarist and their intended audience.

There is a large emphasis on the materiality of the diary in this chapter, and a focus on the original manuscript diaries draws attention to the innovation and experimentation inherent in women's diary writing from Ireland, including the creativity displayed in some of the detailed title

---

1 Felicity Nussbaum, 'Eighteenth-Century Women's Autobiographical Commonplaces'. *The Private Self: Theory and Practice of Women's Autobiographical Writings*. Ed. Shari Benstock. Chapel Hill: University of North Carolina Press, 1988, 147–72. See also Chapter 4.

pages. The insertion of paratextual apparatus within a diary, from glossaries to corrections, additions, and marginalia, offers us evidence of an implied audience. Engaging with manuscript sources and exploring the diaries' paratexts helps us better understand life writing's connections with the individual reader and with posterity.[2] Alongside paratext, we also find attention to presentation, historical contextualisation, and the employment of textual strategies, in a diarist's bid to secure and communicate with implicit or explicit future audiences. These strategies, including the ostensible espousal of modesty by certain diarists, were required to encourage a diary's initial survival, its subsequent perusal, and its receipt of approval by later generations of readers.

These later generations of readers are envisaged or referenced across the full corpus of Irish diaries, and a direct address to this future, unspecified reader is not uncommon. Internal evidence for the circulation and readership of the diaries in manuscript form is frequently apparent, as different diarists mention how they entrusted their life writing into the hands of carefully selected friends or family members, alongside often simultaneous attempts to shield their writings from the eyes of others. Given the various women diarists' awareness of current real and potential readers, combined with probable future readers, the diary form could provide those who sought it the opportunity to contribute to the shaping of their own narrative, as well as that of others. While rooted in the self, women's diaries could also function primarily to contribute to a family record, or to offer details of a communal identity, highlighting connections between diaries and female agency. This chapter demonstrates how diaries could capture the family environment within which they were written, charting both a mental and physical landscape, as well as relating the power dynamics at play. Diaries could also serve to either promulgate or challenge family myths and to contribute to larger attempts to construct a legacy for a family or certain key representative family members, ensuring a certain image was conveyed to external eyes. This gave these women writers a degree of agency and bestowed upon them authority as real players in constructing a family's public history.

2 Gérard Genette, *Paratexts: Thresholds of Interpretation*. Trans. Jane E. Lewin. Cambridge: CUP, 1997; Aino Liira and Sirkku Ruokkeinen, 'Material Approaches to Exploring the Borders of Paratext'. *Textual Cultures* 11.1–2 (2019): 106–29. While studies of published paratext must consider the '*producer* (publisher, printer, translator, editor etc)', a focus on manuscript paratext instead prioritises the author's relationship with the '*consumer* – the individual (or collective patron, owner or reader)'. Matti Peikola, '2 Manuscript Paratexts in the Making: British Library MS Harley 6333 as a Liturgical Compilation'. *Discovering the Riches of the World*. Eds. Sabrina Corbellini, Margriet Hoogvliet, and Bart Ramakers. Leiden: Brill, 2015, 44–45.

This chapter considers the writing practices and aspirations of those diarists who actively sought a large audience, but did not achieve fame, as well as examining the audiences, practices, and experiences of more famous writers. A core example of the former is the figure of Elizabeth Edgeworth, sister of the bestselling author, Maria. Elizabeth's diary epitomises the female diarist's quest for an audience and a young woman's decision to prioritise the recording of her father's merits, and his role in the 1798 Uprising, over other private developments in her own life.[3] She is considered here alongside recognised diarist-authors, examining the various diaries (1769–1826) and early literary aspirations of Mary Shackleton Leadbeater, for example, as well as the diaries (1791–1827) and other writings of the poet and author Melesina Trench. The role the diaries played in these two women's literary careers and reputations is examined, considering the diaries both as fully formed life writing and as a pathway towards other kinds of writing, including poetry. The writers' literary afterlives are also investigated, assessing the import and impact of the nineteenth-century publications of their life writings, particularly the 1862 edition of Trench's diaries, and the editorial decisions taken by her son, Richard Chenevix Trench, who altered the content of the manuscript diary, bowdlerising whole sections. The legacies of Trench and Leadbeater have been shaped by the posthumous publication of their life writing, often leading to findings that are not supported by the original source material. The simultaneous examination of original diary text and paratext proves revealing for exploring questions of audience, agency, and literary aspiration.

Paratext and Family Audiences

A footnote in the life of her famous sister, Maria (1768–1849), we know very little about Elizabeth Edgeworth beyond the details in her diary and the few surviving letters pertaining to her or written by her to her relation Harriet Beaufort.[4] The first child of Richard Lovell Edgeworth's third wife, Elizabeth Sneyd (b. 1753, m. 1780), who died of tuberculosis in 1797, Elizabeth Edgeworth was born in 1781. She was 13 years younger than Maria and eighth in order of the 22 surviving siblings, with 16 of these born

3 Elizabeth Edgeworth, Diary of Elizabeth Edgeworth, sister of Maria, with occasional entries for period December 1797–February 1800. NLI MS 18,756. All subsequent quotations from Elizabeth Edgeworth's diary in this chapter are taken from this manuscript.

4 There are at least nine surviving letters from Elizabeth Edgeworth in the NLI collection (1798–1799), eight to Harriet and one to Frances, née Beaufort, the final wife of Elizabeth's father, Richard Lovell Edgeworth, written in French. NLI POS 9027.

by the time of the diary's creation.[5] Elizabeth's diary ends suddenly on 25 February 1800, with no indication of ill health of any kind, or any notion of an intention to cease writing. It is another hand that explains that the diarist 'died at Clifton' in England that year.[6] Elizabeth Edgeworth grew up in Enlightenment Ireland's most famous literary household, receiving an innovative and influential education and bearing witness to a wide range of intellectual activities. The Edgeworth household was a centre for elite sociability in the midlands of Ireland, with neighbouring gentry visiting to partake of its rich associational life and to celebrate the achievements of its famous writer.[7] Single-author salons were held in the Edgeworth family's impressive library, frequently serving as a platform for discussion and appreciation of Maria Edgeworth's own work, whether published or unpublished. Edgeworth's diary offers substantial evidence to support our sense of Edgeworthstown as an intellectual hub and centre for educational advances, with children awarded a progressive role. However, it also simultaneously charts how Elizabeth and her siblings' position within this hub fluctuated greatly, shifting from the centre to the periphery, and from active participants in educational matters to onlookers and minor actors. Although the diary was written before Maria Edgeworth's full ascent into literary celebrity, by the time of its commencement, Maria had already attained significant success, including for *Letters for Literary Ladies* (1795) and *Practical Education* (1798), and it seems that both Elizabeth's life and her diary took place in the shadows of Maria and their father, Richard Lovell Edgeworth (1744–1817). Obtaining a reader for one's own literary creations at Edgeworthstown was not straightforward. While it was undoubtedly an intellectual centre, opportunities for composition were not always available and disseminating one's writing could prove difficult. Alternative audiences seemed unavailable for the literary outputs of the other Edgeworth family

5 Although the records note that 16 had been born at this point, six had died, either as infants, during childhood, or in their 30s. There were thus ten surviving children at the time of the diary's composition, before the birth in 1799 of the first child of the fourth marriage. Richard Lovell and Frances Edgeworth would go on to have six surviving children in total.

6 The annotator notes that Elizabeth died on 30 April, while the *Memoirs of Richard Lovell Edgeworth* state August 1800. Maria Edgeworth and Richard Lovell Edgeworth, *Memoirs of Richard Lovell Edgeworth, Esq.* 2 vols. London, 1820, II 262. Elizabeth Edgeworth is also frequently mistakenly recorded as surviving until 1805. She died from the same disease as her mother.

7 Amy Prendergast, '"Members of the Republic of Letters": Maria Edgeworth, Literary Sociability, and Intellectual Pursuits in the Irish Midlands, c.1780–1820'. *Eighteenth-Century Ireland* 31 (2016): 27–44.

members, and the diary form filled the gap by affording a space for both the recording of literary projects and the courting of alternative audiences.

Maria and Richard Lovell Edgeworth were centre stage within the household, so other family members often found themselves marginalised, regardless of intellectual ability or creative output.[8] Both literally and metaphorically, the Edgeworth siblings acted as minor characters in their sister's life, performing their main role as assistants to Maria in her unfolding career, employed in copying the corrected errors for Maria's larger projects, rather than pursuing their own writings.[9] The Edgeworth siblings were frequently met with a lack of opportunities and platforms for their own creations, and were mostly employed as scholars and recipients of knowledge, or as assistants to Maria, ensuring and maintaining the quality of her work. One wonders about the fostering and promotion of creativity within the household and at the availability of alternative platforms for those other men and women with literary tastes and tendencies. These 'secondary' family members frequently had to seek more marginal routes to carve their own paths, promote their writings, and commit their thoughts to paper. The diary form provided a space for this. The myriad circumstances of intellectual and sociable marginalisation within the household all impacted upon the diary that was subsequently produced by Elizabeth Edgeworth, and on the writer's relationship with her intended audience. The document affords us an insight into how Edgeworth coped with these circumstances as an aspiring writer, and how she attempted to create a piece of writing that might survive within the family, perhaps later receiving some recognition and attention.

A diarist's attempts to simultaneously enable a text's dissemination whilst maintaining their virtue at times led to internal depictions of diaries as inconsequential and lacking substance. The insistence by Anne Jocelyn upon her diary's being simply a 'little insignificant narrative' (12/9/1798), for example, echoes the use of paratext across other genres, particularly the prefatory material to published novels and poems, as writers sought to obscure their intentions of attracting a substantial audience.[10] The diary is presented

---

8 Anne Markey has demonstrated how Honora, née Sneyd (1751–1780), Richard Lovell's second wife, was all but excised from literary history, in spite of her substantial contributions to the development of children's literature in both Ireland and globally; for one salient example, see Anne Markey, 'Honora Sneyd Edgeworth's "Harry and Lucy": A Case Study of Familial Literary Collaboration'. *Eighteenth-Century Ireland* 34 (2019): 50–65. See also Joanna Wharton, *Material Enlightenment: Women Writers and the Science of Mind, 1770–1830*. Woodbridge: Boydell Press, 2018, 73–112.

9 Maria Edgeworth letter to Charlotte Sneyd, 1799. Edgeworth Papers. NLI POS 9027 224.

10 Anne Jocelyn, *The Diary of Anne, Countess Dowager of Roden, 1797–1802*. Dublin, 1870.

as unimportant and inconsequential, certainly not worthy of perusal, while in fact encouraging this very act, and explicitly communicating with its potential audience. We can also occasionally observe the diarist featuring as only a minor figure within the text, presenting herself as just one amongst a cast of other characters, with large swathes of text devoted to the activities, thoughts, and attitudes of others within her network. Such decisions fit into a bid to preserve female modesty, while also responding to the writer's sense of value within their own familial environment.

The entries in Edgeworth's diary were not written exactly contemporaneously. One can speculate that the actual project of diary composition did not commence in earnest until at least autumn 1798, with the preceding months quickly sketched in retrospect. Evidence of Elizabeth casting herself as almost a minor character in her own life is apparent from the very opening. Initially, the diarist begins with mention of her own illness, setting herself centre stage. The first entry commences with the first-person singular, 'In January, I had just recovered from the Small Pox'. However, the diarist later amended the start date to note, 'December 1797 *Simple Susan* Read.' With this addition, Edgeworth significantly changed the narrative emphasis, so that the diary begins with a focus on her sister's short story for children, rather than on her own life. This addition is even more unsettling when one considers that 1797 was the year in which Edgeworth's own mother died. That she chose to include mention of Maria's work, when amending the diary, rather than this fact, crystallises the central role Maria Edgeworth played in her life. There is frequent focus on the activities of others throughout the diary, particularly on the actions of Maria – 'My father went with Maria to Cullon' (4/1798) or, '… the Beauforts all went at the same time that my mother & Maria set out with my father to go to Dublin' (18/1/1799). One senses that this is both strategic, in line with downplaying her own role, as well as a reflection of Maria's centrality within the household. Equally, we get the impression that the diarist was mostly indoors, at home, while other family members engaged with the larger world.[11] There is the sense that Edgeworth perhaps lived vicariously through these other family members, feeling as though she was more involved in their lives and experiences through recording their actions and movements.

While she casts herself in a minor role, one can immediately observe the diarist rendering the text more attractive to an audience, more suitable for posterity, and more likely to draw attention to her other writings. The diary as a whole is especially instructive regarding the material presentation of details for posterity. It is clear that Edgeworth reread her own entries a

---

11 Her sickliness may also have contributed to her exclusion from certain activities.

number of times and inserted explanatory marginalia for a future audience.[12] This usually serves to offer additional information to the reader, elucidating anything she judged to be unclear, and ensuring accessibility. She also amended her language, correcting herself in a bid for greater clarity and precision throughout. Thus, an audience was most certainly envisaged, one who desired grammatical order and precision rather than heightened emotion. Such emendations and marginalia are commonplace in diaries from eighteenth-century Ireland, and many of the surviving manuscript diaries bear evidence of repeated corrections by scrupulous diarists, performing editorial roles. The diary of the young Mary Anne Dawson, for instance, writing in the decade before Edgeworth, features intermittent marginalia, including emendations, such as corrections or additions to geographical details, to ensure accuracy of information (figure 1.1).[13]

In general, Elizabeth Edgeworth's diary is gently paced, methodically recorded, and sparse. However, on occasion, her entries do become more descriptive, and the events depicted acquire a livelier feel. For example, her recordings of the celebratory illuminations in Edgeworthstown ('in honor of an immense victory gained by Admiral Nelson ^now created Lord^') showcase this:

> After Dinner the House was illuminated which made the inside appear like some public building, it cast a fine light out of Doors, & persons passing by appeared like people on the stage, with green grass like a green Curtain for the back ground. We walked out, the people of the town walked round the circular road, like ^as if it was^ a public walk; We walked round the lawn, tho' it was quite dark, [...] it was beautiful, the trees appeared as if frosted, & close to us, as in a Camera Obscura; it seemed as if it was darkness universal, beyond the house which we little beings, had lit to admire, when we came in we stood in the portico, & saw the yeomen dancing as gay, & rural, as they had been steady in the morning. (7/10/1798)

Here, we see the public and private identities of different spaces inverted, with the domestic home becoming 'like some public building', while the outside is transformed as though into a theatrical institution. Echoing this, the road is presented by the diarist as having morphed in the minds of others into a public space. The whole passage is bathed in light and colour, as darkness and light are juxtaposed, casting a magical effect, softened by the echoing green of the grass, figured as a stage curtain. The use of simile

---

12 There is no evidence concerning when these paratextual interventions were made.
13 Mary Anne Dawson, Diary of Mary Anne Dawson, 1782–1784. Clements Papers, TCD MSS 7270–7270a (15/7/1782); (16/7/1782).

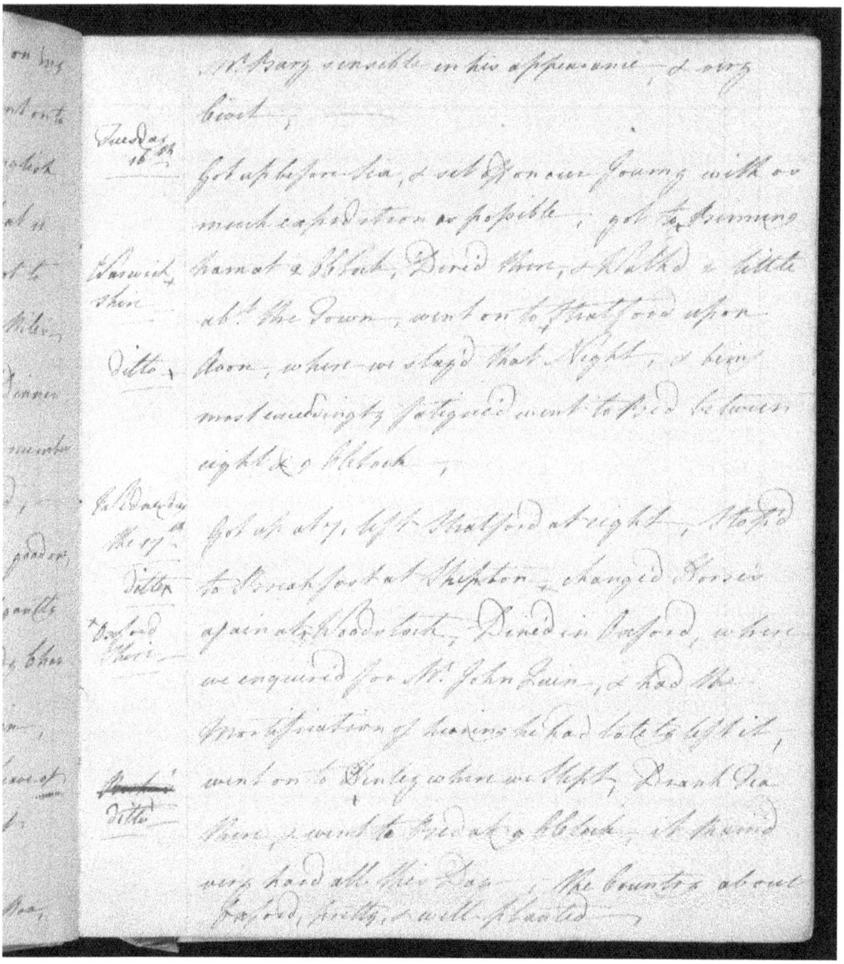

Figure 1.1: Marginalia from the diary of Mary Anne Dawson. TCD MS 7270.

with the camera obscura emphasises this interaction of light and dark and is in keeping with the family's interest in science and the material objects connected with it. Into this setting, Elizabeth inserts the Edgeworth family, beginning two consecutive sentences with 'we walked', signalling the primacy of the family to the scene. And yet, as we see often happen in her diary, she casts these figures as major and minor players, highlighting their centrality while simultaneously delineating them as 'little beings'. The passage's theatricality is further heightened by the performativity of the various players, with the dancing of the yeomen presented as though principally enacted for the enjoyment of the Edgeworth family. Passages such as this offer an indication of the descriptive bouts within the diary, composed by one whose creativity was overshadowed by the success of her famous and justly celebrated sister, but who nevertheless sought to carve out a space and audience for her own writings.

It is clear from her diary that Edgeworth had literary aspirations herself, beyond her contributions to life writing. The diary contains references to her preparations for writing an imaginary tour through England and includes a note in July 1799 stating that she was also writing a story for her brother Lovell, the son who would inherit the Edgeworthstown estate.[14] In the same entry in which she recognises her sister's receipt of praise, she mentions her own writings:

> Maria received a letter from a Mr Ivans, praising Practical Education most highly, & requesting Maria either as a governess or else to recommend one to her – At this time I wrote out my stories into ^a^ small compass – (20/9/1798)

This positioning of herself alongside her famous literary sister implies the possibility of comparison and of equivalence. She immediately establishes a temporal relation between the two and takes ownership of her writing, although qualifying her productions as 'small'. Rather than making larger claims for her writings, both here and in her reference to composing for Lovell, she chooses the descriptor 'stories'. It is clear, however, that she was identifying her literary forays in a medium she intended to be perused by others, perhaps hoping to direct them towards these works. The diary also allowed her to communicate a certain vision of herself as author, or at least to hint at it as one important facet of her articulation of herself.

~ ~

Mary Shackleton Leadbeater also grew up within a well-known Irish Enlightenment family. Mary was the second child of the renowned school-teacher Richard Shackleton and his second wife Elizabeth.[15] Though mostly remembered for its famous male pupils, including author and philosopher Edmund Burke, with whom Mary later corresponded, the Ballitore school,

14 The original heir, Richard, died in 1796, and the first boy named Lovell died as a baby in 1766.
15 There is surprisingly little contemporary biographical or literary criticism devoted to Leadbeater. Apart from featuring alongside Dorothea Herbert in Barbara Hughes's study – *Between Literature and History: The Diaries and Memoirs of Dorothea Herbert and Mary Leadbeater*. Bern: Peter Lang, 2010 – there is no current monograph work dedicated to her. However, she is the subject of several articles and chapters that feature throughout this chapter.

which had been founded by her grandfather, Abraham Shackleton, was also attended by several girls, including Mary and her sister Sarah.[16] The longevity of Leadbeater's diary-writing career, spanning 54 volumes and 57 years, makes her collection of diaries particularly interesting – and extraordinarily useful – in terms of questions of audience: for example, we can compare her adolescent diaries with those written in middle and old age, observing an evolution in matters of audience, with evident shifts over the course of her life writing.

Leadbeater's many diaries engage with the full spectrum of audience engagement and provide a remarkable case study for the examination of issues of audience and paratext. Indeed, within individual diary volumes we can often witness a shift in Mary's attitude to her audience, from being something feared to something desired, while the audience she addresses also changes from her contemporary community to a posthumous one, with her diary writing being alternately hidden and shared, mocked and celebrated. Mary penned her first diary entry as a child in December 1769, wherein she included reference to a personal, unnamed reader: 'I must (I believe) now bid adi^e^u to my reader for this night' (17/12/1769).[17] This anonymous, amorphous reader had fully transformed into a specific, named audience by 1772. Unlike Elizabeth Edgeworth, for whom there is no evidence of siblings reading her diary, Leadbeater's diaries are brimming with comments on the reception of her entries by other named family members, particularly her sister Sarah, 18 months her junior, who also wrote a diary, and with whom she continually shared her writing.[18]

Indeed, striking similarities are discernible between Mary Leadbeater's early diaries and the practices of that most famous of eighteenth-century diarists, the acclaimed English novelist Frances Burney (1752–1840). Burney's diary from 1768, the year she commenced journal writing, includes the statement, 'I have read part of my journal to Miss Young', a figure who had warned her of the perils of diary keeping – describing it as 'the most dangerous employment' – possibly at Charles Burney's request.[19] Writing

---

16 Mary later married another past pupil, farmer and businessman William Leadbeater, originally of Huguenot extraction, who had converted to the Society of Friends. Mary O'Dowd, 'William Leadbeater'. *DIB*.

17 Mary Leadbeater, Diaries covering the years 1769–1789 in 22 volumes. NLI MSS 9292–9314. NLI MS 9293.

18 Sarah Shackleton, Sarah Shackleton's Journal in 4 volumes, 1787–1821. Department of Special Collections. Ballitore Collection. Box 13, F.1. [Microfilm reels available in NLI: n.1009–10, p.1091–2.]

19 Frances Burney, *Early Journals and Letters of Fanny Burney, Volume 1, 1768–1773*. Ed. Lars E. Troide. Oxford: Clarendon Press, 1988, 23. Young's objections are discussed in Stuart Sherman, *Telling Time: Clocks, Diaries, and English Diurnal Form, 1660–1785*.

four years later, Mary echoes this decision to read a section of one's diary aloud to another female listener, stating, 'I read part of my Journal to Sally & [missing] part of to Day in it' (14/4/1772).[20] This activity is reciprocated, and a pattern of communal reading of their diaries emerges, as the two Shackleton sisters shared their entries with one another, assessing their writing, and performing comparative overviews: 'Sister Sally is going to read me her Journal which is concluded & is more agreeable than mine, she is very angry at me for saying so & is beating me' (14/4/1772).[21] The immediacy of Mary's diary writing is also evident here, as she describes events as they unfold, while asserting her ostensible preference for Sarah's diary.[22] As well as representing a receptive audience for Mary Leadbeater's early diaries, Sarah also features within certain diaries as the named addressee. A quasi letter-journal section, appended to the 1774 diary, explicitly addresses Sarah, beginning 'my dear sister': 'Where art thou now? Perambulating the streets of Dublin perhaps & staring about thee till thy foot steps never saw the like before in all they life…'; 'I am as lonesome as can be without thee'; 'I have scarce time to write [. S]ome of the discourse at Polls was about Sweet little Sally but when thou comes home I'll tell the true & full account if thou chuses.'[23] This short period of separation allowed the diarist the opportunity to reflect on the closeness of the sororal relationship, to imagine her sister's activities, and to anticipate the recounting of discussions that had taken place in Sarah's absence. Thus, the letter-journal interlude shifts the emphasis from Leadbeater's own experiences to a focus on Sarah, momentarily removing the diarist to a more peripheral position.

Frances Burney announced that her diary was written '*solely* for my own perusal' (17/3/1768) before quickly renouncing this intention, and her corpus of diaries also includes many letter-journals – directed to her sister Susan Philips, her father Charles, her friend Frederica Locke, and her husband

---

Chicago: University of Chicago Press, 1996. After having read a section of the diary, Miss Young agreed that it was harmless.

20 NLI MS 9295.

21 NLI MS 9295.

22 Later entries, written without the presence of her sister, record a preference for her own diaries: 'Sally & I were reading an old journal of hers ^Sallys^ when Sister Peggy call'd us to work. It was a quier [queer] one, the days very short, though I fancy she thought them long, "Tommy Hamilton is a fine little boy" was in one day' (31/12/1774), clearly making the claim that her diaries are better written and more advanced. NLI MS 9298.

23 NLI MS 9296. Unfortunately, interventions by an earlier NLI preservation team have meant that some of the words and dating material have been obscured at the start of this additional section by the use of tape. The terms 'thou' and 'thee' were forms of address commonly used by the Quaker community.

General Alexandre d'Arblay.[24] Leadbeater's own desire for an audience is to the fore throughout her diary career, even following those moments when she emphasises the secrecy of her diary writing and her ostensible desire to maintain her entire family's ignorance of this writing: 'I can hardly sit alone, if not with a needle with a pen in my hand, for I am wonder^ful^ly taken with my notion of writing a journal, nobody knows of it, but myself, nor I do not intend shall til it is done if I can help it' (28/6/1774).[25] By the very next day, however, the attractions of an audience were asserting themselves to her:

> I have a great mind to show Sally my journal yet I think I will not yet a while however [...] Just now Sally came up & begg'd to know what this was, so I told her & I intend to shew it to her when are settled at the Retreat but if she vexes me, she may be sure I'll put ^it^ in too, if I write while I am angry (29/6/1774)

The diary of Tipperary woman Mary Mathew echoes such commentary in the diarist's reflections upon her own relationship with her female companion, Mrs Mathew:

> I shou'd not take the trouble of writing all this, but that possibly this Book might fall in her way after my death and she [Mrs Mathew] will then see I advise her whoever she happens to live ^with if^ they treat her with kindness, to take the Good and the bad as it comes [...] – but if this falls into other hands, don't let them imagine from this & some other things I have wrote that we don't live in the greatest harmony together [...] (14/11/1772)[26]

Mary Mathew's diary writing explicitly acknowledges the probability of a future audience. Her diary represents a fusion of occasional awareness of such an audience with the communication of candid remarks, including those regarding her companion, which are made in response to immediate circumstances, rather than offering a measured overview of the women's relationship.

Such a posthumous audience is also fleetingly envisioned by Leadbeater in her early diaries, when she comments that 'Perhaps after I am laid in the durt some one may read this... [torn]' (17/4/1772).[27] However,

---

24 Magdalena Ożarska, *Lacework or Mirror? Diary Poetics of Frances Burney, Dorothy Wordsworth and Mary Shelley*. Cambridge: Cambridge Scholars Publishing, 2014, 60.
25 NLI MS 9297.
26 Mary Mathew, Cookery recipes, household accounts and diary by Mary Mathew, 1741–1777. NLI MS 5102.
27 NLI MS 9295.

the majority of Leadbeater's early diaries were composed with a named reader in mind, specifically her sister, as repeated entries make abundantly clear: 'As Sally seems not to have any curiosity to see this journal I think I will keep to myself, as I at first intended – no now I won't for I'm mistaken' (5/7/1774).[28] The immediacy of her writing is continually apparent, as is her ongoing obsession with issues of readership. Such examples, where Leadbeater is in dialogue with herself, almost anticipating later instances of stream of consciousness, continue throughout the early diaries, which maintain such conversational style. There are also some hints at a wider audience for these early diaries, which make clear that Sarah was not their only intended reader. Other female family members are later addressed, beyond the immediate family unit: 'Sally & I went to Cousing Jonathan's [,] chatted with the girls, read them a part of this journal' (5/1/1775).[29] Female family members are often anticipated as readers across the corpus of Irish diaries. Elizabeth Clibborn, a woman who would go on to have at least 15 children, considers the possibility of her diary being read in future by her own daughters, hoping it might provide them with support and advice if they themselves become mothers: 'perhaps my dear girls may in perusing these lines receive some information in rearing their dear offspring if entrusted with any' (11/6/1810).[30]

In spite of her unequivocal desire for an audience, and her willingness and need to share her writing, Leadbeater's early diaries were still viewed by her as semi-private documents. Shortly after her decision to again share her diary with her sister, a dramatic entry from July 1774 describes how Sarah Shackleton stole her diary, demonstrating the perils of diary writing and the possibility of betrayal. The entry states that a lesson had been learned and that Mary would not go visiting without Sarah again. The diarist then went back and struck out much of the page describing the event and ripped out the following one (12/7/1774). After the struck-out material, she states, by way of explanation for her reaction to her sister's deed, 'I tell every thing to my journal'.[31]

While most of the surviving Irish diaries demonstrate an awareness of multiple audiences and are heavily edited and annotated, with certain observations qualified or indeed censored, the full corpus also incorporates a couple of diaries that possess more traditionally 'private' leanings.[32] For

28 NLI MS 9297.
29 NLI MS 9298.
30 Elizabeth Clibborn, Journal of Elizabeth (Grubb) Clibborn (1780–1861). RSFIHL, P9.
31 NLI MS 9297.
32 Of course, many more candid or rebellious diaries may have been written by

example, Elinor Goddard's diary includes explicit detail of those people who provoked her, with little concern for reputational damage.[33] The diary of the adolescent Frances Jocelyn is the most forthright and blunt of all the diaries encountered in this survey, with multiple dismissive and derogatory comments, some of which can occasionally overstep the boundary from candid to cruel. Entry after entry in Frances's diary assesses those figures encountered, with no attempt at either encryption or minimisation: 'I do not like any of the Forsters, but Charlotte the best. Sir Thomas is horrible, & Miss Laetitia so conceited. They really are quite dreadful' (17/9/1810), or '[Lord Monck is] the greatest idiot' (28/7/1811).[34] Despite remarks such as these and others, there is still an awareness of the possibility of the diary's discovery and perusal by Frances Jocelyn's younger sister Anne, who herself would later write a diary: 'My happiness is centred in her [Anne] entirely, she has no faults, heavenly pure angel, but she is a very naughty girl if she reads this' (20/4/1812).[35]

A feared, non-receptive audience is frequently mentioned by Leadbeater in her early diaries, with her anxiety about such readers seeping into her imaginings and causing nightmares: 'I dream'd last night that St. Clair found this journal & carried to my Father & Mother, which vex'd me exceedingly' (5/7/1774), and 'I fell asleep & dream'd my aunt was upon the point of finding out my journal which troubled me' (12/1/1775).[36] These imagined scenarios 'trouble' and 'vex' her, but the diary also includes real instances of non-consensual diary reading and invasion of her private space: 'Rayner took my journal from me & as I look'd over his shoulder he said I trembled, but I did not at last he gave it me' (31/12/1774).[37] On another occasion, a year later, she comments that '[St Clair is] making great game of me and my journal' (27/11/1775).[38] To avoid mockery or censure, the adolescent diaries of both Mary and Sarah were frequently written in secrecy, in addition to being subsequently concealed. Mary describes how

women of all ages but these would seem to be less likely candidates for survival into the twenty-first century. For more on sources and the survival of certain diaries, see the Introduction.

33 This provocation included other people cancelling activities or accusing her of wearing improper clothing. Elinor Goddard, Mrs Elinor Goddard: Journal (1774–1778). NLW 22993A. Consulted on microfilm, NLI POS 9617.

34 Frances Jocelyn, Diary of Frances Theodosia Jocelyn. 1810–1812. NLI MS 18,430.

35 NLI MS 18,430.

36 NLI MS 9297.

37 NLI MS 9298.

38 NLI MS 9298.

Sally kept her journal in 'a dresser box drawer' (24/12/1774), for instance, which she deemed to be a foolish hiding place.[39]

Frances Burney's diaries also showcase the need for secrecy in one's writing, including in relation to the composition of her most famous novel, published when she was 25 years old, *Evelina, or the History of a Young Lady's Entrance into the World* (1778):

> The fear of discovery, or of suspicion in the house, made the copying [of *Evelina*] extremely laborious to me: for in the day time, I could only take odd moments, so that I was obliged to sit up the greatest part of many nights, in order to get it ready (n.d., 1777)[40]

Burney and Leadbeater both wrote their diaries over the course of a whole lifetime, with Burney beginning in March 1768, when 15 years old, and writing her final diary entry in 1840, shortly before her death that same year. The intended readership and purpose of Burney's diary writing changed significantly over the course of her life, fulfilling different needs as she grew older. The diary engages with quite distinct notions of audience, ostensibly beginning as a private document, before being sent at intervals to her sister and then being written intentionally for posterity at the prompting of her husband.[41] This trajectory, though not identical, is very similar to that of Leadbeater, although it was the latter's father, rather than husband, who encouraged her to write in the diary, and to attract a larger audience, as was the case with the diary of 'the Oxfordshire diarist' Caroline Powys, née Girle, 'kept by desire of her father'.[42]

The alteration in Leadbeater's intended audience is reflected in a shift in tone, with an increase in formality over time, and a diminution of the candid nature in evidence across the adolescent volumes, as Leadbeater became aware of her increased influence and audience.[43] The changing physical dimensions and characteristics of each diary volume also capture this shift and mirror the changes occurring. In addition to telling us much about the individual document's origins and provenance, physical archival copies of a diary inform us of the actual spatial dimensions a diarist had to engage with and to write within, as well as how they interacted with or

39 NLI MS 9298.
40 Frances Burney, *A Known Scribbler: Frances Burney on Literary Life*. Ed. Justine Crump. Toronto: Broadview, 2002, 113.
41 Judy Simons, *Diaries and Journals of Literary Women from Fanny Burney to Virginia Woolf*. Basingstoke: Palgrave, 1990, 19–20.
42 Caroline Powys, *Passages from the Diaries of Mrs Philip Lybbe Powys, of Hardwick House, Oxon, AD 1756 to 1808*. Ed. Emily J Climenson. London, 1899, x.
43 Hughes 137.

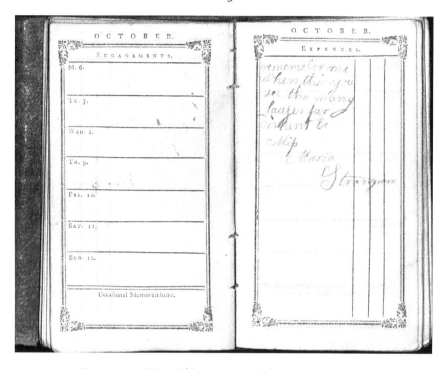

Figure 1.2: Inscription within Mary Hancock diary. PRONI D3513/3/1.

envisaged their audience. One useful example of this is the diary of Mary
Hancock, held at the Public Record Office of Northern Ireland, in Belfast,
which also indicates the intricacies of diary provenance.[44] The diary is
in the form of a pocketbook dedicated to diary entries for the year 1788,
which was printed in Dublin for W. Wilson of Dame Street as *The Lady's
and Gentleman's Memorandum Book. With A Complete Kalendar. For the Year
1788. Forming a Daily Account of their Engagements and Expences Throughout
the Year.*[45] Paratextual material indicates that the pocketbook was given to
Mary Hancock, later Hogg (1773–1828) of Lisburn, Co. Down, by Maria
[elsewhere Mary] Strangman in 1789. However, the earliest horizontal diary
entry, made in the expenses section for January, states that the object (again
identified as 'a trifle') had initially been presented to Maria Strangman
by her brother, before being passed on to the second Mary: 'Mr William

44 Mary Hancock, Diary of Mary Hancock, Sister of Isabella Steele-Nicholson, 1788.
PRONI D3513/3/1.

45 For more on pocketbooks, see Jennie Batchelor, 'Fashion and Frugality: Eighteenth-
Century Pocket Books for Women'. *Studies in Eighteenth-Century Culture* 32 (2003):
1–18.

Strangman presented this trifle to his Sister...'. Though the diary is in fact mostly blank, it is remarkable that the entries, which include verse and general observations as well as comments on individual days, were written by both women. Maria Strangman repurposed one of the October expenses pages to contain a memento: 'remember me when this you see […] Miss Maria Strangman' (figure 1.2). Whether or not this was intended for Mary Hancock or another reader, it is clear that the entries were written with the understanding that they would certainly be read by others.

In Mary Shackleton Leadbeater's early diaries, written on small blank pages, there is frequent reference to her poor handwriting and presentation, with comments such as, '[my diary is] quite illegible so scrawld, so blotted, the letters half finish'd, 'tis not fit even for myself to see' (27/12/1774).[46] Criticism from her sister regarding the diary's material quality is also incorporated into the diary itself, with its physical aspects and poor, illegible writing commented upon (figure 1.3):

> Sally wishes I would write this <u>better</u> & <u>larger</u> & then it would be <u>easier to read</u>, but I commonly write it in a great hurry & with midlin pens & have not time to take pains & writing it large would take up too much room, & Sally says I must get another volume or make this larger & that it will be like the Bible 'tis so thick. (29/6/1774)

Leadbeater's first ten diaries, from 1769 to 1777, also indicate how her writing was sometimes shaped, and to an extent cramped, by the limitations of the medium used. She crossed out sections of 20/2/1770, for example, in order to comment, 'I believe ^I may pass over all^ the rest in silence since this journal is so near an end'.[47] Her eleventh diary, MS 9303, was given to her by her father as a present to mark her eighteenth birthday, as noted on the inside leaf: 'Mary Shackleton Given her by her Father 19th of 1st mo: 1777.' The writing here is smaller than usual as Mary tried to fit the entries around the physical text she had been given by her father – a 'Kalendar' from 1777, printed for Samuel Watson of Dame Street, Dublin. Blank pages were inserted on either side of the printed calendar.[48] A change in emphasis and content is apparent from the very beginning, with the diary commencing with references to Quaker meetings – both the women's meeting and a select meeting. This diary marks a notable shift in emphasis, incorporating more members of the surrounding Quaker community, without commenting on

46 NLI MS 9298.
47 NLI MS 9293.
48 NLI MS 9303. This is not the first calendar used, and NLI MS 9294, an extremely short journal for 1771–1772, is also written in the blank pages surrounding the calendar.

from his uncle to day which I think is unkind
not to acquaint of the Child's health which he
might before we were earnest to know — sweet one
day, I have not got him out of my head yet —
I dare say Sally on thorns as the saying is tis a
this but not an inch of it shall She see till
we are at the Retreat, I intend nor I will not
shew it to her then if she don't ask to see it. my
Aunt sent Sally up in a hurry for something but
She was so charmd with my conversation that
She forgot it, but at last recollected that it was the
Ink — we miss the alcove much is puts us quite
out of sorts especially Betty & Sally who had
more to do with it than I — Sally wishes I
would write this better _or larger_ & then it would
be easier to read, but I commonly write it in a
great hurry & with middlin pens & have not time
to take pains & writing it large would take up
too much room & Sally says I must get another
volume or make this larger & that it will be like
the Bible tis so thick. I wrote from the 10th line
of the 12th page since I came up so think it is now
time to lay by as "Twilight grey
            Has in her sober livery all things clad.
But I cannot conclude to day till I say that Jany
ough came home with Cousin Sam & dined with

these people or including gossip, with the diarist herself no longer centre stage as in the previous ten diaries. Barbara Hughes has also noted the 'abrupt change in style, content, and handwriting which accompanies the gift, indicative of a decidedly different audience'.[49]

Though this wider audience was not actively sought out in the first ten volumes of Leadbeater's diaries, some of these diaries feature remarkably detailed title pages that showcase the diarist's literary aspirations and desire for an audience. Of particular note is the fascinating title page for journal MS 9295, her diary for 1772, which presents the following title to its readers (figure 1.4):

A JOURNAL OR DIARY BY Mary Shackleton. Being THE SECOND VOLUME. AND MUCH MORE Entertaining than the First 1772.[50]

This fusion of manuscript and print expectations is of significance for book history and for our understanding of material culture and manuscript circulation, as well as questions of audience.[51] Leadbeater was mirroring the processes of print culture, manually reproducing a title page for the subsequent work, thus awarding the diary additional weight and prestige. Such borrowings from print culture also occur in MS 9297, her diary from 26/6/1774 to 6/8/1774, which is presented as the 'Journal of the Proceedings of Mary Shackleton'. A similar debt to print culture is in evidence in the stunning memoirs, or Retrospections, of diarist Dorothea Herbert, where Herbert produced an elaborate title page for her writing, as well as multiple intricate illustrations.[52] Meta-discourse is a feature throughout Leadbeater's writing; the strategy of modesty espoused by Elizabeth Edgeworth is completely rejected by Leadbeater, who comments self-referentially on 'This most elegant journal'.[53] Edgeworth's tactic of the diarist featuring as only a minor figure within the text is also rejected here, as it was by Frances Burney, who famously placed herself centre stage throughout.[54]

---

49 Hughes 137.
50 While the terms 'diary' and 'journal' are used interchangeably here, Leadbeater's later diaries do separate the functions, as discussed in Hughes.
51 For more on these topics, see Aileen Douglas, *Work in Hand, Script, Print, and Writing*. Oxford: OUP, 2017.
52 For discussion of these 'emulative practices', see Mary Catherine Breen, 'The Making and Unmaking of an Irish Woman of Letters'. PhD Thesis, University of Oxford, 2012. The Retrospections have been digitised by Trinity College Dublin and can be viewed here: https://digitalcollections.tcd.ie/concern/works/gb19fg671?locale=en.
53 NLI MS 9300.
54 Lorna J. Clark, 'The Diarist as Novelist: Narrative Strategies in the Journals and Letters of Frances Burney'. *English Studies in Canada* 27.3 (2001): 283–302. See also

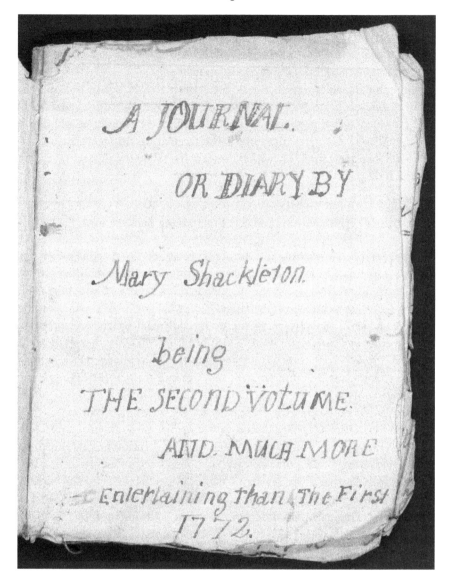

Figure 1.4: Title page for Mary Shackleton Leadbeater 1772 diary. NLI MS 9295.

As Leadbeater's diaries progress we can note the pleasure she takes in the act of diary writing, as well as her increasing awareness of questions

Lynn Z. Bloom, "'I write for myself and strangers": Private Diaries as Public Document'. *Inscribing the Daily: Critical Essays on Women's Diaries.* Eds. Suzanne Bunkers and Cynthia Huff. Amherst: University of Massachusetts Press, 1996, 171–85.

of audience.[55] The below quotation confirms that she was unambiguously and self-consciously writing for an audience and that she was doing so as a 'journalist':

> This evening enter'd into my head the notion of making a journal. I am a great journalist & have made several, but none I expect will be so clever as this, they are mere <u>bagatelles</u> – & pray what is this but a <u>bagatelle</u> too! But I hope to divert myself & two or three of my female friends with it, if I have constancy to finish (27/6/1774).[56]

Leadbeater makes clear that her goal was to expand her audience, extending readership beyond her sister Sarah, to include other female friends whom she hoped to 'divert' with her writings. Mary's shifting awareness of audience and her intention to attract a greater readership aligns with her sense that the diary form could be employed to communicate a specific perspective or narrative to this new audience, whether on life in Ballitore, on her own character, or on the values and achievements of her family, the Shackletons.

Diaries and Family Legacy: The Edgeworths

Following the success of her publications, particularly her didactic *Cottage Dialogues among the Irish peasantry* (Dublin and London, 1811), a work of moral and social improvement, which went through five editions by 1822, Mary Leadbeater composed biographical writings that paid tribute to her parents.[57] She portrays Richard and Elizabeth as virtuous, respectable people in her posthumously published account of Ballitore from 1766 to 1824 – *The Leadbeater Papers. The Annals of Ballitore* (London and Dublin, 1862) – as well as throughout the entirety of *Memoirs and Letters of Richard and Elizabeth Shackleton, Late of Ballitore, Ireland* (London, 1822).[58] In part owing to the commercial success of her other writings, Leadbeater

55 There is much less about the weather and more of a narrative style with connected entries, where each day of the first week tells us more about her new residence and her evolving emotions regarding the sick child David.

56 Caroline Powys also aspired to 'in time, perhaps, have the honorary title of an expert journalist'. Powys 59.

57 Leadbeater's diary for 1812 provides information on her management of the second edition of *Cottage Dialogues*.

58 In the *Annals*, she notes her mother's intelligence (115); her father's role as beloved family man (113); her pride in them both and their remarkable virtue, stating that she wishes to give her own children a similar upbringing (121–22). Frances Burney also produced an idealised memoir of her father, *The Memoirs of Doctor Burney* (London, 1832).

gained access to this additional public platform and had a specific outlet to present her desired image of her family, especially her parents, just as Maria Edgeworth did when completing the memoirs of her father Richard Lovell, published in 1820.[59] Diaries could also be used for shaping or providing the history of a family and of individual family members. Leadbeater's own diaries are full of colourful anecdotes and character portraits of her siblings, parents, cousins, aunts, and uncles, though as these diaries have never been published, such portraits have been largely supplanted by her more hagiographical descriptions of her parents in the two texts mentioned above. For Elizabeth Edgeworth, however, the diary form offered a unique opportunity to record her own portrait of her family and of its most famous representatives, allowing her the chance to contribute to the construction of the Edgeworth family legacy.

A diarist embodies the twin roles of author and editor, identifying certain details for inclusion while jettisoning others; as Dan Doll and Jessica Muns argue, 'a diary can never offer absolutely unmediated experience. There is always a principle of selection that filters and limits what can be recorded on the page'.[60] As with all diarists, Elizabeth Edgeworth had to decide which elements of her life to place most emphasis upon. The first eight months of her diary pass by swiftly before the reader is offered a much lengthier account of the 1798 Rebellion's impact on the lives of those in the Irish midlands. Although figures still vary, rebel deaths have been estimated by twenty-first century historians to have reached 25,000, with approximately 600 military fatalities.[61] Edgeworth's diary focuses on the latter stages of a Rebellion that began in May and had ended in failure by October. A planned country-wide uprising of those seeking greater independence for Ireland, involving both

59 Maria Edgeworth and Richard Lovell Edgeworth, *Memoirs of Richard Lovell Edgeworth, Esq.* 2 vols. London, 1820.

60 Dan Doll and Jessica Munns, *Recording and Reordering: Essays on the Seventeenth- and Eighteenth-Century Diary and Journal.* Lewisburg: Bucknell UP, 2006, 10.

61 The conflict and extreme violence of 1798 marked it as a time of great uncertainty and unreliability across Ireland, with much confusion surrounding fatalities, attacks, and intent. Thomas Bartlett, 'Ireland during the Revolutionary and Napoleonic Wars, 1791–1815'. *The Cambridge History of Ireland, Volume 3, 1730–1880.* Ed. James Kelly. Cambridge: CUP, 2018, 74–101. Diaries from this period offer repeated attempts to make sense of events, with people struggling to establish veracity and to take some control by noting down occurrences. Kevin Whelan, 'Introduction'. Elizabeth Richards, *The Diary of Elizabeth Richards (1798–1825): From the Wexford Rebellion to Family Life in the Netherlands.* Ed. Marie de Jong-Ijsselstein. Intro. Kevin Whelan. Hilversum: Verloren, 1999, 12. Elizabeth's diary attests to the constant confusion surrounding the numbers of rebels, the loss of life incurred, and the movements of both soldiers and rebels.

Catholics and Protestants, the Rebellion commenced with a premature outbreak and then a wave of attacks, leading to reinforcements being sent from Britain.[62] The delayed landing of French Soldiers under General Humbert off Killala, Co. Mayo, to provide support for the Irish rebels, took place on 22 August, prompting the descriptor *Bliain na bhFrancach*, or the Year of the French. Edgeworth's detailed entries on the Rebellion begin almost immediately following this, on 24 August 1798. Descriptions of the concluding episodes and consequences of the Rebellion, and the Edgeworth family's experience of them, account for over a third of Edgeworth's diary, being deemed of greatest significance to her audience. Many of Edgeworth's contemporary diarists also devoted large portions of their diaries to recording the upheaval of 1798, with the Rebellion playing a prominent role in the diaries of Anne Jocelyn, Elizabeth Richards (later Stirum), and Mary Anne Fortescue, for example.

Edgeworth's entries on the Rebellion offer a clear sense of her intended audience and make it abundantly apparent that a future, posthumous reader is envisaged. Edgeworth begins the diary proper on the fourth page of the document. On the third page, recto, of which the top half is blank, the reader receives definitions to allow them to navigate the various groups that will be mentioned throughout (see figure 1.5). This concise glossary is divided into two, with an initial grouping providing definitions for 'Defen[d]ers', 'United Irishmen', 'Rebels', and 'Croppies'. A definition for 'Orangemen' is placed separately and described thus: 'Orangemen Protestants united in opposition to Rebels who wore Green – in [illegible] ^behalf^ of the House of Orange in King William III's reign'. The prominent insertion of such a glossary, at the outset of the diary, immediately suggests that the accounts of the Rebellion are judged by Edgeworth to be of interest to any anticipated reader. One also imagines that this reader is envisaged as one who will engage with the diary after a substantial passage of time, as the diarist anticipates their ignorance of such widely known current events. However, while a glossary is helpful in delineating the different terms for future audiences, it may also have served to elucidate them for contemporaries. Some slipperiness existed surrounding the descriptors Edgeworth employs, with contemporary connotations shifting depending on allegiance, perspective, and emphasis. Croppy, for instance, which denotes a supporter of the Rebellion, 'whose short hair signalled his sympathy with the French Revolution', is generally employed in derogatory fashion in Loyalist songs from this period onwards, as well as to evoke sympathy and compassion in a Nationalist tradition, as

---

62 Nancy Curtin, *The United Irishmen: Popular Politics in Ulster and Dublin, 1791–1798*. Oxford: OUP, 1998; Ian McBride, 'Reclaiming the Rebellion: 1798 in 1998'. *Irish Historical Studies* 31.123 (1999): 395–410.

Figure 1.5: Glossary to Elizabeth Edgeworth diary. NLI MS 18,756.

in the anonymous 'The Croppy Boy'.[63] References to 'croppies' figure three times in Edgeworth's diary proper, but only in the context of accusations of betrayal. A charge is laid against the diarist's father (twice) and Lord Cornwallis, the lord lieutenant, on 15 September. The employment of such nomenclature, as recorded by Edgeworth, shows disapproval of her father's

63 'Croppy'. *The Oxford Dictionary of Phrase and Fable*. Andrew Carpenter, *Verse in English from Eighteenth-Century Ireland*. Cork: Cork UP, 1998.

ostensibly sympathetic treatment of those rebelling, rather than suggesting his membership of the group in question. Edgeworth is very alert to the significance of such naming practices, and what they can imply, as in the following instance:

> My father very anxious how to behave to the people, who insulted his yeomen who came with Hry & to Longford on Tuesday, His arms did not come, he wrote to Athlone for them – Kelly & some others said to ^have^ joind the Rebel army [...] & next day the ~~gentlemen~~ ^yeomen^ & in the whole town of Longford, upbraiding [?] my father & his men, calling them Cropies & Rebels &c &c (5/9/1798)

We can see here that Richard Lovell Edgeworth is being cast in the role of rebel sympathiser and that the word gentleman has been crossed out and corrected to yeomen.[64] Unfortunately, parts of the glossary have also been strenuously struck out, one assumes by a later hand.[65] The definition of Orangemen remains intact, but the four initial definitions have been rendered largely indecipherable in places, obscuring Edgeworth's efforts at interpretation.

Throughout her accounts of the Rebellion, Edgeworth's primary thrust is towards a vindication of the actions and character of her father, as well as the provision of clarity regarding the actions of her stepmother, Frances Edgeworth, who was charged with having prevented a chaise with a wounded man from going to its original destination (10/9/1798). Elizabeth Edgeworth is consistently a minor character throughout the diary, as in her life, and while she tells of the various efforts to ensure her safety, it is other family members whose actions and emotions are dissected, rather than her own. Writing for posterity, she sought to contribute to moulding the legacy of Richard Lovell Edgeworth, and the Edgeworth family more generally, anxious that their performances during the Rebellion be conveyed clearly and their motives understood. While her father was denied his desired Court of Enquiry to address his treatment during the Rebellion, a point referred to several times in the diary, Edgeworth attempted to intervene and provide some exoneration. Multiple details are presented as extenuating circumstances, and this entire section of her diary reads as a defence of the actions of her father, beginning with this minor explanation: 'we saw the *Ray Fencibles* pass thro' the town – My father was gone to Longford, therefore

---

64 'The Irish Yeomanry was a voluntary, part-time military force raised in 1796 for local law-and-order duties'. Allan F. Blackstock, "'A dangerous species of ally'": Orangeism and the Irish Yeomanry'. *Irish Historical Studies* 30.119 (1997): 393.

65 '... who crop[p]ed their hair' is the only part of the first four definitions not struck out.

was not present to give them a glass of wine or something to eat, which he had intended to do' (28/8/1798).[66] On those occasions when Edgeworth does not make her message clear enough, she amends her entries to ensure a coherent narrative. She revises the following sentence – 'we feared the house wd certainly be burned' – to include the explanation '^as my father has taken command of the jail^', lest anyone think mistreatment had been meted out to the Edgeworth tenants. In the end, Edgeworthstown House was left untouched by the rebels, ostensibly saved due to a previous good deed by the housekeeper. However, mistrust then led to accusations being levelled at the unscathed patriarch by other landlords.[67]

Edgeworth's propensity for highlighting the family's achievements and interventions is always to the fore. Both Edgeworth's diary and Maria Edgeworth's letters recount an explosion that occurred on 4 September 1798, for example, and a comparative analysis offers a sense of Elizabeth Edgeworth's priorities:

> Elizabeth Edgeworth diary: we had a few minutes before heard a noise, like thunder which we took no notice of, but it was the ammunition cart, which had burnt & killed three horses on the road, which ^had occasioned this explosion^ Some people were killed, an officer much wounded, my mother went to bring this gentleman ^Mr Rochford^ to Edgeworthstown & linnen was prepared to dry the wounded persons…

> Maria Edgeworth letter to Aunt Ruxton, 5 September 1798: as we were quietly sitting in the portico we heard – as we thought close to us – the report of a pistol or a clap of thunder which shook the house […] The ammunition cart, containing nearly three barrels of gunpowder packed in tin cases, took fire and burst half way on the road to Longford. The man who drove the cart was blown to atoms – nothing of him could be found – two of the horses were killed, others were blown to pieces and their limbs scattered to a distance – the head and body of a man were found a hundred and twenty yards from the spot.[68]

The same event is inevitably framed and reported differently, across different media, by different writers, presenting us with an array of voices, perspectives, and levels of objectivity and emotion. Speaking of the French landing at

---

66 Fencibles were defined by their supporters as 'regular troops but for the internal protection of the country only'. The Reay Fencibles were enlisted in Scotland in 1794 and disbanded by 1802. Ian H. M. Scobie, *An Old Highland Fencible Corps: The History of the Reay Fencible Highland Regiment*. Edinburgh: Blackwood and Sons, 1914, vii.

67 Edgeworth and Edgeworth II 220–22.

68 Maria Edgeworth, *Maria Edgeworth's Letters from Ireland*. Ed. Valerie Pakenham. Dublin: Lilliput Press, 2018, 58.

Killala, the Irishman from Maria Edgeworth's *An Essay on Irish Bulls* (1802) offers some reflections on this inherent quality of life writing: 'During the French invasion of Ireland, two persons of undoubted integrity, who lived in the same house, kept journals of all that passed. When the journals were compared, scarcely a point of resemblance could be discovered'.[69] These differing accounts within 'the same house' are apparent within the life writing in evidence at Edgeworthstown itself, which often takes the same event as its focus, as in this instance. Maria's telling of the explosion is much more visceral and graphically violent, and, although it is probable that Elizabeth was sheltered from many of the violent details of the Rebellion, she was clearly aware of the loss of life experienced here. The figures for these losses are unclear – two horses, the man who drove the cart and others in Maria's account; and three horses and some people in Elizabeth Edgeworth's. The accounts are identical in their experience of the ensuing noise as being like thunder, but the two sisters communicate an entirely distinct picture. Elizabeth Edgeworth chose to focus on the survivors, rather than the gruesome causalities, and, significantly, to highlight the interventions of her stepmother. The entry was further amended to include mention of the driver's name, ^Mr Rochford^, in order to ensure her stepmother's deed was carefully recorded for posterity and the family's image strengthened.

The Edgeworths were an elite Enlightenment family with a public image to uphold and a legacy to build and safeguard. The legend that claims Edgeworthstown House was saved due to a good relationship between the household servants and the surrounding Catholic community contributed to the family's projected self-image, one that blended 'enlightened landlordism' with 'a residual feudalism'.[70] Many of the documents generated from within the household sought to justify the family's ownership of land and property and defend their position within Irish society. This material promotes their sense of their role as enlightened, improving landlords and trusted members of the wider Protestant community, and therefore the best people to govern Ireland.[71] Richard Lovell's attention to questions of the Edgeworth record and afterlife is obvious from his posthumously completed and published *Memoirs* (1820). Combined with the 'The Black Book of Edgeworthstown',

69 Maria Edgeworth, *An Essay on Irish Bulls*. Eds. Marilyn Butler, Jane Demarias, and Tim McLoughlin. London: Pickering & Chatto, 1999.

70 M. Kelsall, 'Edgeworthstown "Rebuilding"'. *Literary Representations of the Irish Country House*. Basingstoke: Palgrave, 2003, 31.

71 Ian Campbell Ross, 'Maria Edgeworth and the Culture of Improvement'. *Still Blundering into Sense: Maria Edgeworth, Her Context, Her Legacy*. Eds. Fiorenzo Fantaccini and Rafaella Leproni. Florence: Firenze UP, 2019, 29–48; Niall Gillespie, 'Irish Political Literature, c. 1788–1832'. PhD Thesis, TCD, 2013.

which charts the family's history in Ireland from the sixteenth century, and the profusion of letters portraying the family that were generated for wider consumption, it is clear that the creation of a family archive and image was held in importance within the household.[72] The well-known conversation piece 'The Edgeworth Family' (1787) by Adam Buck adds additional visual support to the family's wider repository of written images and similarly serves to present a particular vision to the public, communicating a strong image of the domestic education projects underway at Edgeworthstown.

The diary of Elizabeth Edgeworth disrupts and problematises the coherent image promoted in the paintings and writings concerning Richard Lovell, while endeavouring to consolidate it. Writing in the shadows of her more celebrated family members, Edgeworth's diary conveys the experience of marginalisation and her difficulty in carving out her own path, despite the family's efforts to integrate the lives of the children with those of the adults. Her diary reveals the obstacles to her prominence within the household and her apparent failure to secure or command attention. Elizabeth Edgeworth was neither the confidante of her father, like Maria, nor his favourite child, which position was filled by Honora (1774–1790).[73] Her death is recorded in the memoirs of her father as a cause of melancholy, but features primarily as 'another loss to her parents of the promising fruits of careful education'.[74] While she struggled to achieve an audience during her short life, her diary provided her with the means to work towards the acquisition of some degree of agency and authority, in her quest to contribute to and shape her family's recorded history. It courts a sympathetic audience from within her own family members, as well as targeting future generations. By aligning her writing with the narrative being crafted by her father and sister, and eschewing a focus on the personal, Elizabeth Edgeworth sought to ensure her diary's survival and to communicate with posterity.

Melesina Trench and Mary Leadbeater as Authors: Their Diaries, Literary Careers, and Afterlives

Diaries frequently served a dual purpose, functioning as fully formed life writing, as well as a route towards other literary endeavours, whether that

---

72 Toby Barnard, 'Libraries and Collectors, 1700–1800'. *The Oxford History of the Irish Book, Volume 3*. Eds. Raymond Gillespie and Andrew Hadfield. Oxford: OUP, 2006, 111–34, 133.

73 Mitzi Myers, '"Anecdotes from the Nursery" in Maria Edgeworth's *Practical Education* (1798): Learning from Children "Abroad and At Home"'. *The Princeton University Library Chronicle* 60.2 (Winter 1999): 247.

74 Edgeworth and Edgeworth II 262.

be the circulation in manuscript of imaginative literature or publication more broadly. There are suggestions that the diaries of Frances Burney served in this way, for example, and 'may have functioned as a form of apprenticeship that gave her the confidence and practice she needed to become a professional writer'.[75] While Elizabeth Edgeworth appears not to have sought to become a professional writer, the diary form offered her a channel for recording evidence of her other imaginative literary works, as well as affording her a platform for writing generally, allowing her to be creative and to hone her literary skills. Unlike Edgeworth, the diarists Mary Leadbeater and Melesina Trench went on to publish many works, including poetry, essays, and pamphlets, finding additional outlets for their writing beyond their diaries. Neither of these writers stopped writing in their diaries after becoming published authors, and it is clear that there was a symbiotic relationship between their life writing and instances of verse and improvement writing. Their prose writing within their diaries could be used to hone their poetry, for example, and their poetry employed to enhance their prose.[76] The diaries also provided a space in which they could give vent to their emotions and engage with topics that might not be deemed suitable in other forms.[77]

Unlike Edgeworth and Leadbeater with their large familial environments, Melesina Chenevix grew up with neither siblings nor parents, being orphaned by the age of four, and reared by her paternal and maternal grandfather (Richard Chenevix, Bishop of Waterford, and Archdeacon Gervais) in turn.[78] Melesina then found herself widowed by 21, following her marriage to Col. Richard St. George of Hatley Manor, Co. Leitrim, in 1786. The heiress later remarried while in France, to fellow Irish Huguenot Richard Trench, in 1803, the year following the establishment of her lifelong friendship with Leadbeater, which only ended with the death of both women, who died within one year of each other. The friendship between the two women was explicitly underscored by the next generation,

---

75 Clark 284.

76 See Katharine Kittredge, 'The Poetry of Melesina Trench: A Growing Skill at Sorrow'. *British Journal for Eighteenth-Century Studies* 28 (2005): 201–13. Dialogue between diaries and other prose works is not uncommon. Rolf Loeber and Magda Loeber note that Louisa Beaufort's nineteenth-century diary 'was substantially used for the text of an educational novel for children and adolescents'. Louisa Beaufort, 'Louisa Beaufort's Diary of Her Travels in South-West Munster and Leinster in 1842 and 1843'. Eds. Magda Loeber and Rolf Loeber. *Analecta Hibernica* 46 (2015): 134.

77 See Chapter 4 on Trench's mourning journal, for example.

78 Melesina has been described as a silent child. Her grandfather disapproved of diary writing and one would imagine she began writing later than Edgeworth and Leadbeater, though her earlier diaries do not survive to offer a date of commencement.

with Leadbeater's niece highlighting the relationship in the full title of *The Leadbeater Papers. The Annals of Ballitore… And the Correspondence of Mrs. R. Trench and Rev. George Crabbe with Mary Leadbeater* (1862), while Rev. Richard Chenevix Trench, the Dean of Westminster, frequently promoted the connection with Leadbeater, 'one of my mother's most honoured friends', throughout his publication of edited extracts of his mother's life writing in *The Remains of the Late Mrs. Richard Trench. Being Selections from her Journals, Letters, & Other Papers* (1862).[79]

Connections with posterity permitted the eighteenth-century diarist to imagine a situation whereby her diary could be a document connecting her tangentially to literary and cultural authority, thus giving her a degree of agency. The elderly Anne Jocelyn contemplates future attempts to establish a narrative of the Rebellion of 1798 within her own diary, for example, reflecting upon the event's written legacy and considering 'whoever writes the history of this eventful unhappy summer' (12/9/1798).[80] For Jocelyn and her contemporaries, there was the understanding that any historian of 1798 would almost inevitably be male – but might some source material be female in origin?[81] There is a sense within women's diaries from Ireland that such diaries could be employed in the construction of a more public narrative, whether the charting of a family's personal history of the conflict, or a record of the times. Leadbeater was able to preserve portraits of people and places in her surrounding environment throughout her multiple diaries, which circulated widely. These diaries were later drawn upon as a source for *The Annals of Ballitore* (1862), establishing a dialogue with Leadbeater's earlier portraits of Ballitore and placing them in an entirely new format and for a new audience, as a work of social and cultural history.[82] The *Annals* have been described as the 'edited and published' version of Leadbeater's diaries, or glossed as a posthumous publication of the same.[83] However, the

---

79 The association has continued: the two have been analysed together in the work of Stephen Behrendt, '"There is no second crop of summer flowers": Mary Leadbeater and Melesina Trench in Correspondence'. *Forum for Modern Language Studies* 52.2 (2016): 130–43; and Katharine Kittredge, '"I delight in the success of your literary labours": Friendship as Platform for Reinvention'. *The Circuit of Apollo: Eighteenth-Century Women's Tributes to Women*. Eds. Laura L. Runge and Jessica Cook. Newark: University of Delaware Press, 2019, 155–75.

80 Anne Jocelyn 24.

81 The letters of Helen Maria Williams from Revolutionary Paris also presented a form of immediate history. For discussion of British women who did produce histories, see Devoney Looser, *British Women Writers and the Writing of History, 1670–1820*. Baltimore: Johns Hopkins UP, 2005.

82 Hughes 138.

83 Claire Connolly, 'Irish Romanticism, 1800–1830'. *The Cambridge History of Irish*

Annals are a separate piece of life writing, a retrospective work, 'begun in the year 1799'.[84] While there are stylistic and thematic continuities, the *Annals* provide a new, retrospective narrative, based on certain diary entries, with the published work edited and introduced by Leadbeater's niece, Elizabeth Shackleton.

Trench's diaries were published in the same year as *The Annals*. A private edition of Trench's journey to Germany in 1861 was followed in 1862 by a larger offering from her various diaries, reproducing the German section, intertwined with letters and commentary. The aims of the project are plainly stated by Richard Chenevix Trench, who makes his objectives clear: 'I have no intention of writing a Memoir, but record only the events of my Mother's life so far as is necessary for making these *Remains* intelligible.'[85] However, he also stipulates that what the reader is presented with are 'only remains of her "Remains"' as so much of the material is lost by this point.[86] Again, the impact of the material reality of a diary's ephemeral nature reveals itself, having an effect on diary composition, as we have seen with Leadbeater, as well as on a diary's survival. Chenevix Trench bemoans how many of the early diaries his mother kept had gone 'hopelessly astray' by the mid-nine-teenth century: 'the volumes, or fascicles, consisting for the most part of loose sheets of paper, not very carefully sewn together, with or without covers may seem in some measure to have provoked their fate'.[87] This is very far from the only consideration, however, and choices made by Trench's son impacted vastly upon the text that we are presented with and upon which many opinions have been based. Comparative analysis between the *Remains* and surviving manuscript material in the Hampshire Record Office in the UK demonstrate a considerable number of both silent and explicit editorial decisions taken by Chenevix Trench that have influenced our understanding of Melesina, her life writing, and her legacy.[88]

Literature, Volume 1, to 1890. Eds. Margaret Kelleher and P. O'Leary. Cambridge: CUP, 2006, 407–48; Angela Bourke et al., eds., *The Field Day Anthology of Irish Writing, Volumes 4 and 5, Irish Women's Writing and Traditions*. Cork: Cork UP, 2002, IV 515. Conflation of the *Annals* and the diaries has also led many to state that the diaries were commenced in 1766, when they in fact begin in 1769. Both Connolly and *The Field Day Anthology* refer to a 1766 start date for the diary.

84 A manuscript copy of *The Annals of Ballitore* is available in the RSFIHL – Hannah Shackleton, Ballitore Journal 1766–1772, P25 & Second Volume 1772–1784, P26.

85 Chenevix Trench in Trench, *Remains*, 207.

86 Chenevix Trench in Trench, *Remains*, viii.

87 Chenevix Trench in Trench, *Remains*, vi.

88 Hampshire Record Office possess six of Trench's original MS diaries, from 1791 to 1802 (23M93/1), in addition to copies of extracts from her diaries from 1797 to 1820 in her son's hand (23M93/1/6).

Chenevix Trench's comments upon the period of time in which his mother was in Ireland, her country of birth, demonstrate his prioritisation of her more cosmopolitan travel accounts over quotidian details and certainly over the diaries' Irish interludes: 'Of the period, somewhat more than a year, which elapsed [in Ireland, 1801] before her next visit to the Continent, I find few memoranda, *and fewer still which need to be published*' (my emphasis).[89] Comparison between the Irish volume – that is her diary for 1801–1802, or 23M93/1/5 – and this section of *Remains* reveals a difference in content, both domestic and public. Trench's entries for December 1802, excluded from *Remains*, provide insight into a typical day, including Trench's learning German, playing chess, writing letters, and keeping company. Entries for mid-December also record her joy at the return of her son from school, while the new year charts her sense of loss at his departure. In addition to Chenevix Trench's dismissal of these and other details regarding dinner engagements, birthday parties, and visits to different demesnes, he also made the decision to exclude some of his mother's frank opinions, such as her strong disparagement of the middleman system in Ireland (see figure 1.6).[90]

In addition to such omissions, Trench's own emendations are also absent from *Remains*. The manuscript diary shows that the diarist was very particular with language and revisited the diary entries to make alterations that ensured exact reflection of her thoughts in order to precisely communicate her intentions. For example, she altered her commentary on the family of the principal tenant on her farm near Gorey, in Co. Wexford, to declare that 'he has a handsome family' after having struck out the comment 'His family are fine' (13/8/1801).[91] Subsequent to this, within the same entry, she corrected a remark concerning how the family behaved in certain circumstances, changing it to read 'particularly in the presence of their ^those they consider as their^ superiors', placing the origins of this perspective of superiority back upon the family.[92] In deciding what to choose then for inclusion, it quickly becomes clear that Chenevix Trench placed most value upon his mother's dealings with the various celebrities of the day as she travelled across Europe, recalling the diaries of English Bluestocking courtier Mary Hamilton (1756–1816), who carefully tracked her interactions with other members of the elite, including at the court of King George III.[93] Chenevix Trench includes Trench's critical portrayals of several ascendancy figures,

89 Chenevix Trench in Trench, *Remains*, 129.
90 For analysis of this see Chapter 5.
91 23M93/1/5.
92 23M93/1/5.
93 16 manuscript diaries (1776–1797, mostly dating from 1782–1784) belonging to Mary Hamilton are preserved in the John Rylands Research Institute and Library,

Figure 1.6: Melesina Trench diary written during her time in Ireland. HRO 23M93/1/5.

including Lady Holland, who 'has a mixture of imperiousness and caprice very amusing to the mere spectators. Her indolence is also remarkable, and she lies in a very easy posture on a sofa…' (8/9/1800), and Lady Hamilton, who is described as 'bold, forward, coarse, assuming, and vain. Her figure is colossal' (3/10/1800).[94] This focus informed much of the twentieth-century commentary on Trench as gossip and socialite.[95]

Decisions of inclusion, exclusion, and elision such as are evident in the *Remains* are rife across nineteenth- and twentieth-century publications of earlier manuscript diaries and life writings.[96] These later editions present us with selections of texts deemed interesting and appropriate, whether morally or socially, by the mores of the later period and generally overlook any reference

University of Manchester, and have been digitised and are available online. Mary Hamilton, Diary of Mary Hamilton, The Mary Hamilton Papers, HAM/2/1–16.

94 Trench, *Remains*, 101; 105.

95 Jack Russell, *Nelson and the Hamiltons*. New York: Simon and Schuster, 1969; Mollie Hardwick, *Emma, Lady Hamilton*. New York: Holt, Rinehart, and Winston, 1969.

96 This is the case with the letter-journals of Elizabeth Sheridan (later Le Fanu), for example. They were presented to the public as *Betsy Sheridan's Journal* (Oxford: OUP, 1960), with the editorial decision taken by William Lefanu to invoke the writer's diminutive name rather than her given name, as so often used to occur in publications of Frances Burney's writing.

to the material conditions or paratextuality of manuscript editions.[97] A case study surrounding scholarship on the 1599–1605 'diary' of Margaret Hoby (frequently described as the first-known female diarist writing in English) makes clear the problems that can arise from relying on earlier editions of diaries. It identifies the mistranscription, misrepresentation, omissions, and invented meanings resulting from two previous editions of the text.[98] The quality of printed editions of earlier life writings has improved immensely, and many now feature details of editorial conventions, which provide much clarity to a reader navigating them. Some fine contemporary scholarship has subsequently resulted from exclusive engagement with modern scholarly editions.[99] However, where possible, it is always helpful to engage with the original manuscript and to familiarise oneself with all editorial conventions and decisions, considering the implications of these for understanding authorial intention, aspiration, and literary afterlives.

The predominant scholarly narrative for both Trench and Leadbeater is still largely informed by the late nineteenth-century editions of their work. Mary Leadbeater is now named, along with Henrietta Battier, as one of 'the most important Irish women poets of the revolutionary era' in a 2021 survey of Irish women's poetry.[100] However, contemporary critics argue that her fame is almost exclusively posthumous, generated by the publication of *The Annals of Ballitore*.[101] This is in spite of such descriptions of Leadbeater

---

97 See Mary Hamilton's diaries, published by her great-grandchildren, Elizabeth and Florence Anson, in 1925 as *Mary Hamilton, Afterwards Mrs John Dickenson, at Court and at Home. From Letters and Diaries, 1756 to 1816*. Eds. Elizabeth and Florence Anson. London: John Murray, 1925.

98 Juan Pedro Lamata, '"[A]ltered that a little which before I had written": How Margaret Hoby Wrote and Rewrote her Manuscript'. *Renaissance Studies* (2023): 1–20. See also *Diary and Letters of Madame D'Arblay* (1842–46), first published two years after the diarist's death, described as 'an interesting case of a diary being revised by the diarist herself in later years, and then tampered with by other editors'. Ożarska 76.

99 Magdalena Ożarska's monograph is based exclusively and intentionally on scholarly editions, not manuscripts: 'My purpose here is not to investigate written artefacts, i.e. original manuscripts.' Ożarska 5.

100 Catherine Jones, 'Irish Romanticism'. *A History of Irish Women's Poetry*. Eds. Ailbhe Darcy and David Wheatley. Cambridge: CUP, 2021, 106–109. Trench is not mentioned in the chapter.

101 See, for example, Katharine Kittredge, 'Melesina Chenevix St. George Trench'. *Women Writer Biographies*, Chawton House Library, and comments such as 'Leadbeater's fame as a woman writer was, however, posthumous and developed following the publication of her "Annals of Ballitore" by her niece, Elizabeth Shackleton.' Gerardine Meaney, Mary O'Dowd, and Bernadette Whelan, *Reading the Irish Woman: Studies in Cultural Encounters and Exchange, 1714–1960*. Liverpool: LUP, 2013, 73–74. Stephen Behrendt departs from this narrative.

as 'standing conspicuous' 'among the many distinguished Female Writers of the present day' in the *Freeman's Journal* (8 October 1813), for example.[102] Equally, Trench's career is described thus in her entry in the *Dictionary of Irish Biography*: 'Like her favourite author, Madame de Sévigné, Trench *wrote neither for an audience nor fame* but gained both posthumously through letters and journals' (my emphasis).[103] In fact, neither woman was a stranger to either success or recognition during their own lifetimes and it is clear that both actively sought out an audience across the full breadth of their writing.

Trench's diary shows that an audience was constantly in view, with its entries carefully edited by the diarist herself, including the numerous emendations aforementioned. Trench's own thoughts on the posthumous publication of life writing – evident in her intention to edit letters of two childhood friends – indicate her awareness of this possibility of publication: 'Where nothing is published that the dead would have wished to conceal, or that can hurt the feelings of the living, it is a blameless gratification to diffuse and prolong the remembrance of those we have loved' (n.d./9/1811).[104] The origins of the narrative of Trench's seeking neither an audience nor fame seem to be Chenevix Trench's comments in the opening sentence of *Remains*, where he describes his mother as 'one who had no name in literature', before praising her 'sacred obscurity'.[105] He casts his mother in a demure light, establishing Trench as one who did not seek attention, his marriage of words in the phrase 'sacred obscurity' reinforcing the connections between feminine retirement and virtue. However, as with Leadbeater's writing, including her diaries, the literary aspirations of Trench and her quest for an audience are discernible across both manuscript and print circulation of her works.

There remains a need to acknowledge manuscript circulation as valid and important during the long eighteenth century and as a choice that was made by many authors, both male and female.[106] A wide audience could be reached in this manner, and Melanie Bigold's work on Elizabeth Carter, Elizabeth Rowe, and Catharine Cockburn has demonstrated how manuscript circulation was 'an accepted method of engaging with the wider republic of

---

102 *Irish Newspaper Archives*. Her death notice mentions how she was 'favourably known to the public by her compositions, both in poetry and prose'. *Freeman's Journal* (5 July 1826).
103 Bridget Hourican, 'Melesina Chenevix Trench', *DIB*.
104 Trench, *Remains*, 245.
105 Chenevix Trench in Trench, *Remains* v; vi.
106 Melanie Bigold, *Women of Letters, Manuscript Circulation and Print Afterlives in the Eighteenth Century*. Basingstoke: Palgrave, 2013, 8.

letters'.[107] Betty Schellenberg and Michelle Levy have shown how 'print has cast an artificially large shadow over what was in fact a well-established, lively, and accessible culture of manuscript production and circulation'.[108] Leadbeater's diaries make numerous references to her adolescent literary outputs and demonstrate that she was also aware of the prejudices against women who sought an audience for the work: 'What shall I do about my unfortunate verse – I hate to be thought forward'. However, she overcame these scruples very quickly and decided to circulate her poetry amongst both male and female peers: 'I believe I'll go make a verse but then I have several to write for Hannah' (22/12/1774) and '[Hannah] shew'd us a note from Williams to her desiring her to get him two of my verses' (6/1/1775).[109] Modesty was only one reason for choosing manuscript circulation over print, with conservatism and agency two other pertinent factors, as circulation in manuscript form 'left control of the text in the author's hands', recalling Leadbeater's earlier attempts to control who did and did not read her diary.[110]

Equally, the reasons for an author's seeking anonymous publication are not clear cut, though gender considerations are still at play. Leadbeater's earliest printed work, *Extracts and Original Anecdotes for the Improvement of Youth* (Dublin, 1794), in which her first verses appeared, was published anonymously. Trench also embraced this means of reaching an audience. She was the anonymous author of multiple pamphlets on topics ranging from the support of abolition of the slave trade to the education of children and the amelioration of conditions for young boys engaged in chimney cleaning.[111] Trench published several volumes of poetry, all anonymously, including the extended narrative poems, *Lady Mary Queen of Scots, an Historical Ballad; with Other Poems. By a lady* (London, 1800); *Campaspe, an Historical Tale; And Other Poems* (Southampton, 1815); *Ellen, a Ballad. Founded on a Recent Fact. And Other Poems* (Bath, 1815); and the science fiction poem, *Laura's Dream; Or The Moonlanders* (London, 1816). In addition to desiring an audience for her writing, there was also a 'philanthropic impulse' behind numerous publications, as reflected in the full titles of certain works, such as *Ellen, a Ballad... Sold for the Benefit of the House of Protection*.[112]

These women writers were recognised for their achievements during their lifetimes and found encouragement amongst their peers. Trench was

---

107 Bigold 7.
108 Michelle Levy and Betty A. Schellenberg. *How and Why to Do Things with Eighteenth-Century Manuscripts*. Cambridge: CUP, 2021, 1.
109 NLI MS 9298.
110 Bigold 11.
111 See Behrendt 73–74.
112 Behrendt 74.

supported and championed by Leadbeater, as well as by Anna Seward, Eleanor Butler, and Sarah Ponsonby.[113] In reciprocal fashion, Leadbeater's named publications were equally well supported by Trench and other Irish writers. The English edition of Leadbeater's *Cottage Dialogues. Vol. 1* (Dublin and London, 1811) famously featured a glossary by Maria Edgeworth, whose name was very well established by this point, while the prefatory material credits Trench for her revisions and editing. Previous to this, Leadbeater's *Poems, by Mary Leadbeater (Late Shackleton)...* (London, 1808) received support from across the Quaker community as well as from peers. We know that Melesina Trench ordered six copies of this work, and Trench's name features on the subscription list alongside such elite company as the Bishop of Meath, the Countess of Bessborough, and Lord Charleville. Amongst the 164 subscribers to Leadbeater's 1808 poetry collection were multiple Quaker life writers from Ireland, including Elizabeth Clibborn and Dinah Goff. Both Trench and Leadbeater had access to an extensive network of fellow female writers who assisted them in ensuring their work reached a wide audience and supported their endeavours across a variety of genres.

Irish diaries, then, bear witness to an array of readerly apparatus and to a specificity of presentation, as well as a multitude of marginalia, incorporating emendations and annotations. These elements highlight the importance of engagement with manuscript sources where they do survive. As we have seen, such aspects are often absent from published versions of diaries, many of which have also been shown to have been significantly altered or bowdlerised by nineteenth and early twentieth-century editors in particular. This chapter makes clear that many diaries from the long eighteenth century were explicitly composed with an audience in mind, particularly a future or posthumous one, including those written by Elizabeth Clibborn, Mary Mathew, Maria Strangman, Mary Anne Dawson, and Anne Jocelyn. It is also clear that the diary form could offer a space to display one's creativity and literary prowess, and the language used is often very carefully considered. We have seen how diaries were employed to record events, to contribute to the shaping of a family's legacy, and to preserve one's story for posterity. Considerations of the paratextual apparatus of Elizabeth Edgeworth's diary, alongside her processes of selection, omission, and narrative emphasis, provide us with new insight into the strategies that could be embraced in order to ensure an audience for one's life writing. Offering this audience a framework for understanding the material proffered, a glossary serves as an entry point into the diary that follows, encouraging engagement and

---

113 For other examples of women supporting the writing of their peers see Elizabeth Eger, *Bluestockings: Women of Reason from Enlightenment to Romanticism*. Basingstoke: Palgrave, 2010.

facilitating comprehension. It also reaches out to future generations to offer them historical context for the unfolding events in the diarist's lifetime and positions a young woman such as Elizabeth Edgeworth as someone capable both of contributing to larger narratives and of playing a role in curation and future understanding.

Comparative readings of the manuscript diaries of Melesina Trench and Mary Shackleton Leadbeater support such findings and disrupt our understanding of these women as figures who avoided fame and a wider readership, with their diary entries revealing authors conscious of shaping their sentences and writings with an eye to both current and future readers. The diaries' paratext, the diarists' emendations, editorial interventions, and marginalia, alongside the integrated commentary on the publication of life writing and the embracing of the title of journalist, communicate these women's anticipation of and desire for an audience. These diary examples, added to Trench and Leadbeater's myriad literary outputs across verse and prose, clearly establish these women as writers with broad literary aspirations who disseminated their writing across a variety of different avenues, and fully embraced the role of author. With exceptions noted, the corpus of writing considered in this book challenges any interpretation of the diary as a private form of writing not intended for a readership and prompts us to reconsider diary writing as a practice that allowed women to contribute to a wider literary tradition in which they could view themselves as agents.

CHAPTER TWO

Diaries, the Novel, and the Adolescent Self

Diaries offered women in Ireland a platform that proved cross-generational in appeal, with women of all ages engaged in journal-keeping. The breadth of ages is conspicuous across the diaries that survive, with the youngest diarist commencing at 11 and the oldest at 67, with the intervening decades all represented to differing degrees. The most common age for women and girls to begin writing a diary in Ireland was 15 years old, with most women and girls taking up the practice between the ages of 14 and 30.[1] The diary form provides all these generations of women with a vehicle for expressing themselves, but it is particularly germane to these younger writers, developing a voice and shaping a sense of selfhood as they emerged from their parents' protection, seeking models to identify with and which to emulate, and attempting to portray a coherent sense of self. This chapter demonstrates how young women and girls used the diary form to navigate the transitional period from childhood to adulthood, and often from singlehood to marriage, negotiating the marriage market and courtship, and such contingent activities as dancing and flirting. It offers a better understanding of the individual's perception of the lived experience of youth in the eighteenth century, detailing adolescent attachments and rebellion against parental restraints. Though dating from the late nineteenth century, the term adolescent can be applied constructively to earlier periods such as this, allowing recognition of the many continuities in adolescent behavioural patterns and attitudes evident in life writing, particularly those related to an emerging sense of selfhood.[2] The diaries are filled with these young

1 All these ages are based on the Irish diaries that survive for 1760–1810. See Introduction.

2 Mary O'Dowd, 'Adolescent Girlhood in Eighteenth-Century Ireland'. *A History of the Girl: Formation, Education, and Identity*. Eds. Mary O'Dowd and June Purvis. Basingstoke: Palgrave, 2018, 53–54.

people's anxieties and preoccupations, and continuities with today's ideas of adolescence are frequently discernible. Entries charting friendships and flirting coexist with others fearing singlehood or pining for a certain body shape, consistent with our sense of adolescent diaries from later periods.[3]

In addition to this consistency of emphasis and interest, the diaries demonstrate striking parallels in terms of their form. There are immediate transhistorical parallels discernible in the practice of young girls trying to find their own voice and appropriating the voices of others, stretching back to previous centuries.[4] What immediately distinguishes the eighteenth-century adolescents from these predecessors is how they often constructed a narrative voice for themselves by emulating the voices found in those novels that were emerging during that century. There are remarkably close intersections with certain titles, and an examination of the diaries reveals parallels and continuities with sentimental, picaresque, Gothic, and epistolary novels. Key patterns in expression and style can be identified across the adolescent diaries – the widespread espousal of hyperbole, for example, the mode of sensibility, the abundance of superlatives – offering a sense of the style preferred by young people in the eighteenth century. All the diarists endeavour to create a coherent narrative voice, and many also display a cast of secondary characters surrounding them. We see the adolescent diarist present herself to the reader as heroine of the piece, interacting with sympathetic female friends or rebelling against villainous parent figures, for instance. The diarists also engage in fantasising and romanticising elements of their lives. This is particularly apparent in their portrayals of non-threatening relationships through their celebration of key friendships and platonic familial connections. There is often a striking difference between such detailed portraits and the absence of commentary on their prospective future husbands, about whom the young diarists are often resolutely silent.[5]

---

3 Hiltrud Susanna Kirsch, 'The Body in Adolescent Diaries, The Case of Karen Horney'. *The Psychoanalytic Study of the Child* 57.1 (2002): 400–10.

4 Though there are extant examples across other forms of writing, it is difficult to find adolescent diarists from earlier periods. Elizabeth Deleval (1648–1717) and Elizabeth Isham (1609–1654) are frequently referenced as such, but their writing is retrospective, so that they frame the narrative from a more advanced age. With thanks to Edel Lamb for her thoughts on diaries from this period. See Edel Lamb's own project, the Leverhulme-funded, 'Writing Early Modern Girlhood, c. 1544–1704'.

5 Mary Anne Dawson is recorded as having married Windham Quin, only brother of Valentine-Richard, 1ˢᵗ Viscount Mountearl, *Debrett's Peerage*, II 1129. Several online genealogical overviews of the Dawson family suggest that this event took place in 1783, e.g. https://www.thepeerage.com/p4794.htm#c47935.1. There are references to different members of the Quin family throughout the diary. However, no mention is made of

The diarists discussed in this chapter range from those who kept a diary all their lives to those for whom the diary form was only embraced for a few months during their adolescence. While she wrote throughout her life, Mary Shackleton Leadbeater's earlier diaries, from the 1770s, will be considered here, particularly those from when she was between the ages of 14 and 16.[6] Mary Tighe, née Blachford, maintained a diary from at least age 14 to age 30, though the majority of the entries do not survive.[7] Conversely, the diaries of Mary Anne Dawson, Charity Lecky, and Frances Jocelyn were of short duration and pursued from approximately the ages of 19 to 21; 14 to 15; and 16 to 18 respectively.[8]

Frequently dismissed by male contemporaries as preoccupied only with balls and marriage prospects, the voices of young women and adolescents were repeatedly marginalised during this time. This chapter instead champions these figures, recognising the value of their opinions. It demonstrates how we might better understand the evolution of personal identities through inclusion of such source material, as well as gain a better understanding of the development of both imaginative and non-imaginative prose during the long eighteenth century, as the boundaries between both are revealed as exceptionally porous and fluid. The diary offered these young people a space to experiment and rehearse personae, providing them with an alternative platform when their voices were so frequently silenced elsewhere.

The Development of a Novel Voice

The diary (1782–1784) of Mary Anne Dawson is characterised by a meticulous commitment to precision. Mary Anne provides a dry, unsentimental

Dawson's preference for either Windham or the heir Valentine, and there is no allusion to a wedding.

6 Mary Leadbeater, Diaries covering the years 1769–1789 in 22 volumes. NLI MSS 9292–9314.

7 So much of Tighe's diary writing has been destroyed that it is difficult to form any conjectures about its original length or content. Mary Tighe, *The Collected Poems and Journals of Mary Tighe*. Ed. Harriet Kramer Linkin. Lexington: University Press of Kentucky, 2005.

8 Mary Anne Dawson, Diary of Mary Anne Dawson, 1782–84. Clements Papers, TCD MSS 7270–7270a; Anon. [Charity Lecky]. Diary of a Winter in Bath, 1796–97. James Marshall and Marie-Louise Osborn Collection, Beinecke Rare Book and Manuscript Library, Yale University, Osborn c446; Frances Theodosia Jocelyn, Diary of Frances Theodosia Jocelyn, 1810–1812. NLI MS 18,430. Jocelyn is one of the few diarists to note her birthday each year, e.g. 'This is my birthday. 18! How old I am grown!' (11/8/1812). Subsequent quotations from these diaries in this chapter are taken from these MSS.

recording of her timetabled days of learning. The earlier part of her diary in particular presents itself more as a chronicle, offering a register of the events of Dawson's day as they unfolded, producing a form of historical record without a focus on interiority or 'philosophic treatment'.[9] It provides an exact facsimile of a young woman's routine during the late eighteenth century, incorporating details from when Mary Anne gets up until she retires to bed. Her days were full of learning, especially French and Geography, for which she had masters who taught her; walking; visiting and receiving visits; and occasionally going to the theatre or on excursions.[10] The following is an indicative entry and is representative of her unadorned style of writing:

> Got up before 7, translated a Page of the History of Spain into French, Breakfasted at half past eight, taking Lesson with the Geography Master, Read the Psalms & Lessons for the Day –, finished my Letter [...] Spent the Evening at home, Wrote French Exercise, & Read French, went to Bed at 10 (2/8/1782)[11]

Dawson enjoyed a wide-ranging Enlightenment curriculum. Her reading encompassed examples from conduct literature, life writing, History, Geography, and French, with titles including Clarendon's *History of the Rebellion* (1702–1704) and *The Letters of the Late Ignatius Sancho, An African* (1782), for example.[12] It also included many titles by Bluestocking authors, with Dawson citing works by Hannah More; Elizabeth Carter's 'Paper in ye Rambler'; Hester Chapone's 'Letter on the Government of the Temper' (1773); Elizabeth Griffith and Richard Griffith's *Genuine Letters* (1757–1770); and Frances Burney's 1782 novel *Cecilia*.[13] In general, however, there are

9 'Chronicle, n.'. *OED.*

10 Mary Anne's diary can be divided into four sections – Part 1 in Chelsea with Lady Dartrey's family where the diarist is very scholarly but still participates in visiting rituals; Part 2 at Hot Wells, enjoying the Bath scene and more of a leisured timetable with no lessons; Part 3 charting the ill health and eventual death of her mother; Part 4 back in Ireland with the Charlemonts, where she engages widely with associational life, including going to the Castle, assemblies, and national convention.

11 Music is perhaps less a preoccupation of the diarists than one might expect, though there are references in the diary of Mary Anne to Lady Dartrey's singing and playing the harp, and in the diary of Marianne ffolliott to the diarist giving her sister 'a lesson on the piano before breakfast' (23/12/1809). Marianne ffolliott, Diary of Mary Anne Ffolliott, Boyle Co. Roscommon, 1809–1827. PRONI D1995/1.

12 She also records her subscription to a circulating library for one quarter, from which she 'brought home the 1st Vol of Johnson's Lives of ye Poets, & the first of Ld. Lytellton's Letters' (23/8/1783).

13 Carter contributed to nos. 44 and 100 of *The Rambler*, from 18 August 1750 and 7 March 1751 respectively.

few examples of imaginative literature cited, with fewer still instances of novels.[14]

Dawson's diary writing is an outlier amongst that of her peers, who sought to replicate the flow and verve of the novels they were reading and whose entries heave with excitement and energy. The following embodies the general thrust of the 1810–1812 diary of Frances Jocelyn, for example: 'We sat up in Jem's room, and laughed and screamed and also in the tent. [...] I am so pleasant. I shall jump out of my skin, I am so happy' (10/7/1811). The short assertions of happiness, combined with the physicality of the verbs, 'jump', 'laugh', and 'scream' convey the youthful excitement and exuberance that ebb from Jocelyn's diary. The repetition of the intensifier 'so' is a pattern we see throughout her diary entries, further strengthened here by the figurative expression of joy. Unlike Dawson's entries, Jocelyn's diary throbs with expressions of praise for a variety of imaginative literature, particularly novels and poetry. She mentions reading Thompson, 'a beautiful lovely writer' (25/1/1812); finishing 'San Sebastien, the pleasantest Novel I ever read' (28/1/1812); and praises the 3-volume didactic novel by Jane West, *The Infidel Father* (1802), 'which I like very much' (19/5/1812). Jocelyn also mentions reading the poem *Psyche; or, The Legend of Love* (50 copies published for private circulation, 1805) by her fellow diarist Mary Tighe, while others played: 'They played at chess, & I talked & read Psyche' (2/11/1810). While one does occasionally find the rudimentary sense of a general day as chronicled in Dawson's early entries – 'I would not go out. Played, sang, drew, read chemistry all the morning' (Jocelyn, 5/1/1811) – the vast majority of other entries by Mary Anne Dawson's peers are entirely different in both tone and content. One can speculate that the absence of a jocular tone was prompted by the murder of Mary Anne's father, Richard Dawson of Ardee, Co. Louth, on the family property, the same year the diary was commenced, though there is no reference to this in the diary itself.[15] The other adolescent diaries are more playful, less guarded, and one can immediately identify multiple parallels and continuities with eighteenth-century novels across voice, tone, character, narrative technique, and style.

The diary of Charity Lecky is exceptionally useful in exploring intersections with emerging modes of novel writing and offers the possibility of identifying and exploring connections between life writing and realism,

14 Several references are made to Samuel Richardson's *The History of Sir Charles Grandison* (1753).

15 '[H]e was waylaid by two or more Ruffians by whom he was feloniously robbed and so violently assaulted that he soon after died of the wounds that he received by the said ruffians or some of them.' Diarmuid Mac Iomhair, 'The Murder of Richard Dawson'. *Journal of the County Louth Archaeological Society* 15.3 (1963): 249–54.

sentimentalism, the picaresque, and the Gothic.[16] One crucial influence upon Lecky's diary is Tobias Smollett's picaresque novel *The Expedition of Humphry Clinker* (1771).[17] There are many echoes of that epistolary novel throughout Lecky's diary, and the character of Lydia Melford seems to have provided the very model for Charity Lecky's portrayal of herself, such are the similarities in expression, phrases, and markers of both adolescents' youth and ostensible naivety, as well as their later confidence and maturity. Additionally, there are multiple narrative parallels in evidence throughout, including of course the 17-year-old Lydia's visit to Bath but also the journey as a whole. Travel from the periphery to the metropole, whether it be from provincial Ireland or Wales, represents the core motivation behind the two texts, with both the novel and the diary engaging with the experiences of marginality and the realities of the marriage market. While Charity Lecky makes use of the popular Gothic tropes of the 1790s for her descriptions of the dangerous carriage ride, the device of the carriage spill itself is of course central to the plot of *Humphry Clinker*, allowing the eponymous character's true identity to be revealed.[18] The nature of travel permits the fictional letter writer to encounter new environs and new people, and the journey from Wales to Bath undertaken by Lydia – related to us alongside the voices of her brother, uncle, aunt, and aunt's maid – foregrounds issues of nationality and difference, which we also find echoed in Charity's diary writing.[19]

A wide variety of formal mechanisms and narrative structures are drawn upon in creating a diary. It is clear that Charity Lecky was taking much care with her recordings and experimenting with styles. She seems cognisant of the possibility of using the diary format as one in which to hone her style and her method of communication. This is in opposition to her impression of her own clumsiness while speaking, such as when she was the recipient of a gift, which 'I was very thankful for, but, as usual I lost all power of articulation at that time & could scarcely say I was obliged to her' (17/3/1797).

16 Notes on the diary by Centa Thompson, who transcribed the work in the early twentieth century, suggest that the diary is by Centa's grandmother, Hannah Lecky, née McCausland (1751–1826). However, Hannah was middle aged and married with children at the time of the diary's composition. Instead, I would posit that the diary was written by one of the four surviving daughters of Hannah and her husband William (1748–1825), MP for Derry. The diarist refers to letters to Jane and Sydney, which means that she could potentially be Charity or Elizabeth. The latter is too young, being only ten at this point, making Charity, born 1782, the most likely author.

17 With thanks to Aileen Douglas for initially alerting me to the parallels.

18 The event is described thus by Lydia: 'some of us narrowly escaped with life – My uncle had well nigh perished...'. Tobias Smollett, *The Expedition of Humphry Clinker*. Ed. Lewis M. Knapp. Oxford: OUP, 2009, 334.

19 For considerations of this diary and Irishness see Chapter 5.

The written diary allowed her more time to compose her thoughts and communicate her opinions, judgements, and observations, working through her thoughts on questions of self, nation, and age, as she undertook her journey. Charity Lecky's diary presents us with an excited, impressed, and at times mesmerised perspective on Bath. It draws upon a highly charged style of writing, and her account of life there is one loaded with hyperbole, with one superlative following another in a breathless, excited style, so that she describes events and interactions as being the best ever encountered or experienced: 'it was one of the pleasantest entertainments I had ever been at' (24/1/1797); 'the most beautiful elegant dance I ever saw' (3/3/1797). Such superlatives remind us of the writer's youth and suggest one well versed in the novels of the day, rather than an adherent to the abundance of conduct literature targeted at her age group.[20]

Lecky's descriptions of Gothic landscapes with portending precipices and sublime vistas on her way to and from Bath are quintessentially Radcliffean in composition. Her journey is communicated with a sense of danger and menace, so that the writer is confronted by 'a dreadfull rock hanging over as if ready to tumble on the road – so steep that we were in danger of falling over the horses' (11/5/1797), before coming face to face with 'another shocking mountain where we had the open ocean to the right & a tremendous rock to the left' (11/5/1797). Such descriptions set the diarist up as the heroine of the composition, facing such circumstances with courage and strength. She is a Julia or an Emilia overcoming obstacles and avoiding dangerous accidents, all conveyed with a narrative depth akin to that of a novel. Indeed, Charity Lecky's diary repeatedly echoes the tone of the letters written by Smollett's Lydia Melford, emulating their freshness and excitement. Lydia's writing style is also one infused with hyperbole and superlatives: 'We went accordingly to Lough Lomond, one of the most enchanting spots in the whole world.'[21] Her style is similarly imbued with excess sensibility, wherein encounters and friendships with other young women are met with deep joys, sorrows, and aspirations: 'I hope, the friendship we contracted at boarding-school, will last for life ... O, my dear Letty.'[22] The character's epistolary correspondence with Laetitia Willis showcases that privileging of friendship so often associated with adolescence, wherein one notes a

---

20 While other diarists record the titles of novels they read, we are not treated to such details from Lecky. For conduct literature's circulation in Ireland, see Moyra Haslett, "For the Improvement and Amusement of Young Ladies": Elizabeth Carter and the Bluestockings in Ireland'. *Eighteenth-Century Ireland* (2018): 33–60.

21 Smollett 258.

22 Smollett 10.

quest for independence and a rebellion against parental structures.[23] We can observe such highly charged friendships and markers of sensibility in Charity Lecky's diary too. Taking leave of a friend, for example, is recorded with dramatic flair: 'Miss S bid us adieu, I fear for ever, we have but little chance of meeting in this world again' (2/11/1796).

There are stylistic parallels with Lecky's writing throughout the diary of Frances Jocelyn, which also effervesces with hyperbole and superlatives and places great emphasis on friendships. A chapel is described by Jocelyn as 'the most beautiful little thing I ever saw' (13/11/1810), while the diarist 'took a delightful drive, the pleasantest day I ever felt' (14/9/1810). As with Lecky, Jocelyn's movements across Ireland, from urban to rural environments, leads to the landscape being recorded with hyperbolic assiduity, here with underscored superlatives. Jocelyn records having walked 'to the top of Sugarloaf's shoulder, where we saw the most delightful beautiful view I ever remember seeing' (3/10/1810). Jocelyn's evocations of Gothic landscapes depart from Lecky's in her conjuring of the morbid through an existential undercurrent that surfaces intermittently throughout the diary: 'I was standing on a dangerous rock to-day and it occurred to me, suppose I tumbled down and was drowned...' (22/5/1812). The voice and tone of her diary can shift instantly from mundane to histrionic, as when she is in the midst of packing her belongings for a visit, Jocelyn reflects, 'one should always settle one's things before one leaves home. God alone knows how soon I shall return to it, if ever' (27/9/1810).

The melodramatic tone continues in Frances Jocelyn's portrayal of her relationship with her stepmother – Juliana Anne, daughter of John Orde of Weetwood, whom Jocelyn's father Robert had married in 1804.[24] This stepmother is cast as the diary's antagonist. The overblown emotion and exaggeration typical of the Gothic melodrama are apparent throughout the diary, but here the thematic emphases of such plays by Charles Robert Maturin or Matthew Gregory Lewis are also suggested, in which the protagonist rails against authority figures who are also usurpers.[25] Expressions such as 'Mama vexed me to the soul' (15/12/1810) and 'Many and many a bitter moment and tear she [Mama] has cost me' (26/12/1811) are recorded alongside more minor infringements into her personal life by this woman, with whom she has 'a little tiff' (26/4/1812) or a 'long annoying conversation' (23/7/1812). Such encounters often escalate so that we see

23 Thomas J. Berndt, 'The Features and Effects of Friendship in Early Adolescence'. *Child Development* 53.6 (1982): 1447–60.
24 Frances's mother, also Frances Theodosia, née Bligh, of Elphin, had died in 1802.
25 For instance, Maturin's *Bertram; or, The Castle of St. Aldborand* (1816).

dramatic incidents recalled as below, wherein Jocelyn espouses the role of the long-suffering heroine:

> a dreadful scrape with Mama, but it is not my fault. I cannot help what are her opinions. I do not care, but I will not be ill-humoured about it. I cannot help being much vexed. Have I not a dear & tender father & such brothers & sisters as God never produced before, I believe (27/11/1810)

One negation is piled upon another here to both exonerate Jocelyn and to insist to herself and her reader that she will not be impacted by the episode, so that we find 'it is not', 'I cannot', 'I do not', and 'I will not' mounting up alongside her negative insistence on possessing the very best family members, with the obvious exception of her stepmother. Such intergenerational conflict is also apparent in the diary of Mary Shackleton, later Leadbeater. Both Mary and her sister Sarah resided in the home of their maternal aunt Deborah for a lengthy period during their adolescence. In general, the sisters experienced relative freedom and were less chaperoned in mixed-gender settings than those who were not members of the Quaker community.[26] However, on those instances when their freedom was curtailed, the diarist is careful to record the displeasure experienced.[27]

Descriptions of intergenerational disagreement coexist in both Shackleton and Jocelyn's diaries alongside the celebration of female friendship, whether sororal or not. Indeed, Mary's diary includes a visual illustration of female friendship, in a tiny doodle of girls holding hands.[28] As we saw with Lecky, Jocelyn's portrayal of her relationships with various female friends and cousins borrows heavily from the depictions of intense female friendship found across eighteenth-century sentimental novels, from Samuel Richardson's *Clarissa: Or, The History of a Young Lady* (1748) onwards. Moyra Haslett has observed how 'intense bonds between women are most insistently affirmed and idealised, as the affection and support between Clarissa Harlowe and her closest friend Anna Howe is figured as stronger than the ties of family' and considers 'the potentially

---

26 Mary O'Dowd, 'Deborah, Margaret, Mary and Sarah Shackleton.' *Sisters: Nine Families of Sisters Who Made a Difference*. Eds. Siobhán Fitzpatrick and Mary O'Dowd. Dublin: Royal Irish Academy, 2022, 112–35.

27 For example, after Mary was 'refused leave' on one occasion, she explains how she responded thus: 'fell a crying, ran to the Retreat told Betty', then 'Betty told me my Aunt said as much to her as she would not let us go at all to Polls I walk'd about in great grief & cry'd'. Aunt Deborah eventually granted permission, and Mary concludes the incident with the remark, 'I dry'd up my tears...'. NLI MS 9296 (6/1/1774).

28 NLI MS 9296 (20/5/1774).

unsettling possibilities of female bonds'. [29] Frances Jocelyn's diary eulogises female friendships, with the diarist luxuriating in the intensity of her attachments. The arrival of the Jocelyn cousins precipitates expressions of excitement, for instance: 'Dear Miss Jermyn & I are to sleep together. I am so delighted. I shall kill myself with laughing, dear creature. I quite love her, she is so goodnatured' (24/9/1810). Jocelyn's partiality for repeating the intensifier 'so' is in evidence here, as is her predilection for short, declarative sentences in which she sets down her emotions and her preferences. Our sense of this adolescent writing style is further enhanced by the inclusion of direct quotations in Mary Leadbeater's diaries, which replicate the dialogues of young people, allowing us to gain further access to the period's adolescent speech patterns. Mary records the following exchange, for instance: 'Molly ask'd if Peggy Widdows drank tea with them "No she was at the Coffee house" "Where's that?" "Betty Lyons's" "Who was with her?" "Some of the boys I suppose" "Was Hannah there?" "I suppose so" (8/1/1775).[30] The repetition of the verb 'suppose' indicating hesitant agreement, and suggesting nonchalance, is a linguistic echo of the behavioural responses and relationship dynamics charted above.

While Jocelyn's note of affection for her cousin Miss Jermyn was prompted by the former's anticipation of the latter's arrival, the diarist is especially fond of conveying the depth of her friendships through expressions of sorrow upon parting from friends in a manner that echoes Charity Lecky's earlier leave-taking of Miss S: 'I was obliged to tear myself away from my beloved friends' (7/1/1811) and 'with great sorrow came away & shook hands a thousand times with them, how I did long to see them again dear loves & to kiss them' (11/2/1811). Strong emotions were elicited in Jocelyn by the arrival and departure of this multitude of different female friends and family members, but she reserves her most heightened emotion for one named friend in particular, Frances Howard (d. 1813) of Castle Howard, Co. Wicklow, recalling the observation by Frances Sheridan's eponymous sentimental heroine Sidney Bidulph that, 'We can have but *one friend* to share our heart,

---

29 Moyra Haslett, 'Fictions of Sisterhood in Eighteenth-Century Irish Writing'. *Irish Literature in Transition, 1700–1780*. Cambridge: CUP, 2020, 292. Haslett's work has elsewhere demonstrated how, though more infrequent than the multiple satirical depictions, positive fictional depictions of female assembly are more prevalent than had been thought. Haslett showcases how eighteenth-century depictions of girls' schools, for instance, can 'celebrate the possibility of supportive, affectionate bonds between girls'. Moyra Haslett, '"All pent up together": Representations of Friendship in Fictions of Girls' Boarding Schools, 1680–1800'. *Journal for Eighteenth-Century Studies* 41.1 (2018): 81–99, 94.
30 NLI MS 9298.

to whom we have no reserve, and whose loss is irreparable.'[31] The recently married Frances is singled out in particular as the recipient of Jocelyn's love: 'How much I felt at parting from Fanny, the friend of my bosom, the chosen one of my affections' (28/2/1811). As above, communication of Jocelyn's affection for Frances was prompted by their forced parting: 'This is the last walk I shall take with my beloved F for an immense time, I much fear. I feel so melancholy at the idea of parting from my dear dear friends, but this is a world of trouble which we sinful mortals must bear' (19/11/1810). She begins with a declarative finality in portraying the activity as 'the last walk', before qualifying this with a liminal descriptor of a lengthy interlude – 'for an immense time' – and softening the finality further through her selection of the verb 'fear' rather than 'believe'.

Such emphases on the passage of time and a sense of finality exist alongside the frequent inclusion of notes of nostalgia by Jocelyn and her fellow adolescents. Surveying the rooms before her at Powerscourt in Co. Wicklow, Frances comments, 'Oh how many pleasant moments came to my mind as I passed through those rooms. Ces jours ils sont passes [Those days are over]' (21/10/1810). There is no sense here that the diary form provides a retrospective function only for older diarists. The adolescent diarists embraced this aspect of life writing and were frequently prone to nostalgia and to using the diary to signify the progression of time and to record alterations in circumstances. We see 16-year-old Mary Shackleton reference 'the days of childhood and innocence' (2/1/1775), while Mary Tighe, then Blachford, begins an early diary entry with the comment, '14 & 4 months old. When I look back & consider my past life (short as it has been) I see in it such an astonishing medley it causes me at times not to know what to think' (16/2/1787).[32] Tighe parenthetically recognises her youth but demonstrates the opportunities for retrospection and the accompanying functions of analysis and recording that the diary form could provide to people of all ages. The 'astonishing medley' of her life furnishes the diary with content, in addition to the events and emotions from the specific day of the week during which the entry was written. The retrospective comments of the three diarists recall the propensity for nostalgia discernible in sentimental novels, such as the following from *The Memoirs of Miss Sidney Bidulph* (1761): 'With what delight do I recall the days of my childhood, which I passed here so happily! You, my dear Cecilia, mix yourself in all my thoughts; every spot almost brings you fresh into my memory.'[33] Sheridan's protagonist contrasts

31 Frances Sheridan, *The Memoirs of Miss Sidney Bidulph, Extracted from her journal* (1761). Cited and discussed in Haslett, 'Fictions of Sisterhood', 296.

32 Tighe 211.

33 Frances Sheridan, *The Memoirs of Miss Sidney Bidulph.* Ed. Heidi Hutner and Nicole

her miserable, married circumstances with the joyous days of childhood female friendship, providing a potential model for the adolescent diarists in their search for an authentic voice to articulate their experiences.

Navigating the Marriage Market

The diarists' navigation of heterosexual relationships and their anticipation of marriage is a notable uniting factor across the adolescent diaries. Marriage was an important goal in the lives of most young women in eighteenth-century Europe, and the diarists' responses to the prospect of courtship and betrothal inspired many diary entries steeped in heightened feelings.[34] These emotions are filtered and selected by the diarists as they attempted to navigate these fraught, transitional moments and environments, and to craft a more cohesive sense of self, with a mature voice. Several days before arriving in Bath in England, where she would spend her winter dancing and being presented to others, Charity Lecky encountered the steps in the city walls of Chester known as the Wishing Steps. Her companions encouraged her to hold her breath until she reached the top and to make a wish. Her diary records that she directed this wish towards the successful acquisition of 'good partners at the Bath balls', ruminating that 'experience will decide whether it has any effect or not' (27/10/1796). Lecky's diary entries portray her as fully aware of the pressures upon her as a young single girl in need of a husband and fearful of becoming an older unmarried woman, or an 'old maid': 'There were 2 sisters lodging in the House when we went to it [,] one of them an old maid [...] (God grant I may not be one)' (2/11/1796).[35] The figure of the unmarried woman is one to be avoided and the various adolescent diarists use their diaries to record and reflect upon their level of success in their interactions with men, whether through flirting, dancing, or conversation.

Details of either pre-marital courtships or engagements are notably absent across the full corpus of diaries, and it is difficult to gain access to any of the diarists' opinions on their future husbands. Elizabeth Richards

---

Garret. Toronto: Broadview, 2011, 283. Tamara S. Wagner argues that '*Sidney Bidulph* is unique among the fiction of the time in openly critiquing the somatics of sensibility. Nostalgia in the novel is a comforting emotion that counteracts resentment'. Tamara S. Wagner, *Longing: Narratives of Nostalgia in the British Novel, 1740–1890*. Lewisburg: Bucknell UP, 2004, 56.

34 Deborah Simonton, 'Earning and Learning: Girlhood in Pre-Industrial Europe'. *Women's History Review* 13.1 (2004): 363–86.

35 See also 13/2/1797.

is one of the few Irish diarists to note her affection for her future husband, the Dutch officer Frederick van Limburg Stirum:

> For the first time I felt pleasure in the listening to a declaration of love, and to my shame I confess it, unwarranted by my mother's approbation. I did not, I could not, conceal from him the pleasure I felt [... my mother] said that nothing would ever induce her to give her consent should Count Stirum offer me his hand (22/1/1801)[36]

However, this candid acknowledgement of unsanctioned attraction and attachment is then followed by a diary hiatus of four years, by which time Elizabeth was a mother, so there is no record of their developing relationship or of Elizabeth's anticipation of the married state.[37] It is difficult to establish patterns regarding the marriage wishes or preferences of such women in Ireland, though in the last two decades historical research has emerged that offers us valuable insights into marriage conditions within eighteenth-century Ireland, including work by Leanne Calvert, Rachel Wilson, Deborah Wilson, and Maria Luddy and Mary O'Dowd.[38] In the case of Elizabeth Richards, we see the young woman use the diary as a confidante, and as a space in which to record her preference for this Dutch émigré as future husband.

Charity Lecky's diary ended while she was still young and single, and so considers courtship, engagement, and marriage in the abstract, often sparking expressions of anticipation and excitement. However, real, impending marriage could prompt recordings of trepidation and anxiety. The diary of Mary Blachford contains a particularly striking account of the diarist's extreme apprehension and distress at her approaching wedding to her cousin Henry Tighe. The day before her wedding day, which was to take place on 5 October 1793, she writes, 'My soul draws back with terror

---

36 Elizabeth Richards, *The Diary of Elizabeth Richards (1798– 1825): From the Wexford Rebellion to Family Life in the Netherlands*. Ed. Marie de Jong-Ijsselstein. Intro. Kevin Whelan. Hilversum: Verloren, 1999, 50.

37 The above entry, from January 1801, is followed by an entry from February 1805, addressed to her husband, the first half in French, stating that it is now two years since Elizabeth became a mother. Although I have not been able to gain access to the original MS, and so have worked exclusively with the scholarly edition, the contents of the diary entry make clear that she was not keeping a diary during the intervening time.

38 Rachel Wilson, *Elite Women in Ascendancy Ireland, 1690–1745: Imitation and Innovation*. Woodbridge: Boydell & Brewer, 2015; Deborah Wilson, *Women, Marriage and Property in Wealthy Landed Families in Ireland, 1750–1850*. Manchester: MUP, 2009. Maria Luddy and Mary O'Dowd, *Marriage in Ireland, 1660–1925*. Cambridge: CUP, 2020.

& awe at the idea of the event which is to take place tomorrow. Oh My god! Let it not be unattended with thy blessing' (4/10/1793).[39] Harriet Kramer Linkin and Averill Buchanan have sketched out the contours of the couple's unsuccessful relationship, as well as Mary's response to other prospective suitors, whom she would have preferred.[40] The absence of love for Henry is one possible explanation for Mary's apprehension, but it is also likely that the terror and awe referenced here were prompted by the 'deflowering' associated with the wedding day itself. In addition to any unease about the physical act of consummation, the cultural value awarded to virginity must have had an emotional impact on those young women on the cusp of exchanging titles – graduating from maiden to wife and giving up what had been their most valued asset from the marriage market in which they had been circulating.[41]

Prior to Mary's wedding, her mother, Theodosia Blachford, had brought her to London in 1789, primarily to improve Mary's health, but also to break off an earlier attachment and to allow her to engage with 'a larger pool of prospective suitors' on the English marriage market.[42] The term 'market' itself has been described as 'highly appropriate' by Kimberly Schutt as 'the potential partners were frequently assessed as commodities for trade or sale rather than as actual people'.[43] Entrance into the marriage market represented a transitional moment in the lives of middle-class young women, as they attempted to gain social advancement and assist their families by marrying well.[44] This was frequently met with anticipation and anxiety, as the whole education and social formation of girls was calculated for their entrance into society, where they were to be displayed by older family members. The opening of Maria Edgeworth's novel *Belinda* (1801) famously disparages the actions of Mrs Stanhope who took every opportunity 'of showing her niece off', as Clarence Hervey expounds, '... for last winter, when I was at Bath, she was hawked about every where, and the aunt was puffing her with might and main...'.[45] Theodosia Blachford herself recognises the pride she had shown at her own daughter's successes: 'Did I enjoy the

39 Tighe 219.

40 Tighe 4–7. Averill Buchanan, *Mary Blachford Tighe: The Irish Psyche*. Cambridge: Cambridge Scholars Publishing, 2011.

41 Corrinne Harol, *Enlightened Virginity in Eighteenth-Century Literature*. Basingstoke: Palgrave, 2006.

42 Tighe 6.

43 Kimberly Schutte, 'The Marriage Market'. *Women, Rank, and Marriage in the British Aristocracy, 1485–2000*. Basingstoke: Palgrave, 2014, 88.

44 Peter Borsay, 'Children, Adolescents, and Fashionable Urban Society in Eighteenth-Century England'. *Fashioning Childhood in the Eighteenth Century: Age and Identity*. Ed. Anja Müller. Aldershot: Ashgate, 2006.

45 Maria Edgeworth, *Belinda*. Ed. Kathryn Kirkpatrick. Oxford: OUP, 2009.

triumphs of her beauty & captivating manner? Every voice that reached me sounded her praises – I took, I suppose, too much delight in these applauses' (c. 1810).[46] The diaries offer us an opportunity to engage with the portrayal of such experiences by the young women and girls themselves, and to chart how such a transitional moment is depicted in their diaries, through the narrative techniques discussed above.

One of the most sustained diary accounts of the eighteenth-century marriage market and the difficulties in navigating it are contained in Charity Lecky's diary. As the market developed in the later eighteenth century, Bath and London became recognised as two of its most popular international centres.[47] Characterised as 'the resort of the inhabitants of all climates and of people of every age and description', Bath provided the setting for the unfolding of various marriage plots and their contingent narrative complications, with the mixing of people from different locales.[48] Consequently, Bath became an invaluable site for comparative analyses and socio-cultural observations across literature, with Frances Sheridan's play *A Journey to Bath* (c. 1765) and her son Richard Brinsley's *The Rivals* (1775) representing key examples, alongside famous novels by Jane Austen, Frances Burney, and Amelia Opie. In addition to its role in the development of the novel and the marriage plot, a visit to the town was frequently the motivation behind the creation of a diary. Indeed, in *Northanger Abbey* (1817), Henry Tilney satirically suggests to Catherine Morland that all young women visiting Bath must possess one: 'Not keep a journal! How are your absent cousins to understand the tenor of your life in Bath without one? How are the civilities and compliments of every day to be related as they ought to be, unless noted down every evening in a journal?'[49]

With Bath a space that promoted pageantry and self-exhibition, its visitors could present themselves to a new audience, while simultaneously observing others do the same, with everyone engaged in the moulding and formation of character.[50] Particularly attractive to young people, Bath afforded the adolescent diarist the opportunity to position herself amongst those from different countries, allowing the crafting of a distinctive narrative

46 Theodosia Blachford, 'Observations on the foregoing journal by her mother, Mrs Blachford'. Tighe 231.

47 For Georgian Bath, see Peter Borsay, *The English Urban Renaissance: Culture and Society in the Provincial Town*. Oxford: Clarendon Press, 1989.

48 Anon., 'Review. *A Winter in Bath; by the Author of two popular Novels*. 4 Vols. Crosby. 1807'. *The Critical Review, Or, Annals of Literature* 3.XI. London, 1807, 291.

49 Jane Austen, *Northanger Abbey, Lady Susan, The Watsons, Sandition*. Oxford: OUP, 2008, Chapter 3.

50 Steven Gores, *Psychosocial Spaces: Verbal and Visual Readings of British Culture, 1750–1820*. Detroit: Wayne State UP, 2000.

voice, based upon a spectrum of affiliation with those encountered from different regions and countries. A certain degree of performativity was clearly possible, as younger diarists responded to other models and examples in their attempts to communicate a sense of self. Presented with this vast marriage market, composed of men and women from across Europe, Charity Lecky embraced the diary form both to better negotiate Bath and to comprehend her own position, employing the diary entries to interpret and scrutinise her encounters. The diary reveals an increasing awareness of the limitations imposed on Charity by both her gender and her age, communicated through a diary voice that closely echoes those of the young women featured in contemporary novels, as she meticulously records her interactions with those of the opposite sex, under parental supervision.

Charity Lecky was primarily viewed as a commodity upon this Bath marriage market, there to be inspected and assessed by all drawn to it from their different countries. Early in the diary, the writer laments the tendency of adults to assess her developing body and remark upon her recent physical changes: 'but then visiting and being visited & the like began, & I was tired of hearing how tall I was grown, & some saying they'd have known me, and others not etc etc' (2/11/1796). This attitude of inspection intensified during her stay in Bath, when it becomes clear that Charity Lecky, and in particular her physical appearance, was constantly being scrutinised, as she was regarded as a potential partner. This process is all the more intimidating as, given Bath's international visitors, it was sometimes conducted in a language Charity did not understand. Her appearance was dissected by the Prince of Orange and his wife, for example, the latter of whom, 'fixed her eyes on me, came close & stared in my face – smiled at me & then patting the Stadtholder made him look round at me – they conversed for some time in Dutch – ever & anon looking steadfastly at me' (3/1/1797). This joint assessment by both sexes was not an isolated incident, nor was the ensuing oral appraisal. On another occasion, Charity was again subjected to intense scrutiny, this time in the English language:

> She examined me from top to Toe [,] at least as much of me as she could see, & then after 3 or 4 hours time she went to a Lady, & directed her to look at me [,] she is cursedly wrong said she pretty loud [. S]he said some thing & then she took another view & turning to her [said] she is ugly for all that (7/11/1796)

Lecky sarcastically notes that, 'this was entertaining', and such comments must have been difficult to internalise. Her diary contains numerous occasions wherein she reflects upon her appearance and the way she was perceived by others. One entry, which was simply recording her day, is intercut with the parenthetical comment, '(I wish I was thin)' (16/3/1797). The linking of personal value and worth with physical appearance seems to be constantly at the back of Charity Lecky's mind, interfering with her sense of self and her daily achievements. This also translates onto her exterior adornments, with the above entry also regretting her outmoded appearance, 'my poor dress not looking fashionable' and her unfashionable hairstyle (7/11/1796).[51] Such notes of regret concerning clothing are also frequently in evidence in the diaries of Mary Leadbeater, then Shackleton, whose religious affiliation precluded her from the wearing of ostentatious dress. This led to frequent laments regarding the plainness of her outfits, supporting Mary's later comment that 'the fondness for dress so natural to youth was pretty much starved'.[52]

Lecky did however engage in some physical scrutiny herself, as in the following remark: 'I sat next General Erwin & examining him from top to toe, & listening to all he said I liked him better than any other man I had seen since I came to Bath' (5/12/1796). Here we see the diarist use the identical expression that had been applied to her, so that the assessment is not quite as one-directional as it first appears. There are also instances of flirtation and welcome recordings of her popularity amongst the opposite sex: 'I had beaus enough and flirted a little' (22/2/1797).[53] Like Smollett's Lydia initially, Charity enjoyed these newfound attentions and freedoms, and certainly appraised prospective candidates. Indeed, while Lecky and her young female peers – including other fictional counterparts such as Edgeworth's eponymous Belinda or Frances Burney's Evelina (1778) – were at a disadvantage and were subjected to constant appraisal, this diary makes clear that Charity herself was in pursuit of a partner, if not always for life, then at least symbolically, for the duration of the ball, and that the partner that she wished for was explicitly an Irishman.[54]

The international composition of Charity Lecky's dancing partners is made clear in the following, which places the Irish partners alongside the men from France and England present in Bath:

51 This is reminiscent of Lydia's description of herself as 'a country hoydon' despite six hours with the hairdresser. Smollett 94.

52 Mary Leadbeater, *The Leadbeater Papers: the Annals of Ballitore...* [Ed. Elizabeth Shackleton.] 2 vols. London, 1862, I 62. Cited in O'Dowd, *'Deborah,'* 120. Mary's diary is also careful to record her and her friends' weight, though she does not make any comments on the respective figures. NLI MS 9296 (4/1/1774).

53 For the role of sex and sexual activity in courtship, see Leanne Calvert, '"He came to her bed pretending courtship": Sex, Courtship and the Making of Marriage in Ulster, 1750–1844'. *Irish Historical Studies* (2018): 244–64, and Mary O'Dowd, 'Adolescent Girlhood', 58–60.

54 Frances Burney, *Evelina, or the History of a Young Lady's Entrance into the World*. Ed. Edward A. Bloom. Oxford: OUP, 2008.

I got plenty of Dancing & most Excellent partners – English Irish & Frenchmen, & here I lamented much not being able to talk French for some of my partners could scarce speak a word of English, & I feared to attempt speaking French, so that we had but little conversation, but the Irishmen made up for it (24/1/1797)

In Lecky's searching out of partners, we repeatedly note an explicit preference for the company of Irishmen: 'I was very well entertained & met a number of acquaintances – a countryman of my own' (21/1/1797). She declined an escort to walk her home, hoping to once again be accompanied by a countryman: 'there was another who I was intimate with who had before engaged to do me that service & was besides an Irish & a married man' (8/2/1797). The man's nationality is underscored by Lecky to clearly communicate this element of his character as conveying a respectability, reliability, and, finally, a degree of suitability, as being one of her own, as she expresses above.

The diaries of Frances Jocelyn and Mary Anne Dawson also include frequent accounts of dancing, though of a less international flavour. Jocelyn's diary records the measures undertaken for a ball in Co. Wicklow for which they had all been preparing for several days – chalking the floors, looking for beaux, putting up variegated lamps. Frances Jocelyn is careful to list all the families present, including the Meaths, Moncks, Grattans, Dalys, La Touches, and Brookes, as well as various officers. She records that she 'Danced setts with different men' (5/11/1811), though she declines to name them on this occasion. Previously, she had used the diary to single out one particular man for disparagement, mentioning the 'odious Captain Balfour' while again noting that she had 'danced with all the officers in turn' (29/4/1811). Mary Anne Dawson's diary also distinguishes one man. In her case it is to bestow praise upon the gentleman: 'several minuets were danced [...] engaged myself for the rest of the Night to Mr Barnham who was introduced to me by Lady Lumn & is a very pleasing Gentleman like Man in his appearance' (29/7/1783). After the death of Dawson's mother Anne, née O'Brien, the diarist notes her intention not to dance, though this is soon reneged upon:

Ball at Mrs William Foster's remarkable pleasant one. I was determined by my black Gloves not to Dance, but was asked by Mr George Sandfort, Mr Pendergast, Col Bronlow & Mr Wynne (18/12/1783)

A sense of pride is discernible here in light of this suite of names, which Mary Anne takes care to insert into the diary. Unlike the diaries written by older women, many of the adolescent diaries are often remarkably candid, and the diarists are frequently frank in acknowledging such perceived successes, recording conquests and congratulating themselves on the attraction of male attention.[55]

Frances Jocelyn's diary is also brimful of examples of flirting and teasing. She records how 'they [Aunt K and Fanny] tormented me about a certain person as usual' (19/1/1811), as well as playfully noting, while at the Opera, that her brother informed her that Sir C Asgill is 'very much in love with me which amuses me vastly indeed' (26/8/1811). Jocelyn's narrative voice is one that exudes confidence, is unrestrained, and indeed celebrates these aspects of her character. The diaries of Mary Shackleton, later Leadbeater, also include uninhibited observations on her peers, namely her fellow pupils at her father's school in Co. Kildare. In her diary, Mary expands on her crush on Billy Hall, while also describing her sister's idolisation of a boy called Elsey. Her descriptions of Billy borrow from romance, and in the following entry she even awards him a martial quality: '– his hair was untied & powdered, he look'd like the pictures of the young warriors who have just taken off their helmets' (30/12/1774). An extended interlude from the following month allows Mary to set herself up as heroine, recounting her response to the suggestion that Billy might be leaving Ballitore and later editing these comments:

> Betty says to me 'Billy Hall is to go to Dublin in a few days.' I immediately felt my face & neck all in a glow. 'O' says I & went on reading a letter I had in my hand, but I knew not what I read […] I affected indifference, but I am a bad dissembler I faulter'd in my speech, but she might attribute that to my usual impediment. What shall I do! I am in such a^n^guish of mind ^alas^ alas should I never see him more (9/1/1775).[56]

Rather than simply record the interaction, Mary evokes the scene for us. She inserts quotation marks and engages in repetition to underscore the difficulty of the situation, recording her actions, then immediately qualifying them: 'I affected indifference, but…'; 'I faulter'd … but…'. The exclamation mark adds an immediacy to the entry and a sense of urgency. The initial single exhortation 'alas' is judged insufficient, and the manuscript shows that a second utterance is later added. The word 'anguish' itself is at first misspelt, adding further to the impression of torment.

Mary's diary from Summer 1774 contains an inverse entry, in which the news was confirmed that Sally's crush, Elsey, would remain at Ballitore school: 'Sally's joy at this is not to be described […] vented her joy in a flood of tears', and 'Elsey is to stay at school still to the extreme joy of a

---

55 For audience, see Chapter 1.
56 NLI MS 9298.

certain person'.[57] The sisters projected their feelings for these two boys onto material objects, for instance hair and paper: 'left Sally in a rhapsody kissing a water paper Elsey gave her' (6/1/1775), and 'How shall I contrive to get a lock of Billy Hall's hair! Sally will not get if for me' (11/1/1775).[58] Alongside these simulacra and the above written effusions, the diaries make clear that Mary and Sarah's interactions with Billy and Elsey had a physical side too. Individual entries record pinching and slapping, for example: 'Billy Hall & I fell to slapping each other' (30/12/1774); 'Billy Hall pinch'd me, I pinch'd him, am I sorry I hurted him? Why? Ask my heart' (5/1/1775).

Mary herself married relatively late, at age 32, while Sarah Shackleton never married. The entry for Mary's 'bridal day', 6 January 1791, has an overwhelmingly religious tone, in which the diarist reflects exclusively on the ceremony itself, specifically the advice offered during it, rather than on the couple's relationship or other elements of the celebration.[59] One of the most immediate markers of Mary's new status is her change of name, noted on the title page of the diary manuscript as, 'The Journal and Diary of Mary Leadbeater Ballitore 1791'. General details regarding the various diarists' wedding days throughout the full corpus of diaries are sparse. The day after her marriage to Henry Tighe, Mary simply states: 'In the presence of twenty people I yesterday plighted my faith – & gave my hand –' (6/10/1793). Anne Weldon, née Cooke, first mentions an encounter with her future husband while in Bath with her mother: 'Drank ye water for ye complaint in my side; got acqueanted with Mr. Weldon by his giving his seat to my Aunt Caldwell at a morning consart at Imson Room' (3/10/1761).[60] Less than four months later, we are presented with an understated, unembellished recounting of Anne's wedding day, which is also dominated by the diarist's change of name: 'This morning change my name at St. James' Church at 9 o'clock in ye morning from Cooke to Weldon. Breakfasted at Mr. Hennery. Mr. Frank Crosby gave me away' (11/2/1762). There is much more detail in the remainder of Anne's diary regarding her love and admiration for her husband than this single sparse entry implies. Indeed, the charting of their relationship is the overarching theme of a diary that ceased with her husband's death in 1773.

Frances Jocelyn discontinued writing her diary three months prior to her own nuptials, but the prospect of marriage looms large throughout the diary. The wedding of her friend Frances Howard – 'the serious event of drst

57 NLI MS 9297.
58 NLI MS 9298.
59 NLI MS 9316.
60 Anne Cooke Weldon, 'Anne Cooke Diary'. *Journal of the County Kildare Archaeological Society* VIII (1915–1917): 104–32; 205–19; 447–63.

Fanny's life' – to William Parnell of Avondale, Co. Wicklow, prompted much reflection. Frances Jocelyn wholeheartedly embraced her role of bridesmaid, helping her friend to get dressed before accompanying her to the church. She later records the minutiae of the morning, how she kissed her friend; they came home; had breakfast; cut cake; passed some pieces of it through the ring; and went for a walk. Crucially, Jocelyn's proclivity for frank reflection moves beyond such mundane recordings to offer her personal response to the event, exclaiming that the ceremony was performed 'not at all well': 'She was not at all affected. I could not help shedding a plentiful abundance of tears when I saw her given away out of her father's & mother's protection to another man' (1/10/1810). The repetition of 'not at all' underscores Jocelyn's dissatisfaction and her sense that the ceremony did not provoke an adequate emotional response. Frances's anxiety at her friend's removal away from parental and into spousal protection is discernible here too and is evident across the generations of women, with maternal perspectives on such transfer also set down in diary entries.[61]

Weddings provoke negative connotations for Jocelyn across her diary, and, in addition to Frances Howard's disappointing ceremony, news of her cousin Harriet Skeffington's betrothal to Thomas Henry Foster inspires only a negative response: it 'grieves me from the bottom of my soul. Poor thing, God almighty will, I trust, put a better face upon things for her' (27/9/1810).[62] We saw earlier that marriage functioned as a precursor to sex, and it was also viewed by young women such as Frances Jocelyn as a precursor to pregnancy, again frequently provoking anxiety. Maternal mortality in childbirth was a clear threat and danger during the long eighteenth century.[63] The diarist Elizabeth Grubb, who married John Clibborn in 1800, two months before her 20th birthday, expounds at length on the dangers of childbirth, drawing on examples from her own life, as well as the dreadful experience of her cousin Lydia Pike. After having given birth to her son, Joseph 'on 1st day week', Lydia 'continued finely for some days' before being 'suddenly seized with delirium, her head was quickly blistered but her state continued truly distressing for several days when she got into a kind of stupor which did not

---

61 This parental anxiety is immediately apparent in the diary of Anne Jocelyn, upon the marriage of 'my beloved Louisa' (1773–1807) to Colonel Orde on 11 May 1801: 'That I have parted with such a child as few people have to boast of is most true: how great the mercy that I had her! I have given her to one who I sincerely believe values her as he ought'. Anne Jocelyn, *The Diary of Anne, Countess Dowager of Roden, 1797–1802*. Dublin, 1870 (24/5/1801).

62 Later Jocelyn notes, 'This is poor dear Harriet's wedding day. God grant it may be a happy one for her, dear girl'. Married 20 November 1810.

63 Infertility, infant loss, and miscarriage are discussed in Chapter 4.

go off until the spirit quit its mortal tabernacle' (11/2/1809).[64] Writing on 28 February 1811, Jocelyn, in frightened mode, laments the 'dreadful crisis' that awaited Frances Parnell, with her friend going on to give birth to her first child that August while Jocelyn paced about downstairs 'in agony of mind', listening to her friend's groanings.[65] Separately, following her cousin Harriet's marriage of 20 November 1810, Jocelyn records her fears for her relative, stating, 'I wish so much that she were safely over her accouchment' (7/11/1811).

Frances Jocelyn's diary is filled with references to these two women and to other dearest friends and cousins, but it is immediately apparent that her closest relationship was with her adored older brother Robert Jocelyn (1788–1870), later 3rd Earl of Roden. The two were married within four weeks of each other, and it is their sibling relationship that motivates Frances to employ her most ornate language and to engage with tropes from her reading of imaginative literature. Frances was besotted with this brother, who she repeatedly refers to as 'my beloved' (5/11/1810). Her evocations of their relationship are much more reminiscent of descriptions of romantic love within contemporary novels, and indeed their relationship is glorified and venerated, coming to stand in for any romantic one within the diary: 'that dear love in whom I feel my soul wound up. If it is a sin to love another too much, I commit a great one [...] How much more you feel for a person you love than for yourself' (19/12/1810). Her brother is awarded the role of diary hero; he is her confidante, her soul mate, her friend: 'the happiest hours of my life I can safely say have been spent in our little tete a tetes'. Frances acknowledges that her brother was an unusual recipient of such affection and rhetorically muses, 'I often wonder if many sisters doat upon their brothers as I do upon him' (6/6/1812), recognising her idolisation of Robert and her glorification of their relationship.

Frances Jocelyn's diary is one of the few that feature a pseudo-narrative arc, with the sibling protagonists undergoing several crises and Frances's platonic love story inevitably ending in disappointment. The first instance of a threat to the pair's relationship is Robert's proposal of marriage to Sarah Lennox (20/2/1812). During the intervening period (before the proposal is in fact rejected), we hear of the intense 'anxiety' that Frances experienced regarding this proposal and how 'it haunts me day and night' (25/2/1812).

---

64 Elizabeth Clibborn, Journal of Elizabeth (Grubb) Clibborn (1780–1861). RSFIHL P9.

65 The couple had two children, a son John Henry, born 14 August 1811, and a daughter Catherine. Frances Howard Parnell died in 1813. These dates suggest the possibility that her death was related to childbirth. David Murphy and Sinéad Sturgeon, 'William Parnell (-Hayes)'. *DIB*.

After Robert was turned down, Frances announces, 'The thought of my darling's excellent heart and feelings being so deeply wounded embitters my moments, but I trust he will not feel the disappointment much' (28/2/1812). By the end of the year, Robert had found another potential wife in the form of Maria Frances Stapleton, daughter of Baron le Despencer, a woman one year older than Frances. Sentiments of jealousy, of curiosity, and of envy are all apparent in Jocelyn's remarks regarding this fiancée: 'I quizzed him a great deal which I believe he did not quite like. I read several of her letters, little love, I am sure she is all our hearts could wish', and 'I hope his Maria will value such supreme perfection as she will possess in him' (24/10/1812). Jocelyn's diary entries show the diarist becoming increasingly melancholy about her brother's upcoming marriage – crying after he falls asleep, wiping her eyes on his cravat. She recognises that the current dynamics of their relationship cannot survive – 'I shall never enjoy him again beloved Angel so much at least' (25/10/1812) – and so the central love story crafted by the diarist must cease, and with it the diary itself.

The diary ends suddenly, months before Frances's own wedding, and there are only a couple of cursory mentions of encounters with her future husband, Richard Wingfield. Less than one week after her brother's demotion from leading man in her diary, Wingfield makes a muted appearance: 'Lord Powerscourt called therefore I missed him which I think I was rather glad of. I felt so nervous at the idea of seeing him I have been so plagued' (1/11/1812). This low-key, inconspicuous entry is a complete contrast to the earlier ones eulogising her brother and comes apropos of nothing. Indeed, if a reader did not know about the potential nuptials it would be very difficult to discern any affection or connection from this description. Two days later, Jocelyn's future husband is again referenced and in a manner entirely juxtaposed to the language previously employed to describe Robert: 'I met [Lord Powerscourt and Mr Blackford] just at the door without any witnesses luckily, I felt much agitated but I hope I did not show it, he appears very pleasing I like him rather' (3/11/1812). Both occasions seem to have provoked strong emotions in the diarist, with Frances portraying herself as having been nervous, plagued, and agitated. She is measured in her approval of Wingfield. In what appears a remarkable shift in pace and tone, this man is described simply as 'very pleasing'. One can speculate that the muted approval of the man intended to be her husband is due to the real nature of the match. This is not a relationship that could remain in the realms of the platonic. It would be one that would need to be consummated and that would be expected to produce an heir.

One week after the above entry, the diary ceases abruptly and in doing so gestures towards the transformative event that was to take place in Jocelyn's life, remoulding the diarist so that the chatty, frank, exuberant young woman the reader has gotten to know could become a wife and then mother. The diary closes with the elliptical comment, 'I spent a very good day considering!!' (10/11/1812). Unlike the expansive entries from before, here the diarist engages in elision and intimation, causing her reader to speculate and guess at the cause for this qualified 'very good day' and marking a distinct departure from the diarist's candid nature, moving instead towards a greater awareness of audience. Two months later, Frances's brother Robert married Maria Frances Stapleton (on 9 January 1813) and had six surviving children. Frances herself married Richard Wingfield, 5th Viscount Powerscourt, on 6 February 1813. Her first child and namesake, Frances Theodosia, was born and died the year following her marriage. She had a son, named after his father, who became the 6th Viscount Powerscourt, in 1815, and a second daughter, Catherine Anne, in either 1816 or 1817. Frances died seven years after her marriage, on 10 May 1820, before she reached the age of 25, on her return from Madeira, where she had travelled with her husband and her sister and fellow diarist Anne, for health reasons.[66]

'Young girls are not admitted': Mixed-Gender Sociability and Age

All the young women and girls under discussion here were marginalised by their age as well as by their gender. Female adolescents in the long eighteenth century were routinely advised by parents, guardians, and conduct manuals not to appear too learned or intellectual, and the diarists' writings capture the disparagement endured by young women in a society that dismissed and devalued their opinions.[67] The diary form was used by these different writers in a bid to gain agency and as an alternative voice and platform when they were denied such outlets in the rest of their lives. While mixed-gender associational life in eighteenth-century Britain and Ireland was limited for women of all ages, who were generally denied access to societies, clubs, coffee houses, and taverns, diaries from Bath showcase the many opportunities for mixed-gender socialising to be found in that city. The diary of Mary Anne Fortescue, for example, attests to her attendance at balls in the Upper and Lower assembly rooms and records bands performing in the pump room, as well as music performances in the Harmonic Society.[68] The

66 Anne's own diary includes an account of this journey and of her grief following Frances's death.
67 See Elizabeth Eger et al., eds., *Women, Writing and the Public Sphere, 1700–1830*. New York: Cambridge UP, 2001.
68 Mary Anne Fortescue, 'The Diary of Marianne Fortescue, 1797–1800. Ed. Noel Ross. *Journal of the County Louth Archaeological Society* 24.2–3 (1998): 222–48; (1999): 357–79.

surviving letter-journals by author Elizabeth Sheridan, written from Bath to her sister Alicia Le Fanu in Ireland, frequently mention intergenerational conversations between men and women, with most discussions involving her own father, the actor and theatre manager Thomas Sheridan.[69] Sheridan also records other literary family duos present there from Ireland, such as Charlotte and Henry Brooke, best known as the authors of *Reliques of Irish Poetry* (1789) and *The Fool of Quality* (1766–70) respectively.[70] More unusually perhaps, Charity Lecky's diary offers glimpses into the diarist's incursions into mixed-gender conversations on the traditionally male topics of religion and religious dissent, as well as politics.[71] Aileen Douglas has argued that Smollett's Lydia Melford gains insight and independence as the summer progresses, and in Lecky's diary we see the diarist develop increased self-control, command, agency, and, perhaps, even maturity.[72] One entry notes her own error in judging others, for example, 'I must not forget to mention how very wrong I am in giving way to prejudice & forming an opinion of anyone by their 1st appearance – took him to be a 'would-be gentleman' but much sense & spirit, express himself with piety' (1/11/1796), while on another occasion she recognises her naivety after being avoided by one who had promised her a dance, declaring, 'this affair will make me in future doubt those who brag or talk much or make many offers' (21/11/1796).

Charity Lecky was extremely proud of her inclusion in conversations with men who did not dismiss her opinions outright, recounting how she found herself in conversations where it was generally thought that young women should not be permitted. During her own visit to Bath, Lydia Melford mentions her exclusion from intellectual discussions on account of her youth *and* gender: 'Hard by the Pump-room, is a coffee house for the ladies; but my aunt says, young girls are not admitted, inasmuch as the conversation turns upon politics, scandal, philosophy, and other subjects above our capacity.'[73] However, Charity Lecky records over ten accounts of explicitly mixed-gender conversation in her diary, with religion the subject of debate on at least three occasions, as well as the abovementioned politics: 'Mr Tassoon almost as he entered the room began to speak on Religious subjects & politics' (15/12/1796). Charity notes the respect with which her

---

69 Elizabeth Sheridan, *Betsy Sheridan's Journal*. Ed. William Lefanu. Oxford: OUP, 1986.

70 Sheridan 47.

71 Mr Lion, from Queen's County, 'talked politics at a great rate' (7/1/1797).

72 Aileen Douglas, *Uneasy Sensations: Smollett and the Body*. Chicago: University of Chicago Press, 1995, 170.

73 Smollett 40.

opinions were greeted by a few men who did not dismiss her views out of hand: 'Dr Bridges sat beside me & conversed as if he considered me more on a line with himself, or rather as a being who had a soul & some rationality than as an insignificant trifler which is the light men seems to me to view the younger part of our sex in general' (21/12/1796).[74] The quotations from both diary and novel explicitly differentiate younger and older women, with the former seen as overly erratic and with limited mental capacity, while it seems the latter may be admissible in certain circumstances. This is almost a direct inversion of the spatial realities of the assembly rooms in Bath, whereby the infamous rule stated that older women be relegated along with those who had not yet reached adolescence: 'elder ladies and children be contented with a second bench at the ball, as being past, or not come to perfection'.[75]

Charity's transgression into these realms caused her to witness reflections on religion and politics that inevitably led to heated and controversial debates. One remarkable diary entry from Christmas Day 1796 encapsulates the different strands of the adolescent's own sense of self, as well as her interaction with and treatment by others in Bath, as highlighted in the following transaction:

> he got very warm speaking against the Roman Catholick Religion & said he would as soon trust himself with the Devil as with one of them, I could not help saying (for the honour of Ireland) that there were many of whom I had as good an opinion as to their truth, honesty & fidelity in that Religion as any other, & said everything I could in their favour. he turning sharp on me replied – I was too young to know anything about Religion, that no doubt plays Balls, Cards Concerts took up my time too much to have any to spare on the one thing needful (25/12/1796)

Here we see the diarist taking pride in Ireland and championing its citizens. The Catholic Irish are to be defended explicitly for the sake of the country's honour, as they form part of the make-up of the wider community. This sees Charity Lecky align herself with those of a different religion as she seeks to protect their reputation. The qualities she holds up for praise are truth, honesty, and fidelity. In the midst of many falsehoods circulated in the 1790s, several women sought to convince others of the fallacies being promulgated and instead aimed to highlight the decency they perceived in

---

74 Lydia also notes the dismissive attitude paid to young women, but Smollett counters this by placing men as the victims of cunning females with her assertion that, 'We complain of advantages which the men take of our youth, inexperience, sensibility, and all that, but I have seen enough to believe, that our sex in general make it their business to ensnare the other...'. Smollett 259.

75 John Wood, *A Description of Bath*. 2 vols. London, 1765, II 413.

the Catholic population. The correspondence of salon hostess Elizabeth Rawdon, Lady Moira (1731–1808), for example, frequently refutes claims of Catholic violence and asserts the fabrication of events by others: 'and that the Roman Catholics are to cut the throats of all the Protestants – In the course of the forty years I have belonged to this kingdom, that alarm has been yearly spread, without the least appearance & probability of such a danger.'[76] Disallowed from making speeches in the Irish parliament in the fashion of her husband or son, both of whom engaged in politics to differing degrees, Lady Moira asserted her opinions via the written and circulated word, utilising the letter as a means to communicate her views and obtain an additional and powerful public platform. One of Ireland's foremost salon hostesses, an older woman at the apex of elite Irish society, Lady Moira's opinions carried a certain weight with those of high social standing at the close of the century. In 1790s Bath, Charity Lecky's youth and gender contributed to her opinion being immediately and summarily dismissed as that belonging to a young girl, one ostensibly too fixated on the associational life on offer to adequately understand the situation in Ireland. Her account of this altercation with an elder male portrays the two as pseudo-villain and pseudo-heroine, defaming and protecting Ireland respectively. The exchange also shows Charity Lecky willing to defy conduct book notions of propriety by expressing opinions on such a subject. It is the diary form that affords the young woman a platform to develop and further express these opinions, to create a narrative voice, and to record her defence of the Irish Catholics, as part of her understanding of both nation and national identity, despite her status as a young, unmarried girl. Her diary writing enables her to construct a sense of self and to process such encounters and dismissals, as part of her attempts at negotiating the transition into adulthood.

The diary form could function as a platform for adolescents such as Charity Lecky to record their beliefs and judgements, and to commit these opinions to the page when deprecated in person. Charity's diary allowed her to formulate her thoughts and create a voice throughout the myriad entries. It provided a platform too for her peers – for Mary Blachford to note her anxiety prior to her wedding, for Frances Jocelyn to ruminate on the circumstances of her recently married friend, or for Mary Shackleton to negotiate mixed-gender adolescent gatherings. Gender and age inescapably formed part of the lived experiences of these young diarists and the diary form allowed all of them to mediate their daily experiences, whether at home or away from it, and to situate themselves in their respective environments. The diaries also allowed them to establish a more defined sense of self

76 Elizabeth Rawdon, Undated letter from *c.* 1783. Rawdon and Hastings Correspondence, Granard Papers, Castle Forbes, Co. Longford, T3765/M/3/14/16.

prior to anticipated marriages. By writing about their daily experiences and thoughts, they were better able to understand their own sense of selfhood and to navigate their place in the world, their written records assisting them in this transition from childhood to adulthood.

This chapter has also shown how the various entries come together within each young person's diary to communicate a lively narrative that replicates the cadences of those novels popular in eighteenth-century Britain and Ireland. Often embracing the tone, expressions, and even plot emphases of contemporary novels – from Smollett's *Humphry Clinker* to Sheridan's *Sidney Bidulph*, from Richardson's *Clarissa* to Edgeworth's *Belinda* – the young diarists used the novel to help them to both understand *and* describe their lives. Whether embracing the mode of nostalgia to frame past events, employing sensibility to communicate the values of female friendship, or utilising Gothic melodrama to showcase intergenerational strife, they turned to imaginative literature to assist them in making sense of their lives and in achieving a voice with which to showcase their thoughts. The people in their lives are crafted as characters upon the page, and situations created to allow dreams to flourish and to better cope with impending marriages, as we saw with Frances Jocelyn and her idolisation of her brother Robert. Diaries by more mature women, whether middle aged or older, tend to include more self-castigation, remonstrances, and denigration.[77] Here, these adolescents invoke the models they have read in order to portray themselves as heroines who have to constantly overcome a myriad of obstacles – contending with objectifying suitors, frustrating guardians, and difficult relationships – but who will eventually triumph, or, when reality impinges too greatly, will bring their stories and diaries to an end.

77 See Chapter 4.

CHAPTER THREE

Vulnerability and Abuse

Women's Diary Writing as Testimony

This chapter takes as its point of departure marital, familial, and gender violence, including the threat of such violence.[1] All the diaries in this study relate instances that demonstrate women's limited options, curtailed movements, general vulnerability, and frequent lack of agency, while several also note women being violently pursued or receiving unwanted sexual attention. Vulnerability has been defined as 'the quality or state of being exposed to the possibility of being attacked or harmed, either physically or emotionally'.[2] This constant exposure to the possibility of harm is to the fore in many of the women's diaries with incidents of physical or emotional harm repeatedly gestured to in the daily entries. We can observe entries that deal with unwanted propositioning; male pursuit; non-consensual touch; homosocial drunkenness; marital violence; and abandonment. The breadth of age of the women impacted by such circumstances is immediately apparent, incorporating widows, wards, young girls, and married women, although younger women do appear to be disproportionately affected. These women's daily lives were characterised by the need to be accompanied; the requirement to remove themselves from threatening situations; the need to stay alert; and the sense that danger was always imminent.

The diary entries that trace the events of the Rebellion of 1798 evoke a landscape of violence, turbulence, and even torture. John D. Beatty's edited collection, *Protestant Women's Narratives of the Irish Rebellion of 1798* (2001), allows access to the voices of a range of women who experienced the horrors of the Rebellion, through extracts from their autobiographical writings, especially memoirs.[3] There are portrayals of violence in many of the diaries

---

1 With many thanks to Aileen Douglas for her extensive comments on an earlier draft, which have informed both the content and the structure of this chapter.

2 'Vulnerability', *OED*.

3 John D. Beatty, ed., *Protestant Women's Narratives of the Irish Rebellion of 1798.*

that were written at that time, and, although it has been argued that the rape of women was not a weapon during the 1798 Rebellion, the testimony of figures such as Wexford woman Elizabeth Richards, later Stirum, makes clear that women were often targeted, abused, and certainly punished separately: 'All the morning we listened to the shrieks, the complainings of female rebels. They almost turned my joy to sorrow' (22/6/1798).[4] While acknowledging the increased vulnerability of women during such moments of warfare and violence, and the scholarship dedicated to its examination, this chapter will instead focus on ordinary rather than extraordinary violence, exploring the articulation of quotidian female vulnerability in the long eighteenth century.[5] Equally, while this chapter offers further evidence of the difficulties faced by women, its main emphasis will be to scrutinise *how* these women expressed their experiences in their diaries, rather than offering them to the reader as a historical catalogue of ill treatment. It will navigate issues of power dynamics, rhetorical strategies, and women's struggles to find the appropriate language to depict events. The chapter is also particularly alert to the predicament of diarists who, for reasons of age, or other factors, simply lacked the vocabulary to describe their experiences.

Foundational work on the difficulties faced by women during this period in an English context was conducted by Anna Clark in *Women's Silence, Men's Violence: Sexual Assault in England, 1770–1845* (1987). Clark's findings regarding the suppression of women's speech about sex, the distortion of the reality of women's experiences through public discourse, and the blocking of 'women's efforts to articulate rape as a crime' have informed much of our understanding of women's experience of sexual violence in the period in question.[6] James Kelly's work on the crime of rape in eighteenth-century

Dublin: Four Courts Press, 2001. See also Catherine O'Connor, 'The Experience of Women in the Rebellion of 1798 in Wexford'. *The Past: The Organ of the Uí Cinsealaigh Historical Society* 24 (2003): 95–106; and Susan B. Egenolf, '"Our fellow creatures": Women Narrating Political Violence in the 1798 Irish Rebellion'. *Eighteenth-Century Studies* 42.2 (2009): 217–34.

4 Elizabeth Richards, *The Diary of Elizabeth Richards (1798–1825): From the Wexford Rebellion to Family Life in the Netherlands*. Ed. Marie de Jong-Ijsselstein. Intro. Kevin Whelan. Hilversum: Verloren, 1999, 48–49.

5 Michael Durey, 'Abduction and Rape in Ireland in the Era of the 1798 Rebellion'. *Eighteenth-Century Ireland* 21 (2006): 27–47, though there are some interpretations of domestic and ritualised rape in particular in this article that sit uncomfortably with our more recent understandings.

6 Anna Clark, *Women's Silence, Men's Violence: Sexual Assault in England, 1770–1845*. London: Pandora, 1987, 8. While influenced by Clark, my research departs substantially from elements of this work, including her dismissal of the role literature can play in expanding our understanding of women's experiences of unwanted pursuit, for instance,

Ireland acknowledges the difficulties involved in ascertaining accurate figures, including the 'disincentives to women reporting and prosecuting male sexual assault', with the problem of the 'idealisation of female virtue' firmly to the fore.[7] Research by Katie Barclay has explored consent in an eighteenth-century context and illustrates how the importance placed on female resistance as the only available response to sexual activity shaped both men and women's sexual behaviour, and became portrayed as sexually enticing.[8] Numerous diary writers in Ireland did not have the vocabulary available to vocalise certain experiences, including instances of non-consensual touch, for example, nor did they always fully understand what was happening to them. As we will see, many of the younger diarists, such as the adolescent Mary Shackleton, later Leadbeater, were particularly ill-prepared for the world in which they found themselves, and their vulnerability is palpable in their attempts to express themselves and to communicate incidents that had occurred. Another example is 15-year-old Marianne ffolliott, who presents herself as very much aware of the potential violence surrounding her, employing the diary as a means of setting down repeated instances of excessive male drinking.

The chapter examines how certain diarists were able to draw upon a variety of literary sources – from the Gothic tradition to amatory fiction and novels more generally – in order to comprehend and then vocalise their experiences of a patriarchal world in which assault, abduction, incarceration, and rape were frequent events.[9] It illustrates how Dorothea Herbert, writing in her 30s, for example, was able to frame her experiences and present her

'This book will not discuss such novels (*Pamela*; *Betsy Thoughtless*) in any detail, for it is unclear if they have any relevance to women's actual experience of rape', Clark 19.

7 James Kelly, '"A most inhuman and barbarous piece of villainy": An Exploration of the Crime of Rape in Eighteenth-Century Ireland'. *Eighteenth-Century Ireland* 10 (1995): 79.

8 Katie Barclay, 'From Rape to Marriage: Questions of Consent in Eighteenth-Century Britain'. *Interpreting Sexual Violence, 1660–1800*. Ed. Anne Leah Greenfield. London: Pickering & Chatto, 2014, 35–44; and Katie Barclay, *Love, Intimacy and Power: Marriage and Patriarchy in Scotland, 1650-1850*. Manchester: MUP, 2011. Ciaran O'Neill and Juliana Adelman have ensured Irish voices have been added to the current discourse on historical consent, offering a microhistory on the 'lived experience of sexual culture' in Victorian Ireland. Ciaran O'Neill and Juliana Adelman, 'Love, Consent, and the Sexual Script of a Victorian Affair in Dublin'. *Journal of the History of Sexuality* 29.3 (2020): 388–417.

9 For abduction, see, James Kelly, 'The Abduction of Women of Fortune in Eighteenth-Century Ireland'. *Eighteenth-Century Ireland* 9 (1994): 7–43; and Toby Barnard, *The Abduction of a Limerick Heiress*. Dublin: Irish Academic Press, 1998. One of the most famous incidents of incarceration was that of Lady Cathcart in the attic of Castle Nugent, Co. Longford, where she was imprisoned by her husband for over

diary in response to perceived violence.[10] Herbert's diary writing draws upon and echoes many of the experiences and emotions of the protagonists from the works of earlier eighteenth-century writers, in particular those by the bestselling English author Eliza Haywood (c. 1693–1756). The threat of assault, rape, and general persecution are themes that endure throughout the literature of the long eighteenth century, and the final decade of the century closes with the Gothic undercurrents of Mary Wollstonecraft's writing and the various pursued or incarcerated heroines of Ann Radcliffe's Gothic novels, all of which find echo in Herbert's 1806–1807 diary.

For all these women, regardless of linguistic mastery or literary knowledge, the diary could operate as testimony, as a formal written statement of what they had experienced. The diary form could function as a space in which maltreatment, abuse, or the threat of violence could be recorded when official channels were not always supportive or interested. Diaries also provided simple evidence for oneself that an event had occurred, to allow the diarist to process an encounter and acknowledge that something negative had happened. The diaries being examined in this chapter often provide the sole surviving description of the mistreatment of certain figures, with Elinor Goddard's diary the key source on Sir William Fownes's pursuit of Sarah Ponsonby, for instance, and Dorothea Herbert's account of her sister Sophia Mandeville's abuse at her husband's hands the sole contemporary description of this that I have encountered.[11] The diaries in this chapter prompt us to consider the relationship between public trust and women's voices and statements – and encourage us to explore in what ways the diary could function as testimony for women and girls during the long eighteenth century.[12]

'That odious commerce': Articulating Disapproval in the Diary

Eighteenth-century women have been described as 'underprepared for the sexual economy in which they circulated' with their upbringing having denied them 'the language for both self-defence and accusation'.[13] The

ten years, until his death in 1766. W. A. Maguire, 'Hugh Maguire'. *DIB*. *Gentleman's Magazine*, 59 (August 1789), 766–67.

10 Dorothea Herbert, Dorothea Herbert 1806–1807 Diary. On deposit at TCD.

11 Elinor Goddard, Mrs Elinor Goddard: Journal (1774–1778). NLW 22993A. Consulted on microfilm, NLI POS 9617.

12 Síobhra Aikin, *Spiritual Wounds: Trauma, Testimony and the Irish Civil War*. Dublin: Irish Academic Press, 2022, has challenged the narrative of silence of Irish men and women during the early twentieth century by presenting overlooked examples of life writing as testimony.

13 Laura Fasick, *Vessels of Meaning: Women's Bodies, Gender Norms, and Class Bias*

virtue, or chastity, of young women at this time was relentlessly promoted to the detriment of their general understanding about life, sex, and the sexual economy. Ignorance was preferred to any form of sexual education in an attempt to ensure modesty and to minimise sexuality and accusations of female desire. These societal failings are repeatedly referenced in the memoirs of eighteenth-century Ireland's 'fallen women' – Laetitia Pilkington, née van Lewen (*c.* 1709–1750) and Margaret ('Peg') Leeson, née Plunket (1727–1797) – whose writings engage with issues of chastity, double standards, and female agency and vulnerability throughout.[14] The Irish diaries under discussion here also attest to this miseducation and expose the damage done to young women and girls in both underpreparing them for the realities of society and for probable sexual advances. Importantly, this educational oversight also frequently deprived the diarists of the words to communicate uncomfortable interactions or instances of assault, or indeed the language to record or articulate positive sexual experiences.

Mary Shackleton Leadbeater's account of non-consensual touch in her diary from 1774, when she was 16 years old, is replete with intermingled confusion and frustration:

> I went to it [the arm chair] for that purpose but Dick Jacob seats himself in it & pulled me in his lap. I did not like it at all. (& Cousin Sam & Jonathan Gegehall were facing us) so I desired him to let me up, for I was not an infant therefore did not chuse to be nurse. But all was in vain, till in his struggling to hold me, he like to overturn the screen & then I got loose, after a bit they took leave, & went, to my joy. (18/12/1774)[15]

In the above entry, Mary unambiguously records how she was forcefully pulled on to the lap of another young person. She then uses a succinct sentence of seven words to note her dislike of the young man's actions, ending with the intensifier 'at all'. Again, without any equivocation, she makes it clear that she did not consent to being held and explicitly demanded to be let go. However, her subsequent choice of self-descriptor is revealing for its innocent and misplaced connotations. The young Mary Shackleton,

---

from Richardson to Lawrence. DeKalb: Northern Illinois UP, 1997, 58; and Emily J. Dowd-Arrow and Sarah R. Creel, '"I know you want it": Teaching the Blurred Lines of Eighteenth-Century Rape Culture'. *ABO: Interactive Journal for Women in the Arts, 1640–1830* 6.2.2 (2016): n.p.

14 Laetitia Pilkington, *Memoirs of Laetitia Pilkington.* Ed. A. C. Elias, Jr. 2 vols. Athens: University of Georgia Press, 1997. Margaret Leeson, *The Memoirs of Mrs Margaret Leeson. Written by herself...* Dublin, 1795–1797.

15 Mary Leadbeater, Diaries covering the years 1769–1789 in 22 volumes. NLI MS 9298.

as she was then, held against her will upon the lap of another adolescent, invokes the image of a nursing infant to describe her situation. Though her diary demonstrates that she has experience at this point of her life of flirting, kissing, and playing questions and commands (an eighteenth-century version of truth or dare), she does not have access to terminology surrounding unwanted physical touch.[16] Her use of the infant metaphor highlights both the danger of her situation and her inability to articulate precisely what has happened.

Mary also references the discomfort experienced by her younger sister Sarah, who was similarly pulled onto the lap of another adolescent at the same age: 'Sally and I were left in the parlour. Bob pulled Sally in his lap & says to me "I never kiss'd Sally" & kissed her. Sally got up & ran out. Bob brought her back' (2/1/1776).[17] This incident has been characterised as 'horseplay', but there is every possibility too that Sarah's previous rejection of Bob and her physically indicating her opposition to the kiss twice, by both getting up and then running out of the room, could be interpreted as an absence of consent.[18] This seems probable as Elsey is clearly identified as the object of Sarah's affection throughout Mary's adolescent diary volumes for this period, not Robert (Bob) Baxter.[19] Unlike elsewhere, where Mary expounds at length, here she chooses short declarative sentences. In contrast to the descriptive accounts and rhapsodies discernible elsewhere in her diary entries, this is a blunt, unadulterated report and does not seem to convey approval.

16 This game is referenced in *The Spectator* – 'While other young ladies in the house are dancing, or playing at questions and commands, she [the devotee] reads aloud in her closet.' *The Spectator*, 354 (16 April 1712). This replaced the more childlike games described in Mary's earlier diaries, where one finds role playing and masters and scholars. By 1774, Mary portrays herself as much more mature, less interested in gossip, and not engaging in as much playacting, though she does mention hide and seek with Sally and Rayner, with the closet under the stairs identified as their favourite hiding place. NLI MS 9297 (3/7/1774).

17 NLI MS 9301. Mary O'Dowd, 'Deborah, Margaret, Mary and Sarah Shackleton'. *Sisters: Nine Families of Sisters Who Made a Difference*. Ed. Siobhán Fitzpatrick and Mary O'Dowd. Dublin: Royal Irish Academy, 2022, 122.

18 'When they were on their own without adult company, kissing and sitting on each other's laps seem to have been a normal part of the horseplay between the two sexes.' Mary O'Dowd, 'Deborah,' 122.

19 See Chapter 2. Bob is later described by the adult Mary Leadbeater thus: 'Robert Baxter, from Monaghan, was a parlour-boarder at my father's at this time. He was but sixteen, yet he was six feet high, and lusty in proportion.' She also states that he was 'affectionate, artless, and unassuming, and we soon loved him'. Mary Leadbeater, *The Leadbeater Papers. The Annals of Ballitore...* [Ed. Elizabeth Shackleton.] 2 vols. London, 1862, I 97.

While Mary Shackleton's diary records her and Sarah's crushes, and instances of kissing and fondling, there is a complete silence regarding sexual pleasure within the corpus of Irish diaries. Marital love and affection are obvious across numerous diaries, particularly in that of Elizabeth Richards, but there is an absence of commentary on sex or sexuality. More scandalous examples of life writing from eighteenth-century Ireland do succeed in acknowledging and conveying sexual desire, such as Margaret Leeson's *Memoirs* (1795–1797) wherein the memoirist expounds on her experiences working in Dublin's brothels, recalling how 'Sally Hayes and I lived in Drogheda-Street, in an endless round of pleasures'.[20] Early in the memoirs, when Leeson is recounting her childhood and adolescence, she reflects on the admittance of her first lover, 'wherein I saw my seducer had triumphed, yet how could I call him seducer when I met the seduction half way', knowingly alluding to examples from amatory fiction.[21] Such acknowledgement of sexual consent is discernible in the earlier poetry of someone like Aphra Behn, notably 'The Willing Mistress' (1673). Behn's description of the two lovers in their shady grove lightly employs euphemism to invoke 'that which I dare not name', clearly conveying consent and sexual pleasure from the poem's very title, but ostensibly not articulating these within the poem itself.[22]

Many eighteenth-century novels describe the dangerous environment to be navigated by young women and girls who were unprepared for the world in which they moved. One common trope is the predicament of the young woman who is placed in a dangerous position due to external misinterpretations of her class or status, which gives us an insight into the relevant protection afforded to wealthier women.[23] Frances Burney's eponymous Evelina is pursued into the long alley in Vauxhall, for example, where she struggles to 'disengage [herself]' from her assailant due to a shift in how she is perceived: 'He seems disposed to think that the alteration in my companions authorizes an alteration in his manners.'[24] While visiting England from Co. Derry with her mother in the winter of 1796, the young diarist Charity Lecky (then aged 14) was propositioned by a man in Bath, who also mistook her status, as described in the following diary entry:

20 Leeson II Chapter 14.
21 Leeson I Chapter 3.
22 Aphra Behn, 'The Willing Mistress'. *The Norton Anthology of Literature by Women*. Eds. Sandra Gilbert and Susan Gubar. New York: Norton, 1985, 111. With thanks to Moyra Haslett for this reference.
23 We should bear in mind that victims of crimes such as sexual assaults in Ireland 'came primarily from the lower classes'. Kelly, '"Most inhuman and barbarous"', 81.
24 Frances Burney, *Evelina*. Ed. Edward A. Bloom. Oxford: OUP, 2008. Originally published 1778.

[Mr Casin] said he had been introduced to so many Ladys he did not remember their names, he begged the favour of mine, blushing up to the eyes [...] in the course of the conversation I said where my mother & I was to spend the Day, why said he, have you a mother with you – what he had taken me for I don't know.[25]

Lecky's description of the encounter is full of voids. She understands that a mistake has taken place and that her position in society has been misinterpreted, but she does not have access to adequate language to articulate this. Rather than even employ euphemism, she literally states that she does not know 'what he had taken me for'. There is the possibility that Lecky was ignorant of the suggestion of prostitution and the dangers into which she was potentially placing herself, but the more likely interpretation is that that she did fully understand the implication of the man's words but could not articulate them herself, employing the construction 'I don't know' to gesture towards that which she cannot politely say.[26]

In addition to such instances of vulnerability during balls or within the home, there are interspersed references to male drunkenness in several diaries, a state which frequently causes anxiety amongst the women and girls.[27] A young Frances Jocelyn employed her diary to note her own sense of discomfort and unease when she encountered a drunken man on the following occasion in Co. Wicklow: 'I was a little frightened of a drunken man whom I met coming back from the cottage' (14/10/1810);[28] while Frances ffolliott, née Homan, records her good luck when travelling in England to have avoided a drunken coachman, in a diary entry from 1808: 'We very fortunately came post from Shrewsbury, as the horses of the Stage tired and fell, the Coachman was quite drunk' (20/8/1808).[29]

25 Anon. [Charity Lecky]. Diary of a Winter in Bath, 1796–97. James Marshall and Marie-Louise Osborn Collection, Beinecke Rare Book and Manuscript Library, Yale University, Osborn c446.
26 With thanks to the participants at BSECS annual conference, Oxford 2022, who offered extensive feedback on this passage.
27 There is reference to an inebriated woman in the diary of Elinor Goddard, but the fear here is that the woman concerned would vomit on the diarist, rather than pose any danger to her: 'I did [travel] so in the same stage with one gentleman a little livery boy a Methodist Abigail and a drunken woman that I feard wd puke in my cap'. NLW 22993A/NLI POS 9617 (12/7/1781).
28 Frances Jocelyn, Diary of Frances Theodosia Jocelyn. 1810–1812. NLI MS 18,430. This is in contrast to the shelter and protection usually afforded by the premises themselves, as outlined in Chapter 5.
29 Frances ffolliott, Typescript copy of a few pages of the diary of Mrs John Ffolliott, mother of Maryanne Young. 1808. PRONI D3045/6/1.

These brief encounters shift to repeated occurrences in the diary of Frances ffolliott's daughter Marianne, which features sustained references to drunkenness.[30] The initial portion of the diary (1809–1810) was composed exclusively at the family home at Hollybrook House in Sligo and includes excursions into Boyle and to surrounding country estates of counties Sligo and Roscommon. At the centre of Boyle stands King House, 'one of the earliest surviving substantial townhouses in the province of Connacht', sold by the King family in 1795 to the War Office in London, to be used as a barracks.[31] During the early portion of ffolliott's diary, the barracks was occupied by the Clare Regiment. The diary features sustained references to military figures, and places much emphasis on associational life, for instance: 'Papa and Mamma went into Boyle to visit the Ladies of the new Regiment. The Gentlemen that were visited on Sunday returned their visit on Thursday' (4/5/1810). David Fleming's work on the political culture of provincial Ireland for earlier in the eighteenth century stresses that 'social interplay – in the form of hunting, horse racing and other sporting events, as well as less formalised convivial gatherings – tended to create bonds of friendship and camaraderie [between locals and soldiers and officers]'.[32] ffolliott's diary makes clear that these incidents of associational life between the military and civilians involved substantial consumption of alcohol.[33] Research on drinking patterns in eighteenth-century Ireland demonstrates that alcohol 'was integral to the forms of sociability and the patterns of association that shaped and defined how people interacted' and 'became a staple commodity for middle- as well as upper-class households' by the later eighteenth century.[34] This is certainly borne out by ffolliott's diary, where

30 Diary of Mary Anne Ffolliot, Boyle Co. Roscommon, 1809–1827. PRONI D1995/1. With thanks to Catriona Kennedy who originally alerted me to the usefulness of this source. Subsequent quotations from Marianne in this chapter are taken from this MS unless specified otherwise.

31 Nollaig Feeny, 'King House, Boyle, Co. Roscommon' *History Ireland* 5.21 (Sept/ Oct 2013). For the location of barracks throughout Ireland during the eighteenth century, see Ivar McGrath et al, *Army Barracks of Ireland*. https://barracksireland. wordpress.com/

32 David Fleming, *Politics and Provincial People: Sligo and Limerick, 1691–1761*. Manchester: MUP, 2010. See also Catriona Kennedy and Mathew McCormack, eds., *Soldiering in Britain and Ireland, 1750–1850*. Basingstoke: Palgrave, 2013.

33 On alcohol consumption and the military, see Martin R. Howard, 'Red Jackets and Red Noses: Alcohol and the British Napoleonic Soldier'. *Journal of the Royal Society of Medicine* 93 (2000): 38–41.

34 James Kelly, 'The Consumption and Sociable Use of Alcohol in Eighteenth-Century Ireland'. *Proceedings of the Royal Irish* Academy 115 (2015): 220, 232; Lucy Cogan, 'Fountains of Wine: The Drunken Excesses of Georgian Ireland and the End of

there are frequent references to the private consumption of alcohol. ffolliott describes multiple instances of mixed-gender associational life at her home, including when the Bishop and his family were guests at Hollybrook House, such as the following example, which places alcohol at the centre of the interaction, subsequent to some hunting by the gentlemen:

> I thought I should have avoided that odious commerce but I was obliged to join in second pool as the Bishop came up early. the rest of the Gentlemen did not come up till late and had drank freely [.] Creagh took my hand and lost every thing for me in a short time. I was very glad of it as by that means I got out. Creagh was very tormenting to the Bishop but at last he took him to play chess and kept him very quiet. Joseph [Stock] tormented both Miss Stock and me very much at Supper forcing us to drink Punch which was strong enough to catch our breath [...] He devoured an entire bottle which had been a standing dish for a fortnight. (20/12/1809)

This portrait of excess drinking begins when the homosocial world of the gentlemen enters the space occupied by the ffolliott women. The men had 'drank freely' prior to joining the rest of the family to play cards and chess. In addition to the men's own drinking, ffolliott records that both she and Miss Stock were 'tormented' by Joseph Stock and 'forced' to drink punch that she judged to be very strong. Her verb choices of 'torment' and 'force' immediately communicate that these acts happened against her will and demonstrate her unhappiness at the encounter. She records how Joseph meanwhile continued to consume large quantities of drink in the women's presence.

ffolliott's diary reveals a repeated pattern of male excess drinking throughout the following months: 'Patterson got quite drunk and was the most disgusting looking object I ever saw in my life, but thank the fates I did not dance with him in my existence I never beheld such a figure' (28/12/09). Here the drunken state of Captain Patterson actively repels ffolliott, prompting her comment that she is delighted that she did not dance with him: she instead dances with an old and young Mr O'Hara and Captain William Scott, whom ffolliott records as leaving the community to become High Sheriff of Clare. Her revulsion at Captain Patterson is implied as emanating from his drunken state, which transforms him into a 'disgusting' object, with her double use of superlatives conveying the extent of her abhorrence. The following month she again recounts how the homogenous homosocial group branded 'the Gentlemen' (with the stated exception of

an Era'. *Irish Times* (21 September 2021). See also Lucy Cogan's Wellcome Trust-funded project, 'Drinking Cultures: The Cultural Reception of Medical Developments Related to Alcohol in Ireland, 1700–1900.'

Mr. Garret), again drank excessively ('<u>too</u> much'), with the descriptor 'too' underlined by the diarist herself to avoid any confusion (15/1/1810).

This propensity for excessive drinking extended to one Major Creagh, mentioned in the above 20 December 1809 entry, who was constantly at Hollybrook House, and for whom Marianne developed a fondness. She generally paints him in a positive light and, when he does drink excessively, either excuses him or avoids adding further details: 'Creagh drank too much but he was only comical' (11/4/1810) or 'We went to Bed before they came out of the Parlour Creagh got very drunk' (28/3/1810). On another occasion she simply records, 'Creagh had drank a great deal too much …'. The use of ellipses here by ffolliott reveals her generosity and her decision to excuse him from the repugnance she directs at his fellow military men. These three dots imply that his behaviour may not have been appropriate and that it possibly echoes that of the other men recounted previously, but ffolliott makes clear she will not be the judge of this behaviour. Her preference for him is made particularly plain when the Clare regiment was replaced by the Carlow regiment in April 1810. She explicitly laments Major Creagh's departure and states that the two regiments are 'not to be compared', with the new captain described as effeminate and prone to 'sentimental discourse', in juxtaposition with the 'intelligent dark Eyes and Manly conversation' of Creagh. She comments that it is perhaps better that he is leaving as she recognises that she has become overly fond of him: 'it is very well for me I think that Creagh is going away for if he was to be as pleasant as he has been since the throute [?] came I should like him too much' (15/4/1810). This implies either that her affections might become obvious to others, thereby endangering her reputation, or that she might be drawn into an unsuitable relationship.

ffolliott's own understanding and appreciation of female vulnerability in terms of both reputation and violence is further revealed in some interpolated gossip and offhand references to servants' anxieties throughout the diary entries. An entry from 24 April 1810 recounts the elopement of a Miss Crofton, for example:

> she is just 16 – her mother gave her up to the guidance of her Paternal Grand Mother entirely who spoiled her by excessive indulgence. She allowed her at 7 years old to go to every Ball in the neighbourhood [...] She has gone off to Gretna Green with a young ensign who has not a Farthing but his Pay.

This match was clearly one frowned upon by the community, including Marianne, who was a direct contemporary of the young woman. The low rank of the military man is emphasised here as well as the lack of wealth attached to the union, making it a most unsuitable one, the cause of which is related back to the mismanagement of Miss Crofton's upbringing by her mother and grandmother.[35] Intermittent references to the servants of Hollybrook House throughout ffolliott's diary include the recounting of a story of the Devil 'which has set all the Servants in the House nearly mad' (16/1/1810). ffolliott tries to convince the servants that the 'Devil could not come on earth to [illegible] a Girl in marriage', but in her diary follows this comment with the parenthetical remark '(tho certainly some one like ^him^ often does)'. This comment is revealing of her awareness of the dangers existing in the world for a young woman, that someone like the devil, explicitly gendered male, 'often' threatens girls. Her diary as a whole makes clear that drunken men were a constant feature of the mixed-gender associational life she was exposed to. Her diary reveals the strategies taken to avoid interaction with these men, such as going to bed early. It also allows her a space to record her discomfort and frequent repulsion towards exhibitions of drunkenness as she was not able to speak openly about her feelings when such displays occurred. The diary enabled her to give expression to these feelings of disquiet and allowed her, at the very least, to acknowledge the interactions.

Constantly robbed of a means of articulation, young diarists such as ffolliott, Lecky, and Shackleton could record their experiences of unease and mistreatment in their diaries, either in an attempt to make sense of the confusing events that had taken place, or to work though their anger, frustration, and revulsion at the situations they were presented with. Their diaries afforded them the space to make better sense of the world in which they found themselves and provide testimony of the experience of growing up in an environment in which young women's vulnerability was constantly made apparent.

The Power Dynamics of Euphemism

One of the most famous instances of female vulnerability and agency from this period is that involving Sarah Ponsonby, now known as one of the two 'Ladies of Llangollen', who escaped from her Co. Kilkenny home in 1778 with her partner, Eleanor Butler, to spend the remainder of their lives together in Wales. The women's relationship attracted widespread attention from its inception, with the pair gaining instant celebrity status

---

35 David Fleming's work makes clear that marriage between military men and local women in eighteenth-century Ireland was common and that 'the army undoubtedly provided a pool of mostly protestant men to which daughters could be matched. Officers were sought after by eager well-to-do locals.' Fleming 225. Fleming calculates the total number of military marriages in Limerick's parishes to be 61% by the 1750s. Fleming 229.

and attracting people to their home. Indeed, visits to the couple feature in several Irish diaries, including that of Mary Anne Dawson, who writes, 'I walked to see Miss Ponsonby Butler, two Irish Lady's who have join'd their Names, as well as Hearts in one, their story is very remarkable' (15/7/1782).[36] Ponsonby and Butler have since received significant treatment as an eighteenth-century example of an openly lesbian couple, with the nature of their union provoking much debate.[37] While the primary motivation for Sarah's leaving Woodstock, Co. Kilkenny, was certainly the desire to reside exclusively with Eleanor and to establish a household with her, the catalyst for the women's departure was the unwanted sexual attention from Sarah's ostensible guardian, Sir William Fownes. Orphaned at a young age, Sarah was entrusted into the care of William Fownes's wife, her aunt Betty, née Ponsonby, with whom she was very close. The 1774–1778 diary of Elinor Goddard, née Shuldham, a friend of Lady Betty Fownes, appears to be the main source of evidence for Sir William Fownes's unsolicited and unwanted attentions towards Sarah, thus offering a form of testimony regarding his advances and her predicament.

Goddard's diary recounts the following uncomfortable exchange between the 69-year-old man and his 23-year-old ward, in the presence of the diarist, immediately following Ponsonby and Butler's initial failed attempt to depart from Woodstock:

> S[ir] W[illiam] joined us, kneeled implored x twice on the Bible how much he loved her, wd never more offend, was sorry for his *past folly what was not meant as she understood it*, offer'd to double her allowance of £30 a year or add what more she pleas'd to it even tho' she did go. She thanked him for his past kindness but nothing es. hurt her now or wd. she ever be under other obligations to him, said if the whole world was kneeling at her feet it should not make her forsake her purpose, she wd. live and die with Miss B, was her own mistress, and if any force was used to detain her she knew her own temper so well it wd provoke her to an act what wd give her friends more trouble than anything she had yet done. (my emphasis; 2/5/1778)

In addition to the value of the entry owing to its communication of the bravery, determination, and resolution of Sarah Ponsonby and her explicit,

---

36 Mary Anne Dawson, Diary of Mary Anne Dawson, 1782–84. Clements Papers, TCD MSS 7270–7270a. 7270.

37 For example, Susan Valladares, 'An Introduction to the "literary person[s]" of Anne Lister and the Ladies of Llangollen'. *Literature Compass* (2013): 353–68; Ellen Crowell, 'Ghosting the Ladies of Llangollen: Female Intimacies, Ascendancy Exiles, and the Anglo-Irish Novel'. *Eire-Ireland* 39.3–4 (2004): 202–27.

intense feelings for and commitment to Eleanor Butler, this passage is useful for interpreting the discourses and power structures surrounding sexual harassment. Rather than acknowledge impropriety or even inappropriate conduct, Fownes instead chooses to express his advances as 'his past folly', using euphemism to minimise his behaviour and lessen the impact upon the recipient of his unwanted actions. Euphemism has been characterised as 'a powerful language tool' that can 'alter the visibility and meaning of the phenomena it signifies. It also can provide a shield behind which individuals can justify and/or deny their actions and silence reservations about moral wrongdoings'.[38] By describing his behaviour as mere 'folly', Fownes tries to assign this behaviour a benign signifier. The linguistic power dynamics at play here are further reinforced by Fownes's attempt to diminish the relevance of Sarah's interpretation of his behaviour. Sarah's negative experience of Fownes's actions is characterised as inaccurate and as explicitly secondary to his personal intentions – 'his past folly what was not meant as she understood it', implying that it is Sarah who has misunderstood and misinterpreted his supposedly innocuous actions.

Fownes's use of minimising language is echoed in the three following examples taken from Elinor Goddard's own references to his conduct from her diary entries from May:

> breakfasted with Mr Z to whom by Miss Pon's desire I told the direct transaction between her and Sir William (1/5/1778); Mem it was at Miss P's desire I went to and told Mr Z of what had pass'd between her and Sr W (4/5/1778); I at Mr Ham's where I heard Sir William's gallantry to Miss P was beginning to be whispered. (15/5/1778)

These descriptions veer in tone and content from the vague to the implied. Here we are presented with a rhetorical absence, and we can speculate that much of the oral communication of the offending behaviour was also transmitted via euphemism and other minimising language tools. Then, as now, such discursive strategies can allow the audience to be spared the discomfort of taboo topics, but they can simultaneously distort or obfuscate the truth, as here, so that the readers of Goddard's diary cannot know the exact nature or the extent of Sir William's so-called 'gallantry'.[39]

Such euphemism and minimising language are in stark opposition, however, to Goddard's condemnation of Fownes's actions. William Fownes

---

38 Kristen Lucas and Jeremy P. Fyke, 'Euphemisms and Ethics: A Language-Centered Analysis of Penn State's Sexual Abuse Scandal'. *Journal of Business Ethics* 122.4 (2014): 551–69. See also Miguel Casas Gómez, 'The Expressive Creativity of Euphemism and Dysphemism'. *Lexis* 7 (2012): 43–64.

39 The *OED* defines 'gallantry' as 'amorous intercourse or intrigue'.

became seriously ill on 31 May 1778, one month following the revelations of his inappropriate behaviour towards Sarah, later suffering a paralytic stroke and losing his speech and ability to swallow. Without knowing what the result of his initial illness would be, Goddard is explicit in her expression of her disgust at his past intimidation, unequivocally recording that 'Sr W told me before Mrs Tighe his illness, *as I sd* was his own fault what he was punished for' (my emphasis; 6/6/1778). Goddard is forthright in her disgust at his offensive advances and candidly echoes Sir William in laying the blame for his illness at his feet. On the day the pains commenced, when the 'whole house' was woken by his roars, she had taken 'an opportunity to tell him the cause was in his mind'. By 10 June 1778 the diarist records that he 'died after an agony of 12 hours'. Goddard's echoing of Sir William's allocation of blame through her expression, 'as I sd', is omitted from nineteenth-century reproductions of the diary.[40] While it is possible that this could be an oversight, the majority of the transcription is accurate and the three words are clearly visible in the original manuscript diary. One imagines that the diary was edited in order to soften Goddard's denigration of Sir William four days before his violent death.[41] However, this comment is included in the diary, uncensored, reflecting the immediacy of a diary that is impervious to later developments unknowable to the writer and highlighting Goddard's disgust at Fownes's behaviour.[42]

Rhetorical absences surrounding the behaviour of Sir William Fownes are also apparent in the diary of the woman at the centre of the affair, whose account provides no explicit mention of the events. The 'Account of a Journey in Wales', is described by its author as being undertaken by 'Two Fugitive Ladies', clearly fleeing an enemy, albeit an unnamed one. Elizabeth Edwards, the modern editor of the diary, describes it as an 'account of a flight from troubled circumstances' and notes that the 'fair copy manuscript's dramatic visual appearance adds a sense of authority' to the account.[43]

40 E. Owens Blackburne, *Illustrious Irishwomen, being Memoirs of some of the Most Noted Irishwomen from the Earliest Ages to the Present Century*. 2 vols. London, 1877, II 307.

41 For considerations of nineteenth-century editions of diaries and their omissions and bowdlerising practices, see Chapter 1.

42 While Goddard's diary affords us many details regarding the vulnerability of the orphaned ward Sarah, it also provides reflections on widowhood and offers new perspectives on the limits of women's choices, even within widowhood itself, which has been generally perceived as the state in which many women were most free and least vulnerable. See 6/11/1774 and 27/10/1779 for examples.

43 Elizabeth Edwards, 'Introduction'. Sarah Ponsonby, 'Account of a Journey in Wales; Performed in May 1778 by Two Fugitive Ladies'. Ed. Elizabeth Edwards, *Curious Travellers Digital Editions*. editions.curioustravellers.ac.uk/doc/0004.

Beyond the title, however, there is no other allusion to the distress suffered by Ponsonby at home, and, while the diary spans the period from 10 May to 25 June 1778, there is no reference to, or acknowledgement of, the illness and death of Sarah's erstwhile guardian on 10 June. Instead, the work is 'Dedicated to her most tenderly Beloved Companion By the Author' and marks a rupture with the women's previous circumstances as a new life is carved out by both.

'[I] fear her Evidence will not be strong Enough': Abandonment, Abuse, and Testimony

Such happy outcomes were not experienced by all diarists, and Dorothea Herbert's ill-fated infatuation with John Roe, heir to the Rockwell estate, Co. Tipperary, is well documented in her autobiographical masterpiece – her memoirs, 'Retrospections Of An Outcast, Or the Life of Dorothea Herbert...' – as well as in contemporary scholarship by Barbara Hughes and Frances Finnegan.[44] The diarist first met the 'mysterious, moody and attractive' Roe in 1789, with Finnegan mentioning 'a repetition of unsatisfactory annual visits' to the family's nearby glebe-house in Knockgrafton over the next six years.[45] The nature of their relationship is ambiguous, but Herbert's writing makes clear that she was certainly enthralled by Roe. This ambiguity is partially owing to Herbert's declining mental health, charted in her life writing. Rather than focus on Herbert's ill health and the veracity or inaccuracy of her accounts of the connection with Roe, as Hughes and Finnegan have done so well, drawing on the modern terminology of schizophrenia, for example, I want instead to focus on Herbert's mastery of language and her knowledge of other literary genres. This will enable exploration of how her diary fuses different modes in order to convey her perspectives on abandonment, mistreatment, and spousal abuse. Though her surviving diary has been overshadowed by her 'Retrospections' (which she alternately titles 'A Help to Memory'), the work is remarkably literary and often playfully so.[46] This can be seen through the use of unexpected pairings

---

44 Dorothea Herbert, Retrospections, on deposit at TCD. Dorothea Herbert, *Retrospections of Dorothea Herbert*. Ed. Geoffrey Fortescue Mandeville. London: Howe, 1929–1930, republished in the twenty-first century as *Retrospections of Dorothea Herbert, 1770–1806*, with an Introduction by L. M. Cullen. Dublin: Town House, 1988, 2004. Barbara Hughes, *Between Literature and History: The Diaries and Memoirs of Dorothea Herbert and Mary Leadbeater*. Bern: Peter Lang, 2010; and Dorothea Herbert, *Introspections: The Poetry & Private World of Dorothea Herbert*. Ed. Frances Finnegan. Kilkenny: Congrave Press, 2011.

45 Finnegan in Herbert, *Introspections*, 3.

46 The 'Retrospections' have been described as 'largely based on journals' and 'probably

and oppositional structuring – for example, the domestic paired with the destructive in a phrase such as 'cards and a quarrel' – or the merging of adverb and adjective, as in the brisk 'All patiently lonesome', where juxtaposition is used to heighten both the sense of loneliness and the hope and expectation of its cessation. Herbert's diary writing engages with a range of literary material, drawing upon the early novel, 'amatory fiction', and the Gothic mode. Written when she was in her late 30s, her diary of the 1800s is particularly in dialogue with the Gothic tradition as she meditates on her own purported incarceration and the perceived villainy of her family. Equally, the interpolated accounts of the experience of her younger sister, Sophia Herbert Mandeville (1776–1857), give the narrative new emphasis and raise questions regarding both female vulnerability and female agency, as Herbert details the litany of cruelty her sister suffered from her husband, from threats to starvation to enforced separation from her children.

Herbert's account of her relationship with Roe draws explicitly on the narrative formulae of amatory fictions and invokes the experiences and exhortations of their heroines. 'Amatory fiction' is generally described as writing by and for women, concerned with sexual and romantic love, commonly following a formula 'in which an innocent woman becomes the passive victim of a deceitful, experienced man', and portraying 'female resistance to male sexual aggression'.[47] Indeed, instances of sexual violence, abandonment, and the trope of seduction feature centrally across multiple eighteenth-century novels with the inexperienced young woman deceived everywhere to be seen, including for example, the virtuous Olivia Primrose who is betrayed into what the family's landlord, Squire Thornhill, believes is a sham marriage in Oliver Goldsmith's *The Vicar of Wakefield* (1766), her decision eventually being regarded as 'a mark of credulity, not of guilt' by her beloved father.[48] Evoking the innocence and betrayal of this multitude of wronged literary women, Herbert identifies Roe's mistreatment of her

---

written in a fairly short period about 1805/6'. Bridget Hourican, 'Dorothea Herbert'. *DIB*. The only diary that has survived is that from 1806 to 1807, addressed here. Dorothea Herbert, Retrospections, and Dorothea Herbert, 1806–1807 Diary, both on deposit at TCD.

47 Ros Ballaster's work, *Seductive Forms: Women's Amatory Fiction from 1684 to 1740*. Oxford: Clarendon Press, 1992, remains the standard reference for amatory fiction, though its use of the descriptor 'seduced' is now viewed more problematically. Barclay 35–44. Though amatory fiction was for many years divorced from the history of the novel and seen as inferior and reductive, more recent scholarship has sought to incorporate it into the genre of the novel more generally, pointing out the various similarities between the two genres, rather than focusing on what ostensibly sets them apart.

48 He originally exclaims, 'Had she but died! But she is gone, the honour of our family contaminated…'. Oliver Goldsmith, *The Vicar of Wakefield*. Ed. Arthur Friedman,

following his receipt of a letter, lamenting in her memoirs, 'Unkind John Roe! My Passion and Despair at that moment should have bound you to me for Ever! A poor timid Creature was I! Inexperienced in Worldly Craft, and bound down to Silence by Fear, Modesty, and Education!'[49] These later reflections on her unworldliness as a younger woman explicitly connect her to the experiences of someone like the young Mary Shackleton. Again, drawing on the examples of her literary fore-sisters – from Eliza Haywood's Glicera in *The City Jilt* (1726), discarded and 'betrayed by the deluding artifices of deluding Men' following a change of circumstances the night before what would have been her wedding day[50] to Amelia Opie's abandoned heroine Agnes Fitzhenry from *The Father and Daughter* (1801) – Herbert laments Roe's behaviour and highlights both her understanding of how he ought to have behaved and her belief that he should have been 'bound' to her forever.[51]

While the relationship plays a more secondary role in Herbert's 1806–1807 diary to the accounts of her familial situation and the ostensible abuse and incarceration received at her family's hands, the scattered references to Roe in the diary clearly draw on published fictional examples of abandonment and betrayal, such as in the following instance when Dorothea refers to a document she created for Roe to sign:

> Copy of a Certificate to be signed by John Roe of Rockwell Esqr. which if he will freely sign of his own accord will indulge Dorothea Herbert I certify that in what little acquaintance I had with Miss Herbert I never had a thought of making her my wife – nor ever entertaind any partiality for her – On the Contrary I wish the privacy of her Family regarded her as a suspicious or vicious Character whom I was hereafter to judge and punish by making her a common Spiritual Whore to the Whole World. To pres[erve] an authority over her I afforded her a sort of nominal protection which I here relinquish at her request signed by me. Please to direct the above when signed to Miss D Herbert Carrick on [] I think I owed Mr John Roe such a rebuke (19/1/1807)

Oxford: OUP, 2008, 80; 135. Stephanie Insley Hershinow, *Born Yesterday: Inexperience and the Early Realist Novel*. Baltimore: Johns Hopkins UP, 2019.

49 Herbert, *Retrospections*, 250.

50 Eliza Haywood, *The City Jilt*. London, 1764. 'In an unguarded Hour, when most he found her melted by his Pressures, and wholly incapable of repelling his amorous Efforts, did he attack her with all the ruinous Force of fatal Passion', leaving her pregnant with a child she later miscarries, 3; 11.

51 For discussion of the novel in this context see Susan Staves, 'British Seduced Maidens', *Eighteenth-Century Studies* 14.2 (1980–1981): 109–134. Staves defines 'seduced maidens' as 'young women of previously fair fame who are persuaded to illicit intercourse', 114. It is unclear whether Roe and Herbert had a sexual relationship.

While one must immediately acknowledge that this entry bears firm evidence of Herbert's decreasing mental capacity, it also again borrows from and coalesces with fictions of the long eighteenth century.[52] Herbert here ventriloquises Roe and bestows upon him the rake's admission that 'I never had a thought of making her my wife', recalling examples from early fiction, including Samuel Richardson's Mr B ---, who only gradually accepts marriage as the honourable means of a sexual relationship with his servant Pamela (1740), and, in an earlier example yet, the Prince's attempts upon the virtue of Marinda in the anonymous *Vertue Rewarded; Or, The Irish Princess* (1693). Celadon's conversation with the Prince makes the terms particularly explicit: 'your Highness does not design any more than a Jest in't; for though her Person deserves a higher station in the World, yet, since Fortune has given her neither Quality nor Riches suitable to it, you are not so prodigal a Lover as Mark Antony was, to quit your Principality, and your Honour besides for a Mistress'.[53] In Herbert's so-called certificate we find the meekness and inexperience referenced in her earlier lament are absent and instead she casts herself as the judged and punished character, trying to disseminate her version of events and to compose a narrative for herself and her audience. Her 'rebuke' and 'action' echo Laetitia Pilkington's famous mid-century defence of her behaviour and her rejection of her husband Mathew's version of events in her bestselling *Memoirs* (1748). As with Pilkington, the fragility of women's reputations is centre stage in Herbert's diary, and she conveys her understanding of herself as she is portrayed in wider society, as 'Spiritual Whore to the Whole World' (19/1/1807). Richard Graves famously lambasted Pilkington, alongside Constantia Philips and Frances Vane, for their 'immortalisation' of their fame in 'The Heroines: or, Modern Memoirs' (1751): 'Without a blush, behold each nymph advance, / The luscious heroine of her own romance; / Each harlot triumphs in her loss of fame, / And boldly prints – and *publishes* her shame.'[54] Triumphant she

---

52 Unfortunately, the diary as a whole charts an escalation of ill health: 'I have spent these 2 Days fighting the Mob about me and Asserting My Right to the Villain John Roe who is I am convinced My Husband if he married 50 women.' Recognition of her fragile mental state by the diarist herself emerges on 29 August – 'the greatest misfortune that could now happen me – namely the loss of that readiness of Mind and Capacity that always furnishd me with some ingenious Employment' (29/8/1806). These phrases are echoed in comments such as 'so disordered I can do nothing with any pleasure' (2/9/1806) and her reference to 'destracted brains' (22/9/1806).

53 Samuel Richardson, *Pamela: Or, Virtue Rewarded*. Eds. Thomas Keymer and Alice Wakely. Oxford: OUP, 2008; Anon., *Vertue Rewarded; Or, The Irish Princess*. Eds. Ian Campbell Ross and Anne Markey. Dublin: Four Courts Press, 2010, 49–50.

54 Richard Graves, 'The Heroines: or, Modern Memoirs'. *A Collection of Poems in Six Volumes. By Several Hands*. Ed. Robert Dodsley. London, 1763.

is not, but Herbert here recognises the reputational damage that could be caused by a broken courtship and seeks to commit her defence to writing, as she does throughout her diaries and her memoirs.

The focus of the diary is not exclusively on 'the Outcast Dolly Herbert' (2/5/1807), a label she assigned to herself, but incorporates threads of abandonment, ignorance, and naivety from other sources, in particular drawing attention to the experiences of the diarist's sister, Sophia, who married John Shaw Mandeville of Ballyna, Co. Tipperary, in December 1803.[55] The account of Sophia's misfortunes supports the diarist's own narrative, adding further layers of textual authenticity regarding the vulnerability of women and the malevolent capacities of others. Herbert's diary provides a lengthy description of the arrival of her sister at the Herbert family home in April 1807, having just left her husband:

> Mrs Mandeville arrived on foot from Ballyna a Walk of upwards of Nine Miles. Glad to es[cape] with her life but quite distracted at the loss of her 2 Children who he forced Away from her. He followd her some Way on the Road accompanied by Six other Men – Mr & Mrs Mandeville had a violent Altercation on the Road, and Even his Six friends said he behaved shamefully, she asked to see her Children before she came away but he refused – And she arrived here in her Night Cap and Morning gown – fearing she would be pistol'd or poniarded if she staid – for he never paid her a visit without being armed with a gun or a sword – If she had her little Boys, the loss of such a Husband would be no great matter. (19/4/1807)

The violent capabilities of Mandeville are repeatedly signalled here, conveyed by the distance covered on foot by her sister and by Sophia's state of *déshabillé*; by past events; and by the current 'violent altercation' which was apparently condemned by the man's own friends. The above extract begins and ends with chief emphasis on the woman's forced separation from her two young sons, described in both instances as 'a loss'. Sophia's fear is also underscored and her husband's predilection for weapons made clear. It should be borne in mind that 'moderate physical correction in their households' was legally permissible, with William Blackstone noting, 'the law thought it reasonable to entrust him [the husband] with this power of restraining her, by domestic chastisement, in the same moderation that a man is allowed to correct his servants or children'.[56] What is at issue here is the extent rather than the

---

55 Hugh Montgomery-Massingberd, ed., *Burke's Irish Family Records*. London: Burke's Peerage, 1976, 575–79; 779–81. Sophia is referred to as Mrs Mandeville throughout the diary.
56 Mary O'Dowd and Maria Luddy, *Marriage in Ireland, 1660–1925*. Cambridge: CUP, 2020, 304.

existence of the violence, as Mandeville was going far beyond what might be legally sanctioned at the time, causing intimidation and creating fear.

Sophia Mandeville is described as having also provided her own written account of events, which is detailed and drawn upon at length in the diary. I have not been able to trace the original document, but Herbert's assessment of it and her evocation of its sentiments enable us to gain mediated access to Sophia's 'horrible tale':

> Spent the Evening in reading Mrs Mandevilles History [...] The barbarous way Mandeville Tore her little Boy from her and the savage way he used the Child would melt the most hardend Heart – what then must the Mother have felt – hearing the little creature continually screaming in a locked up Room under the Blows he received crying poor Mamma come and take poor Amby – Whole days did the Villain keep the little creature not more than two years and a half old Locked up in a Cold room without fire suffering from the Bruises it received and totally destitute of food – Whilst the Mother & the Young Child at the breast were perishing in another room with cold and hunger [...] in short nothing can be more horrible than the facts stated in her truly piteous tale which compose a large volume (10/6/1807)

Herbert's evocative summary emphasises the physical violence inflicted upon both mother and child, the deprivation, and the cruelty performed, with reference to 'bruises', 'blows', and the perishing cold. Sophia was 'exposed' both literally and figuratively, to Mandeville's insults and to the cold, but also to society at large. The barbarity and savagery mentioned are epitomised by the child's screaming. Ambrose's shrieks express pain, and hearing that pain is part of the mother's torture. Documented domestic abuse cases in eighteenth-century Ireland chart wives having been beaten, viciously kicked, and knocked down by husbands who were later charged for doing so.[57]

These portrayals of Sophia's mistreatment by her husband, and her forced separation from her children, mirror the experiences of Mary Wollstonecraft's eponymous Maria.[58] The Gothic setting and atmosphere of the posthumously published, unfinished work *The Wrongs of Woman: Or, Maria*

57 O'Dowd and Luddy, 311. Such physical violence was generally described metaphorically within prose fiction. There is the example within *The History of Miss Betsy Thoughtless* (1751), where Eliza Haywood has Munden murder Betsy's pet squirrel by violently throwing it against a wall, which seems likely to have been a way for Haywood to hint at physical violence towards his wife also. With thanks to Moyra Haslett for these observations.

58 Mary Wollstonecraft, *Mary and The Wrongs of Woman*. Ed. Gary Kelly. Oxford: OUP, 2009.

(1798) is conveyed not through any supernatural presence but by the horrors of domestic tyranny and the setting and atmosphere of the asylum in which the protagonist is imprisoned by her husband. Again, the account details a wife abandoned and a marriage decimated, but one of the most traumatic elements for Maria is her forced separation from her daughter. As with Herbert's characterisation of Sophia, it is the loss of her child that is most lamented by Maria. The reader is told that 'the infant's image was continually floating on Maria's sight' and there is a physical pain involved in the separation, conveyed through Maria's bodily frustration – 'a bosom bursting' – at not being able to breastfeed, a possibility that it seems was still open to Sophia and her younger son Nicholas, although two-and-a-half-year-old Ambrose was kept locked up separately (10/6/1807).[59]

Across Wollstonecraft's writing, women are not without blame or a share of responsibility for gender inequality – both genders are famously portrayed as having contributed in different ways to such inequality in her *A Vindication of the Rights of Woman* (1792) – and there is much evidence of complicity in *Maria* too. Women are here portrayed as clearly being at fault in supporting patriarchal structures and are implicated within them through their collusion. In *Maria* we are told of the mistreatment by the prison guard Jemima (herself a victim of a litany of horrific sufferings) of another pregnant woman, which leads to the discovery of the latter's stiff cold corpse, and witness the novel's frustrated laments, including, 'How difficult it was for women to avoid growing romantic'. Herbert's diary reveals the misplaced propensity for the internalisation of misogyny by women, evident in her characterisation of her sister in earlier entries from the diary. She berates Sophia's departure from society's gendered expectations and lays the blame and responsibility for an earlier account of mistreatment firmly at her sister's feet:

> Spent a horrid Day with my treacherous Mother and that lump of pride and deceit the Lying in Lady. She was set up by the hunting Bucks of Kilkenny Waterford and Carrick. the dirty Suss[60] had the art to make herself conspicuous by affecting a Manlike courage in Manlike amusements (12/1/1807)[61]

In this less-than-charitable entry from early 1807, Dorothea engages in name calling, denigration, and the upholding of gender norms, supporting

---

59 Wollstonecraft 69. It was in fact this nephew, later Rev. Nicholas Mandeville, who would inherit Dorothea's diary. Finnegan in Herbert, *Introspections*, 212.

60 A 'suss' is defined by the *OED* as a 'Slattern or slut'.

61 Barbara Hughes focuses on this as evidence or symptom of her madness: 'Herbert's socially alienated position finds expression through a taboo language whose marginality reflects her own', 121.

the status quo in a manner Wollstonecraft would have abhorred, before fully inverting such descriptions three months later to cast her sister as a victim of male abuse more akin to herself.

Herbert's depiction of her own alleged incarceration also draws on Wollstonecraft's conflation of literal and figurative prisons, wherein Maria's asylum functions as 'the mansion of despair' with the 'world a vast prison'.[62] By the time she was writing her surviving diary, Herbert was convinced that her family were imprisoning her within the family home, in 'my solitary Cell'. Her diary echoes the portrayals of incarceration, villains, and despotism conveyed throughout Gothic fiction of the late 1790s and early 1800s, particularly recalling Ann Radcliffe's cast of imprisoned heroines, including the orphaned Emily who is confined in the eponymous castle in *The Mysteries of Udolpho* (1794), and the young protagonists' mother Louisa, incarcerated by her husband and his new wife in *A Sicilian Romance* (1790). Maria's nightmares about being attacked, her manacled arms, her portraits of tyrants and domestic despots, and Louisa's 'subjective experience of biological, psychological and social confinement and dispossession' all find parallels in Herbert's narrative of incarceration and the 'brutal attack[s]' upon her bruised body by her 'barbarous family'. [63] For example:

> A bold and General Assault made by the Whole family to deprive me of life and blow me to Hell – Grenadier Matty Chief Leader – I am still alive tho they set me in such a ferment that I have ^been^ up Mad about the House those two nights. (13/10/1806); Mr Nick at Breakfast made another assassination Attempt on Me. Seconded by his Mother and Miss Matty. My Arms are dreadfully bruised by his Iron grasp. (29/2/1807)

The military terminology employed here insists upon the extent of the violence performed upon her, led in the first instance by her sister Martha but involving the entire family, pushing her to madness and 'ferment'. The second entry centres on the actions of Dorothea's brother, the Rev. Nicholas Herbert, who she alternatively portrays as explicit Gothic villain, demon, and assassin, recalling the reminiscences within *Maria* wherein the eldest brother is described as 'deputy tyrant' of the household.[64] It is he whom Herbert most associates with the attempts to suffocate her (2/1/1807) and the general plot of assassination. The tyranny is not just confined to her immediate family, and the Gothic mode is again explicitly drawn upon

62 Wollstonecraft 69; 73.
63 Ruth Bienstock Anolik, 'The Missing Mother: The Meanings of Maternal Absence in the Gothic Mode'. *Modern Language Studies* 33.1/2 (2003): 31. Herbert, 1806–1807 Diary (13/8/1806); (12/11/1806).
64 Wollstonecraft 111.

to cast a family servant as a 'Red Giantess' who 'ran after me and dragg'd me through the Dirty channels shaking and assaulting me' (14/10/1806), demonstrating how Herbert's style was coloured by her likely reading.

Throughout Herbert's accounts of familial violence, multiple questions are raised. Who is the reader to trust and who the diarist? Where does power lie? Herbert states that the motivation for Sophia's writing of her history of events was so that she could sue for a separate maintenance (22/4/1807; 10/6/1807).[65] At the time of the diary's composition, women could bring forth a case for separation via a consistorial court.[66] These courts of ecclesiastical lawyers would only consider written evidence rather than hearing evidence and cross examining, which may explain the reason that Sophia was writing up notes on the abuse she experienced as her 'history of events'.[67] Immediately following the initial recommendation that Sophia sue for a separate maintenance, Herbert states that 'Council has been already consulted so we shall have sad work [and] fear her Evidence will not be strong Enough' (22/4/1807). Throughout, Herbert's diary clearly presents us with vexed matters of trust that echo the trope of the unreliable narrator in fiction and which particularly anticipate additional features of later Gothic novels, such as James Hogg's *Private Memoirs and Confessions of a Justified Sinner* (1824). What is particularly striking is the explicit confirmation of Herbert's awareness of the fallibility of public documents such as Sophia's. She acknowledges that the townspeople had already declared that Sophia's description of events was a fabrication. The fear that Sophia's 'evidence will not be strong enough' seems well founded in light of how wives' versions of violent encounters were perceived.[68] Diane Urquhart's research has shown that although the grounds for separation at the time were adultery or cruelty for both men and women, that cruelty was still connected with

---

65 Hughes posits that the dispute between the couple arose due to the financial demands of John Mandeville, owing to Sophia's full dowry not having been lodged in his account, 51–53.

66 Diane Urquhart, 'The Widening Definition of Marital Cruelty'. *Irish Divorce: A History*. Cambridge: CUP, 2020, 14. For more on the topic see David Fitzpatrick, 'Divorce and Separation in Modern Irish History'. *Past & Present* 114 (1987): 172–97; and Deborah Wilson, 'Separation and Divorce'. *Women, Marriage and Property in Wealthy Landed Families in Ireland, 1750–1850*. Manchester: MUP, 2008, 134–36.

67 I am indebted to Diane Urquhart for her guidance and opinions on separation generally and her comments on the Mandeville case in particular, which have informed this paragraph. Urquhart 14.

68 Additionally, petitions for divorce could only be brought forward by husbands. Urquhart also makes clear that 'the sexual double standard impacted what constituted cruelty towards a wife' and that toleration of 'wifely physical chastisement' continued throughout the nineteenth century, 107; 108.

earlier interpretations as 'action endangering life and limb' and needed to be witnessed.[69] This further underlines the fragility of Sophia's written version of events and the obstacles she faced in communicating the abuse she suffered. The fact that her history appears in such an intricately layered document as the diary of Dorothea Herbert makes us further consider the diary as a possible repository of women's experiences, whether those of the writer or those close to them, and how it provided a platform for the diarist's recording of their own perceptions of such distressing events.

Whether recording and working through experiences of non-consensual touch or unwanted propositions, abandonment or male drunkenness and pursuit, the diaries allowed women and girls such as Mary Shackleton and Charity Lecky, Marianne ffolliott and Dorothea Herbert the opportunity to offer a written declaration of what had happened and to testify to their experiences. Equally, the diaries also provided a space for the recording of the difficult experiences of other women and girls, thus becoming a receptacle for the recording of collective female ills. Sophia Mandeville's experiences find an audience today through Dorothea Herbert's writings, while Sarah Ponsonby's abusive treatment by William Fownes is detailed for us in the diary of Elinor Goddard. In our contemporary world, we are progressively gaining access to a language that allows people to articulate their experiences of a range of unwanted interactions. Reading these eighteenth- and nineteenth-century diaries, we are constantly reminded of the form's silences, absences, lacunae, and omissions, and we have seen in this chapter how imaginative literature could be drawn upon to allow the diarists to both understand and then communicate a wide range of experiences they had difficulty in articulating. Across the full language spectrum, from euphemism to explicit detail, drawing on examples from amatory fiction, novels, and the Gothic mode, all these diaries offer their writers a platform for the recording of experiences ranging from unpleasant to atrocious. The diary genre allows for the provision of testimony, furnishing a record of these experiences for the diarists and indeed for future readers.

69 Urquhart 106.

CHAPTER FOUR

'A means of my doing better'
Diary Writing as a Tool for Individual Improvement

Ideas of improvement have come to be central to eighteenth-century studies, and engagement with the discourses of improvement remains omnipresent across all disciplines.[1] Although it is defined and interpreted in multiple ways and incorporates numerous strands, 'improvement' is generally understood as the opposite of revolution, as a project undertaken for 'gradual, piecemeal, but cumulative betterment'.[2] Across the different branches of estate management, agricultural practice, education, and personal character, whether a person was striving for individual or social improvement in eighteenth-century England, their method was one charac-terised by regularity and steadiness, eventually producing an aggregate. Though many of the tenets of improvement were embraced across Europe, particularly in France, the word itself proved rather untranslatable and its espousal by English-speakers is more readily traceable.[3] Improvement in an Irish context takes on a distinct dimension, with the importation of this fundamentally English concept into Ireland.[4] James Kelly has charted

---

1 Sarah Tarlow discusses the ubiquity of the term but persuasively argues for its continued relevance for scholars in *The Archaeology of Improvement in Britain, 1750–1850.* Cambridge: CUP, 2007, 14. See also Richard W. Hoyle, ed., *Custom, Improvement and the Landscape in Early Modern Britain.* London: Routledge, 2017; Robert C. Allen, *The British Industrial Revolution in Global Perspective.* Cambridge: CUP, 2009; and the Leverhulme Project, *Networks of Improvement: Literary Clubs and Societies, c. 1760–c. 1840,* University of York. https://networksofimprovement.wordpress.com.

2 Paul Slack, *The Invention of Improvement: Information and Material Progress in Seventeenth-Century England.* Oxford: OUP, 2015, 1.

3 See William Douglass, *A Summary, Historical and Political, Of the first Planting, progressive Improvements, and present State of the British Settlements in North-America.* Boston, 1749–51, for the American Colonies.

4 Ian Campbell Ross provides a helpful overview of the 'untranslatable term' and notes its different implications in an Irish or English context in 'Maria Edgeworth and

the negative consequences of this ethos in terms of 'its disruptive impact on the economies of the poor, and the ensuing instances of agrarian and food protest', and the term remains a loaded one in Irish history, frequently conveyed by the use of quotation marks to recognise the perspective of those theoretically being improved: '["Improvement"] stood for the extension of metropolitan manners into the provinces, but also for the reformation of the "barbarism" that characterized an alien people.'[5] Improvement was embraced as a creed by many Protestants of English descent in Ireland in their ostensible attempts to enrich and better the Irish environment, imposing their measures upon those of a different social and religious background, and, as such, became integral to their quests to civilise and reform the Catholic majority.[6]

Most improvement essays across both Britain and Ireland were implicitly targeted at men, primarily of wealth and means – those in a position to embrace new methods of husbandry or pursue policies of land enclosure, for example – unless gender was the explicit feature being addressed. Those improvement texts that were directed at women, such as David Hume's essay 'Of Refinement in the Arts' (1752), included women in order to demonstrate how the female sex could serve to polish, refine, and thus improve men through their inherently female qualities. Then as now, there were various dimensions of improvement available to aspire to – physical, emotional, social, spiritual, and intellectual – and Sarah Tarlow has argued for improvement as a 'cross-cutting ethic', concerned with the spheres of agriculture and the human environment, as well as directed at the 'moral, intellectual and physical improvement of the self'.[7] This latter dimension is particularly apparent across the women's diaries from Ireland, regardless of Protestant denomination, with many of these incorporating elements of improvement discourse in terms of personal betterment. This will be

the Culture of Improvement'. *Still Blundering into Sense: Maria Edgeworth, Her Context, Her Legacy*. Eds. Fiorenzo Fantaccini and Rafaella Leproni. Florence: Firenze UP, 2019, 29–48.

5 James Kelly, 'Introduction'. *The Cambridge History of Ireland, Volume 3, 1730–1880*. Cambridge: CUP, 2018, 1–7. Ian McBride, *Eighteenth-Century Ireland*. Dublin: Gill & McMillan, 2009, 6.

6 See James Livesey, 'Improvement and the Discourse of Society in Eighteenth-Century Ireland'. *Civil Society and Empire*. New Haven: Yale UP, 2009, 54–89; Wes Forsythe, 'The Measures and Materiality of Improvement in Ireland'. *Journal of Historical Archaeology* 17.1 (2013): 72–93; and Toby Barnard, 'The Hartlib Circle and the Cult and Culture of Improvement in Ireland'. *Samuel Hartlib and Universal Reformation: Studies in Intellectual Communication*. Eds. Mark Greengrass, Leslie Michael, and Timothy Raylor. Cambridge: CUP, 1994, 281–97.

7 Tarlow 16.

the focus of this chapter, while we will return to demesne landscapes and agricultural improvement in Chapter 5.

The men and women who aimed at improvement during the long eighteenth century – be it economic and national, or educational and moral – recognised that theirs was not a project leading to instantaneous results. Such recognition is closely aligned to the genre of the diary itself, with its individual entries accumulating over time to produce a final text. Built upon autonomous though interconnected entries, the diary form was an ideal one to employ to participate in this ethos of slow progress and to facilitate any scheme based on gradual and cumulative betterment. Eighteenth-century diaries are perfectly adapted to assist their writers in contributing to the ethic of improvement, owing to their fragmentary, sequential nature. At the same time, the diary enables a habit of self-command, through a combination of commitment and discipline, and a dedication to frequent (ideally daily) writing, assisting in the process of betterment of the individual self.

Women in this period were habitually the target audience of manuals, conduct books, and literary collections with 'improvement' in the titles, designed to initially create and then reinforce polite ideals of femininity, rather than to improve the individual person.[8] The improvement diaries depart from such intentions, instead acting as self-care interventions that see these women privileging ideas of individual betterment. Their goal is not linked exclusively to the securing of a specifically gendered identity – an ostensibly improved femininity – and this is particularly true of older or married diarists. All generations could employ the diary as an instrument of betterment. However, projects of self-improvement take on a different characteristic depending on the life stage of the writer, often being tied up with the role and societal expectations inherent in the figure embodied by the woman writer at the time of its composition. A focus on older women enables us to concentrate on self-improvement divorced from the acquisition of accomplishments and those elements of polite education required by younger, single elite women, which represent valid though separate instruments of achieving and participating in the pervading culture of improvement. This chapter departs from a concern with the promotion of the achievement of gendered subject positions to instead consider these women's attempts at wholistic betterment of the self. It aims to explore how we might consider Irish diaries as an unfamiliar aspect of the ethic of improvement more generally, demonstrating how these diarists drew upon

8 Soile Ylivuori, *Women and Politeness in Eighteenth-Century England: Bodies, Politeness, Identities, and Power.* New York: Routledge, 2019.

but challenged the discourse of improvement and contributed to a larger tradition of improvement writing.[9]

While there are many examples of improvement discourse across the Irish diaries, the 1772–1773 diary of Mary Mathew, the middle-aged unmarried daughter of a conforming Tipperary landowner, and the 1797–1802 diary of Anne Jocelyn, née Hamilton, the Countess Dowager of Roden, both record and track these writers' subscription to the ethos of improvement and are themselves projects of self-improvement.[10] Acknowledgement should be made that any analysis of self-betterment during this period must also be considered in relation to religious beliefs, which pervaded and informed all aspects of European life at this time.[11] Though distinct from spiritual diaries, diaries of improvement engaged fully with the spiritual literary tradition, being particularly in dialogue with narrative trends in religious life writing and conversion narratives. Those diaries that have been designated with the descriptor 'spiritual' were 'not intended to record daily events faithfully' and had as their core aim the desire to 'achieve a deeper communion with Christ'.[12] However, all of these diaries – both spiritual and improvement-focused – foreground self-examination, and consideration of 'improvement diaries' in relation to the spiritual tradition – including diaries such as those of Limerick Methodist convert Elizabeth Bennis, née Patten and the Quaker, Elizabeth Shackleton, née Carleton – reveal many continuities between the two forms of diary writing.

Approaching diaries as projects of self-improvement transforms our understanding of women's participation in this movement. It also allows us to reimagine the landscape of mental health and wellbeing in the long eighteenth century. This proves to be inextricably intertwined both with the ethos of self-improvement being espoused and with the diary form itself. Eighteenth-century diaries can be considered as projects aligned with many of our contemporary theories on mental wellbeing; the manner in which these eighteenth-century women employed their own diaries to 'manage anxiety, reduce stress, and cope with depression' reveals a centuries-old

---

9 For a study of that larger tradition, see Helen O'Connell, *Ireland and the Fiction of Improvement*. Oxford: OUP, 2006.

10 Mary Mathew, *The Diary of Mary Mathew*. Ed. Maria Luddy. Thurles: Co. Tipperary Historical Society, 1991; and Mary Mathew, Cookery recipes, household accounts and diary by Mary Mathew, 1741–1777. NLI MS 5102. Anne Jocelyn, *The Diary of Anne, Countess Dowager of Roden, 1797–1802*. Dublin, 1870. Subsequent quotations are taken from these diaries.

11 Maria Luddy, 'Irish Women's Spiritual and Religious Life Writing in the Late Eighteenth and Nineteenth Centuries'. *A History of Irish Autobiography*. Ed. Liam Harte. Cambridge: CUP, 2018, 69–83.

12 Luddy 72.

tradition of using diaries in a bid to achieve better mental health.[13] Āsa Jansson explains that 'the use of the term depression to denote a low mental state, such as profound sadness, has featured in the English language at least since the mid-seventeenth century', and we see this sense of being pressed down feature in the diaries.[14] Many women employed diaries in response to emotionally challenging events, such as the death of a spouse or a pregnancy loss, and to moderate extreme feelings, as well as to chart those aspects of their lives for which they were grateful. The improvement project diaries of Jocelyn and Mathew frequently foreground such aims, but many of the other diaries from across Ireland also encourage such a thesis of viewing certain diaries as mental health tools. The diary of Anne Jocelyn's namesake, her granddaughter Anne (c. 1797–1822), for example, is careful to chart her moods and track her emotions to better understand them; Theodosia Blachford turned to diary writing to come to terms with the early death of her husband and commemorate their shared lives; while both Mary Leadbeater and her fellow author Melesina Trench used the diary form to respond to bereavement, employing it as a means of dealing with grief arising from the loss of their children.[15] This chapter will demonstrate how women's diaries from Ireland both drew on and contributed to the wider culture of improvement, including the discourse of improvement, and how these women writers inserted themselves into a long tradition of diary writing for better mental health.

'[T]here are duties to be performed, and improvements to be aimed at': Diaries as Projects of Improvement

A year after finding herself widowed upon the death of her beloved husband, Robert, first Earl of Roden, whom she had married in 1752, Anne Jocelyn (née Hamilton) expressed her regret at the limitations placed on her capacity for improvement by his passing, while recognising that some elements were still within her grasp:

> I bitterly feel the useless, insignificant life I lead at this time, excluded
> from my own place, where the active duties that the possession of an

---

13 'Journaling for Emotional Wellness'. *Health Encyclopaedia*, https://rb.gy/1yba5z.

14 Āsa Jansson, *From Melancholia to Depression*. Basingstoke: Palgrave, 2021, 10.

15 Anne Jocelyn, Diary of Anne Jocelyn. 1822. NLI MS 18,430. Theodosia Blachford, Journal of Theodosia Blachford (née Tighe), covering the years 1773–1774. NLI MS 38,639/1/7. Mary Leadbeater, Diaries covering the years 1769–1826, 54 vols. NLI MSS 9292–9346. Melesina Trench, *The Remains of the Late Mrs. Richard Trench. Being Selections from her Journals, Letters, & Other Papers*. Ed. Dean of Westminster. London, 1862.

estate requires, were my pleasure; and though I am still upon *my* own possessions, yet I am cramped in many things I wish to do: but, for all this, I ought to recollect that there are duties to be performed, and improvements to be aimed at, still in my reach, of the utmost importance, in which I exert myself with vigilant attention. I may hope my time may not be accounted lost. (30/1/1799)

Though her diary records various mornings passed signing leases and conducting minor estate business throughout the five years of the diary's duration, particularly when she became heir to her brother's estates, Jocelyn laments the cessation of her more active role in estate management and improvement as wife of the Earl.[16] Employment of improvement methods to purportedly better the lives of one's tenants and their general living conditions in eighteenth-century Ireland was tied up with paternalistic Enlightenment ideas, with it being viewed as an element of one's duty to ostensibly reform the Irish Catholic population, contributing to a larger scheme of 'good government, economic productivity, and social well-being'.[17] Elite women had different roles in its application, whether as wives, widows, spinsters, or daughters, with Maria Edgeworth the most noted example of the latter incarnation.[18] In the above quotation, Anne Jocelyn's use of possessive pronouns and the employment of past and present tenses underscores the juxtaposition experienced in her current role and heightens her sense of loss of status. Her choice of the verbs 'cramped' and 'excluded' gives a physical dimension to her lived experience of widowhood. However, the

16 For example, 'great part of this morning signing leases with Mr. Moore' (4/10/1800). See also (11/7/99); (17/7/1800); (26/11/1801). These leases are in Louth County archives. Both Caroline Wyndham, Countess of Dunraven (1790–1870), who kept diaries from her 18th birthday onwards, and her mother, Anne Ashby, subscribed to this ethos of improvement and contributed to the processes of estate management and active involvement, with both women leaving behind 'a lasting material legacy'. Odette Clarke, 'Caroline Wyndham-Quin, Countess of Dunraven (1790–1870): An Analysis of Her Discursive and Material Legacy'. PhD Thesis, University of Limerick, 2010, 28.

17 Forsythe 90. For extended consideration of this landed elite's attempts to maintain a balance between 'coercion, defence, and an absence of credible pretenders to power', see S. J. Connolly's *Religion, Law, and Power: The Making of Protestant Ireland 1660–1760*. Oxford: Clarendon Press, 1995.

18 For the Edgeworth family and improvement see Ross. For more on women's diaries and involvement in estate improvement in a later Irish context, see Janet K. TeBrake, 'Personal Narratives as Historical Sources: The Journal of Elizabeth Smith 1840–1850'. *History Ireland* 3.1 (1995): 51–55; and Clarke. For improvement and female estate management in Georgian England, see Briony McDonagh, 'Improving the Estate'. *Elite Women and the Agricultural Landscape, 1700–1830*. London: Routledge, 2018, which estimates that over 10% of land in Britain was owned by women.

extract also makes clear that she felt she could still contribute to the culture of improvement through diary composition. Through careful accounting of one's time and the regulation of one's feelings, diaries of improvement allowed women the opportunity to participate in the culture of improvement via a different avenue and to illustrate their commitment to self-discipline and to gradual and collective self-betterment.

Improvement was viewed by many Protestant men and women across Ireland as a moral and civic duty, but it was also a religious one. Accounting for one's days and one's life as a whole in order to 'improve' through self-examination and self-confession of sin was a key aspect of many eighteenth-century diaries.[19] While these diarists both recorded and wished to strengthen their personal relationships with God and their own spiritual character, this was clearly not their exclusive aim. Though imbued with religion, and in conversation with various forms of spiritual life writing, these secular diaries are first and foremost for the diarists' own improvement, understood as 'psychological introspection for the purposes of moral self-perfection and cultivation of feeling'.[20] This is in contradistinction to the diary of Elizabeth Bennis, for example, wherein Bennis makes clear that her goal is: 'to record the author's ongoing journey of faith', with her modern editor Rosemary Raughter describing Bennis's writing as 'the record of a spiritual odyssey', underlining 'its focus on matters of faith and disregard of the mundane'.[21] Born a Presbyterian, Bennis converted from her husband's Church of Ireland faith to Methodism at a young age, playing an influential role in its development in Munster and to a smaller degree in Philadelphia. Her life's core project was to dedicate herself to God. In the spiritual diaries, one's relationship with God is to the fore throughout, and each day's success or failure is measured by how much time the diarist has been able to devote to Him.

Following the famous seventeenth-century example of that of Anglican Mary Rich, née Boyle, Countess of Warwick (1624–1678), spiritual diaries chart interactions with God in different environments, as the diarists record how they meditate in the wilderness, offer prayers, go to chapel, and hear

19 Avra Kouffman, for example, describes journals as 'a mechanism by which women learned to monitor their own actions and thoughts in the absence of external overseers'. '"Why feignest thou thyselfe to be another woman?": Constraints on the Construction of Subjectivity in Mary Rich's Diary'. *Women's Life-Writing: Finding Voice/Building Community*. Ed. Linda S. Coleman. Ohio: Bowling Green State University Popular Press, 1997, 13.

20 Irina Paperno, 'What Can Be Done with Diaries?' *The Russian Review* 63.4 (October 2004): 563.

21 Rosemary Raughter, 'Introduction'. Elizabeth Bennis, *The Journal of Elizabeth Bennis 1749–1779*. Ed. Rosemary Raughter. Dublin: Columba Press, Blackrock, 2007.

sermons.[22] Elizabeth Shackleton's diary (1753–1763) is composed almost entirely of details regarding Quaker Meetings – quarterly, women's, and women's and men's – their locations in the Irish midlands, and Shackleton's observations on them: 'good counsel given'; 'felt the humbling tenderness & power of truth' (3/10/1753; 14/10/1753).[23] Sara Heller Mendelson notes that over half of the 23 surviving diaries and occasional memoirs by the British and Irish Stuart women surveyed in her study were 'initiated for spiritual purposes' and the need to enforce a devotional regime.[24] The diary of English nonconformist Elizabeth Bury (1644–1720), of Clare in Suffolk, for example, 'often advised with herself and others, upon the properest and most effectual Means to promote and carry on her spiritual and pious Designs; and at last determin'd upon this one, *To keep a daily Memorial of what she did;* which should be *a Witness betwixt God and her own Soul'*.[25] For these women, their time with God is depicted as their most valued and most valuable. All other activities, reflections, achievements, and gatherings are explicitly secondary to this core interaction.

The diaries of improvement engage with such spiritual diaries both implicitly and explicitly, as well as drawing upon spiritual autobiography; evangelical texts; the Bible; sermons; and religious discourse; while simultaneously retaining their secular character.[26] God is the addressee of early sections of Anne Jocelyn's diary – 'O my God, I am thankful; help Thou my unthankfulness' and 'Assist me, O merciful Father' – while many entries themselves read as a personal prayer, or, even, a sermon, drawing directly upon her Church of Ireland faith.[27] The Countess Dowager's diary begins with a divine address and immediately establishes the intertwined reflective and spiritual sense of the diary, which is written to improve the self and

---

22 Mary Rich, Countess of Warwick, *Memoir of Lady Warwick, Also Her Diary from AD 1666 to 1672…* London, 1847. See Ann-Maria Walsh, *The Daughters of the First Earl of Cork: Writing Family, Faith, Politics and Place.* Dublin: Four Courts Press, 2020 and Ramona Wray, 'Recovering the Reading of Renaissance Englishwomen: Deployments of Autobiography', *Critical Survey* 12.2 (2000): 33–48.

23 Elizabeth Shackleton, Elizabeth Shackleton Diary (holograph, signed) 1753–63. Ballitore Papers, OSB MSS 50, Box 4.

24 Sara Heller Mendelson, 'Stuart Women's Diaries and Occasional Memoirs'. *Women in English Society, 1500–1800.* Ed. Mary Prior. London: Routledge, 1985, 139.

25 Mendelson 139. See S. Bury, *An Account of the Life and Death of Mrs. Elizabeth Bury.* Bristol, 1720.

26 In her diary, for example, the Countess Dowager includes a very lengthy extract from Archbishop Tillotson's sermons and quotes from Blair's sermons.

27 This repeated dialogic address to God and Jesus is also apparent in the Swedish diaries of Metta Lillie and Christiana Hiärne. Christina Sjöblad, 'From Family Notes to Diary: The Development of a Genre'. *Eighteenth-Century Studies* 31.4 (1998): 517–21.

promote progress, in a bid to 'endeavour by the grace of God to improve in His favour' (opening entry, n.d., 1797). However, throughout the diaries of Jocelyn and Mathew, we see these diarists seeking to record their daily activities and movements, in addition to charting their religious meditations and prayers, with the diaries acting as a more holistic, encompassing project of self-improvement, incorporating the spiritual, but embracing other facets of one's life too. Both diaries include details of when the women wake and rest, eat and walk, whether they were curtailed by poor weather or not, and how best they were thus able to pass their time. They record who visited them, who they visited, where and with whom they dined, and offer occasional observations on all these interactions. Mary Mathew made meticulous records of who visited her in her diary, for example, and occasionally noted whether the visits were by invitation, as status was conferred by receiving visitors rather than visiting others.[28] Mathew viewed these visits as duties and often prioritised them over attending church, explicitly choosing to entertain those of a higher social standing.[29]

In addition to religious inflections, the gendered nature of improvement discourse is immediately apparent in the diaries too. Much of the proto-feminist writing of the long eighteenth century served to demonstrate and persuade the reader that women were also capable of reason and could subordinate passions to achieve it. Arguments for women's capacity for Reason and Enlightenment were frequently interwoven with references to self-improvement, beginning with Mary Astell's challenge to 'those deep background philosophical and theological assumptions which deny women the capacity for improvement of the mind' in her *A Serious Proposal to the Ladies, Part II* (1697).[30] By the later eighteenth century, the popularity of the Bluestockings' pious, didactic, and prescriptive literature, explicitly for the improvement of young women, was exemplified by Hester Chapone's bestselling *Letters on the Improvement of the mind*, which was published or reprinted 57 times between 1773 and 1851.[31] The Bluestocking agenda was one of intellectual and social improvement, bound up with 'progression in

28 Rachel Wilson, *Elite Women in Ascendancy Ireland, 1690–1745: Imitation and Innovation*. Woodbridge: Boydell Press, 2015, 103. Mathew frequently portrays herself as grateful for receiving the attention of these others whom she implies are more in the beau monde/public eye than herself.

29 As in December 1772 when Thomas Vesey of Abbeyleix, Lord Knapton, came to breakfast.

30 Mary Astell, *A Serious Proposal to the Ladies, by Mary Astell*. Ed. Patricia Springborg. Peterborough: Broadview Press, 2002, 21.

31 Gary Kelly, ed., *Bluestocking Feminism: Writings of the Bluestocking Circle 1738–1790*. London: Pickering & Chatto, 1999, 257. Norma Clarke, 'Bluestocking Fictions: Devotional Writings, Didactic Literature and the Imperative of Female Improvement'.

wisdom, goodness and holiness'.[32] Moyra Haslett has demonstrated the reach of Bluestocking improving literature across Ireland, and several diaries from the country feature references to young women reading such texts, including the following entry from the diary of Mary Anne Dawson: 'Sat down in her [Aunt Quin] Room & read in a Treatise I found there on "ye Improvement of ye Mind"' (4/10/1782).[33] What is important to bear in mind with the improvement diaries considered here is that the texts are focused primarily on these women being active agents for improvement, across many of the highlighted dimensions, for themselves and for society, but the project being embraced is not a prescriptively gendered one. The diaries with which this chapter is concerned are those written by older women, not seeking out husbands but consciously engaged in the development of one's abilities for multiple purposes, combining both public and private goals, independent of attracting a husband or presenting themselves as ideals of femininity.

The widow Anne Jocelyn's diary, for example, is very much guided by her family motto, *faire son devoir* ('do one's duty'). An improvement project informed by faith, Enlightenment, the death of her husband, and an impending sense of her own demise, Anne hoped to use the diary to manage her grief while reforming aspects of her character in order to ultimately fulfil her duty as a member of the Irish aristocracy. As an improvement diary, and a tool for self-betterment, her writing is consistently used to monitor her behaviour and provide a space for recollection, affording her 'a daily retrospect of my conduct' (8/11/1798). She frequently reminds herself and her audience of her project's aims, with assertions such as, 'The exact scrutiny of my own conduct is of the greatest importance to me' (8/3/1801) and, 'to consider in everything (however trifling), what is *best* to do, which best often contradicts some present inclination, is still a great duty, as that correction of one's fancy in trifles will form a habit of self command' (19/1/1799). Again and again, verbs such as 'consider', 'reflect', 'scrutinise', and 'correct', and nouns such as 'duty', 'inclination', and 'command' are brought to the fore as the writer strives for control over her emotions and the achievement of self-discipline. Jocelyn is consistently clear about her aims and targets,

---

Women, Gender and Enlightenment. Eds. Sarah Knott and Barbara Taylor. Basingstoke: Palgrave, 2007, 460–73.

32 Cynthia Aalders, '"Your journal, my love": Constructing Personal and Religious Bonds in Eighteenth-Century Women's Diaries'. *Journal of Religious History* 39.3 (2015): 390.

33 Mary Anne Dawson, Diary of Mary Anne Dawson, 1782–84. Clements Papers, TCD MSS 7270–7270a. MS 7270. Moyra Haslett, '"For the Improvement and Amusement of Young Ladies": Elizabeth Carter and the Bluestockings in Ireland'. *Eighteenth-Century Ireland* 33 (2018): 33–60.

as well as the various hurdles her project must overcome before these are reached, though she was not always successful at surmounting them.

Writing two decades earlier, in 1772, 47-year-old Mary Mathew makes clear that her diary is also a project of improvement, composed in order to identify and chart exactly how she passed her time and to what level of productivity:

> Tho' I am going now to write a journal of my life from this day August 1st 1772 I fear I shall by that only see how unprofitably I spend my time god grant it may be a means of my doing better another year.

Commencing with a negative qualifier, this opening sentence immediately establishes the tone of Mathew's narrative, which is frequently self-depre-cating and pessimistic. However, it also clearly communicates the diarist's core aim of 'doing better'. It is with pride that she announces on 25 August, 'I made as much use as possible of the day by being out', and Mathew is careful to record her efforts at intellectual discipline in her and her companion's reading aloud to each other, being 'kept to hard duty' (27/8/1772). She also mentions any minor improvement to the gardens, including many references to her being 'busy planting' elms and lilacs (10/10/1772) in a connection between the mind and the garden signalled by others too, including Mary Tighe in her unpublished novel *Selena* (written *c.* 1801–1803), where a link is drawn between 'the improvement of her own intelligent mind and the cultivation of her curious and beautiful gardens'.[34]

Mathew's diary was part of a larger scheme of improvement that she had decided to cultivate, one that is particularly discernible in her relationship with the Catholic Brien (later referenced as O'Brien) family – father, mother, and daughter – which she charts in the pages of her diary. In the 1770s the Mathews were regarded in the area as a *converso* family, decidedly friendly to the Catholic interest, with Mathew's brother Thomas, the eldest surviving male Mathew descendant, originally conformed in 1755 and again in 1762, as Maria Luddy makes clear.[35] Mathew, a well-connected, unmarried woman of means, is overtly snobbish about the family, especially Mr Brien, her agent, though she also belittles the provincialism of his wife.[36] Although she mocks Mrs Brien's conversa-tional prowess and denigrates her character in the diary, she explicitly

---

34 Mary Tighe, *Selena*. Ed. Harriet Kramer Linkin. Farnham: Ashgate, 2012, 708.
35 Luddy in Mathew iii–vii.
36 'We read out a trifling story for tho' she is a very good woman, not having seen many people besides what the town of Thurles produces conversation could not be supported' (8/9/1772). Maria Luddy describes Mathew as 'relatively wealthy in her own right' with numerous servants. Luddy in Mathew ix.

courts her company. Mathew seems desirous to emulate the pursuits of those above her on the social scale both in Ireland and at a European level and to demonstrate that those of the middling classes in Ireland were also capable of embracing (or feigning) magnanimity and improving the lot of their inferiors: 'Mrs Brien & her daughter dined … I made them both very happy by giving the latter some ornaments for her dress. It pleases one much to see people so grateful as they are for the attentions I have shewed them since they came to this neighbourhood' (21/9/1772). In these entries Mathew constructs a sense of herself as a philanthropic, helpful, generous, improving woman. She repeatedly describes the satisfaction she draws from the seeming pleasure afforded to the Briens' by her actions, including sending them to Dublin in her chaise to see her brother's home, as they 'had never seen a fine house before' (22/9/1772). However, there is a notable tension between the satisfaction that Mathew receives from her dealings with the Briens and her disdain for them, as she repeats how she receives 'no amusement' from their presence 'as they know nothing of the subjects I am used to'. The frequency of their visits is worth noting, however. Undoubtedly, the relationship was cultivated by Mathew, and it continued at her pleasure. One can speculate that Mathew insisted on maintaining and encouraging a connection she apparently disliked because the relationship offered another strand to her project of improvement through its philanthropic nature. It seems likely that the connection solidified her construction of herself as charitable and cultured, and contributed to her internalisation of this portrayal. The power dynamics of the relationship are constantly apparent in the entries and are strengthened by the very existence of Mathew's diary, where it is her perspective that is recorded. Norma Clarke has argued that 'the real freedom [for women] was to move from being a reader to being a writer – this was the shift from deference to authority', and this is clearly at play here: Mathew's diary allowed her to participate in a larger framework of improvement by presenting herself as an Enlightened improver and leader within her social hierarchy.[37]

Through their diaries these women were actively inserting themselves into a wider Enlightenment tradition. Drawing on Diderot and d'Alembert's *Encyclopédie* (28 vols., 1751–1775), Paul Slack has noted how historians of the Enlightenment frequently point to 'a new political economy aimed at "human betterment"' as one of 'its greatest contributions to Western thought'.[38] Women such as Mathew were contributing in their own way

37 Clarke, 'Bluestocking Fictions', 471.
38 Paul Slack, 'Improvement and Enlightenment', *Voltaire Foundation*. https://voltaire-foundation.wordpress.com/2018/03/14/improvement-and-enlightenment/.

towards this 'human betterment', and the surviving diaries offer a strong counterargument to the widespread exclusion of Irish women from Enlightenment scholarship.[39] Rejection of manuscript material, including diaries, as valid source material alters our understanding of Enlightenment output and participants. Eighteenth-century women writers often chose to opt for manuscript circulation rather than print, for a variety of reasons.[40] They committed many of their reflections on current debates, literary musings, and recordings of encounters with recognised Enlightenment figures to papers that were circulated in manuscript form rather than to print. By reinserting diaries into considerations of improvement and Enlightenment discourse, we get a more encompassing sense of women's involvement and their intellectual capacity.

At the core of Mary Mathew's larger project of improvement was of course the diary itself, which she planned to write daily. The diary was intended to record such activities as being charitable towards her servants, translating French, and promoting children's reading abilities by reading aloud, while furnishing evidence of Mathew's prowess at self-discipline and self-command, core elements of mental improvement. In this way Mathew's diary is reminiscent of the famous diary project of British woman Anna Margaretta Larpent, née Porter (1758–1832), of which 17 diary volumes survive. These include a fascinating 'methodized journal' that draws together entries from Larpent's earlier diaries, which commenced at 15 years of age and ceased by 1781, before her marriage to John Larpent, England's Examiner of Plays, in 1782.[41] In the diarist's dedication to her husband and sister in her 'A Methodized Journal AML', Larpent explains that the work may provide insight into how she has spent her life and 'by what means I have formed My Mind'.[42] What follows are meticulous examples of her lifelong quest for self-improvement, with 'lists of all the persons I have lived with, & received …'; 'List ^of^ the publick places I went to'; 'List of the Sermons I heard'; and 'List of all the Books I read'.[43] As John Brewer has noted, Larpent's 'version of the good life is one devoted to self-improvement through literature, the arts and learning'.[44] We can take this further and see

---

39 Michael Brown, *The Irish Enlightenment*. Cambridge, MA: Harvard UP, 2016.

40 Melanie Bigold, *Women of Letters, Manuscript Circulation, and Print Afterlives in the Eighteenth Century*. Basingstoke: Palgrave, 2013. See also Chapter 1.

41 Anna Larpent, Mrs Larpent's Diary. Vols. 1–16. 1790–1830. Huntington Library, California, HM 31201.

42 Anna Larpent, Mrs Anna Margaretta Larpent's 'Methodized Journal', 1773–1780. Huntington Library, California, HM 31201.

43 HM 31201.

44 John Brewer, *The Pleasures of the Imagination*. London: Routledge, 2013, 56.

how, as with Mathew and Jocelyn, Larpent's use of the diary form actually contributes to this wider quest for self-improvement and itself functions as an improvement tool, rather than simply representing a 'mnemonic record of the diarist's life'.[45]

Larpent's diary writing continued until two years before her death and the extant copies show that it was pursued with regularity, though there are gaps in 1791, August 1794, and March 1795.[46] Mary Mathew intended for her own diary to be written up on a daily basis, but there are several references that suggest that she in fact composed these entries a couple of days after the events described, rather than necessarily on that day.[47] As the diary progresses into 1773, one can determine that a great number of the entries are in fact written retrospectively, though each day is accounted for, with the exception of 4 July.[48] There are also fewer reflective entries and more that simply feature mention of the weather. We can see similar patterns in the improvement diaries of young diarists, such as that of 16-year-old Marianne ffolliott, whose diary abruptly ended in July 1810, eight months after it had commenced. Parallels can be drawn between the voices of ffolliott and Mathew and the efforts of this younger diary writer who was also striving for self-improvement. Marianne's frustrated closing remarks indicate her reasons for having initially embraced the diary genre:

> Thus ends a journal which has not answered any one of the Purposes for which it was kept which were to improve me in writing to shew me how my time was spent and stimulate me to spend it properly neither of which things it has done. It is so badly written that I feel inclined to burn it oh that I could write well what a comfort that would be to me. Marianne (25/7/1810).[49]

ffolliott returned to the diary form in 1813 and wrote intermittently until 1835, but her sentiments here echo those of the older diary writers. Her frustration at her irresolution, indolence, and idleness increased during the summer of 1810 as she regrets her failure at 'forming my mind to steadiness'

---

45 Claire Miller Colombo, '"This pen of mine will say too much": Public Performance in the Journals of Anna Larpent'. *Texas Studies in Literature and Language* 38.3/4 (1996): 286.

46 Marilyn Morris, 'Negotiating Domesticity in the Journals of Anna Larpent'. *Journal of Women's History* 22.1 (2010): 85–106.

47 For example, the entry of 1 December.

48 This is apparent from the sentence structure and tense, for example the use of 'was to' and 'had landed'.

49 Marianne ffolliott, Diary of Mary Anne Ffolliott, Boyle Co. Roscommon, 1809–1827. PRONI D1995/1.

(30/5/1810), chastising herself that 'Instead of starting and feeling my blood run cold when the Clock strikes I should feel delighted to think that the hour has been spent to the improvement of myself and others' (30/5/1810). The frequency of diary entries waned dramatically in line with ffolliott's growing sense of frustration, while the daily quality of the diary was abandoned and instead replaced with fortnightly entries at best.

After a solid two weeks spent charting her minor leisure activities, a sense of frustration emerges in the diary of Anne Jocelyn too. As with so many diarists – and certainly echoing the closing of Mathew's diary 12 months after its commencement with the observation that 'I think my time is spent in so trifling a manner 'tis not worth recording' (31/7/1773) – Jocelyn questions the value of her activity: 'How truly insipid is every account of what concerns me now' (29/1/1799). As was the case for ffolliott, Jocelyn was disappointed with her own behaviour, mentioning 'unbecoming and improper expressions', constantly seeing herself as being at fault, and wishing to improve. By spring 1799, she had deviated significantly from the project's original aims, with many entries simply stating, 'as usual', and the majority showing uncertainty about the veracity of her recollected entries: 'I think I was at prayers' (20/3/1799); 'This next week was much the same as the last' (7/4/1799). Jocelyn's lack of resolution and her failure to meet the project's aims are repeatedly charted, and a clear pattern of neglect emerges: 'With my usual irresolution, I have neglected this examination of my conduct for many days' (11/5/1799). In November 1800, evidence of declining motivation is apparent in her recognition of having fallen behind with the project, in terms of both discrete recording and retrospective analysis.[50] For both Jocelyn and Mathew, their projects' shortcomings were tied up with their own personal sense of failure, conveyed in comments such as 'I am far, far indeed from what I ought to be.'[51] These details of personal appraisal are embedded throughout and offer a glimpse into how schemes for self-improvement were also bound up with the quest for better mental health.

'[T]o give a better employment to my mind': Diary Writing and Mental Health

'Health diaries' were employed in the twentieth century, from at least the late 1930s, as a means of data collection and to monitor chronic health conditions, rather than as an instrument or means to achieve better mental health.[52] By the second decade of the twenty-first century, employing a

50 See also 28/6/1799; 7/3/1800.
51 10/3/1800, Jocelyn 74.
52 Donna M. Lawrence and Mary Jane Schank, 'Health Care Diaries of Young

diary for mental health maintenance and symptom management had become a popular method. 'Positive Affect Journaling', or PAJ, is described as 'an emotion-focused self-regulation intervention'.[53] Rather than dwelling on a traumatic incident, a person struggling with the results of such an event is now encouraged to reflect on positive moments in their lives as a mental health exercise that has been associated with 'positive outcomes among medical populations'.[54] Elsewhere, people more generally are encouraged to keep diaries in order to strengthen memory and boost emotional health and general mood, as well as to reduce stress.[55] Various promoters of positive mental health exercises online also illustrate how diaries can be used for personal self-improvement, with tips on how a person can 'track your progress towards goals, good habits and positive behaviors.'[56] Though a recent coining, journalling for mental health, or keeping a diary to regulate one's emotions, was evidently a popular pursuit during the eighteenth century. The opening of Anne Jocelyn's diary signals that her entries were written to 'help to keep off fruitless and unavailing thoughts and give a better employment to my mind' (n.d., 1797). In their overall participation in the culture of improvement, many women also embraced the genre of the diary in order to achieve a more balanced emotional state and gain greater control over their feelings, using the diaries themselves as a tool for symptom management. Women writers also used individual diary entries to recognise and explore negative emotions they experienced, particularly melancholy and anxiety, but also, notably, loneliness and low spirits. Several women explicitly began writing diaries to better cope with bereavement, while expressions of grief and loss are apparent in most of the Irish diaries, and particularly in evidence following incidents of infant mortality, which remained strikingly high during this century.[57]

Women'. *Journal of Community Health Nursing* 12.3 (1995): 171–82.

53 Joshua M. Smyth et al., 'Online Positive Affect Journaling in the Improvement of Mental Distress and Well-Being in General Medical Patients with Elevated Anxiety Symptoms: A Preliminary Randomized Controlled Trial'. *JMIR Mental Health* 5.4 (October–December 2018): e11290. See also Stefan Schneider, 'Ambulatory and Diary Methods Can Facilitate the Measurement of Patient-Reported Outcomes'. *Quality of Life Research* 25.3 (2016): 497–506.

54 Smyth et al.

55 See, for example, Kasee Bailey, '5 Powerful Health Benefits of Journaling'. *Intermountain Health* (31 July 2018; updated 17 November 2023). https://intermountainhealthcare.org/blogs/topics/live-well/2018/07/5-powerful-health-bene-fits-of-journaling/.

56 'How to Keep a Mental Health Journal'. *Mental Health America* (n.d.). https://screening.mhanational.org/content/how-keep-mental-health-journal/.

57 Mortality rates for children up to the age of 15 were between one quarter to one

Anne Jocelyn's diary was specifically written to counter what she herself described as her 'habitual lowness of spirits' (8/3/1801). Her first dated entry evinces a conflict and a struggle to maintain positivity in the face of recent bereavement. The diary was commenced in August 1797, six and a half weeks after the loss of her husband, to whom she had been married for over four decades.[58] Throughout the diary, Anne attempts to fix her thoughts and her interpretation of her situation so as to not become overly despondent, though she does admit that her grief is not eased by the passing of time nor the prospect of her re-joining her husband upon her own demise: 'I find my grief gains upon me. It ought not to be so upon any terms, particularly as the time of separation draws nearer its close [...] I will endeavour, by the mercy of God, to rouse myself from this dejected state' (2/9/1799). The diary quickly becomes a space in which to recognise her failings and to seek to rectify them, and to work against any shortcomings – 'to guard against all peevishness and fretfulness'; 'to conquer the indolence'; 'to raise my miserable mind' (4/9/1797). Throughout the entries, the state of her mental health is unfailingly charted. She constantly diagnoses her own mental health struggles and records any symptoms of this. Jocelyn was aware that she found certain times of the year more difficult than others and was able to precisely identify the onset of melancholy: 'The dreadful misery I have often experienced at this time of year is returning. May it only be suffering and not sin ... my mind is oppressed with melancholy' (22/8/1800).

third. S. J. Connolly, 'Family, Love and Marriage: Some Evidence from the Early 18th Century'. *Women in Early Modern Ireland*. Eds. Margaret MacCurtain and Mary O'Dowd. Dublin: Wolfhound Press, 1991, 285. Meliora Adlercron kept a meticulous record of her children's births, illnesses, and deaths in late eighteenth-century Dublin alongside her 'account of money expended on own & children's acct.'. She notes that she was 'obliged to advertise' for the infection to inoculate her other children after her son William Henry contracted smallpox on 23 January 1780. A later entry from 12/11/1788 records the death of her son Richard William 'after a tedious illness of four years which ended in consumption... at the tender age of 11 years & 7 months'. Meliora Adlercron, Adlercron account books. Household expenses and wages book of Mrs Meliora Adlercron of Dawson St., Dublin, including some notes on births and deaths of members of her family, and references to smallpox epidemics in Dublin, 1782–1794. NLI MS 4481. An extract from the diary of Arabella Ward focuses on an apparition reported by the diarist's ten-year-old daughter Caroline – that of 'a heavenly form' or 'blessed messenger' in the form of her deceased sister. Ward addresses the scepticism of future diary readers stating, 'Let no-one who sees these pages, call this account Enthusiastic. I have taken it from the lips of my children' and exclaims that she is 'ready to believe it a consolation to my sorrow' (12/8/1804). Arabella Ward, Extract from the diary of Lady Arabella Ward, 1804. PRONI D2092/1/10. MIC.

58 Robert Jocelyn died on 22 June 1797.

Those who have charted the evolution from early experiences of melancholia to our current understanding of depression, such as Stanley Jackson and Clark Lawlor, have highlighted the continuities across time and cultures, with the former arguing that melancholia has shown 'a remarkable consistency and a remarkable coherence in the basic cluster of symptoms'.[59] Melancholy has been characterised by its 'core symptoms of chronic causeless sadness and fear' and is recognised as being variously debilitating, incapacitating, anguishing, and disabling.[60] Generally, the diarists encountered in this study were able to identify the cause of their low spirits, but others such as Jocelyn struggled to avoid the mental state and battled with overcoming the overwhelming condition. Jocelyn declares that 'a melancholy cast of mind [...] is to be resisted to the utmost' and that her primary duty is to draw off her mind 'from the dreadful spirit of melancholy which is seizing me fast', using her diary as the primary tool to assist her with this 'great trial' (4/9/1801). Her choice of description of a mind oppressed finds echo in her report of her heart's oppression: 'My heart is oppressed, and the present events have too much overwhelmed me [...] my heart is sinking and almost broke' (23/2/1801). The physical sense of being depressed, as in pressed down or in low spirits, as well as the condition of being oppressed, feature frequently in Jocelyn's diary. Her diary makes clear that it is not just her husband's death that has led to her sense of lowness, but that she had previously suffered 'gloomy and dreadful horrors' in her 'happy days' also. Jocelyn sought solace from the writings of Daniel Waterland, theologian and Master of Magdalene College, Cambridge, on 'religious melancholy', citing his definition of it as being "'but a bodily indisposition ... no fault of the person suffering under it'" (quoted on 3/10/1797).[61] The diarist earnestly hoped that this correlated with her own position, thereby exonerating her to

59 Stanley Jackson, *Melancholia and Depression: From Hippocratic Times to Modern Times*. New Haven: Yale UP, 1986, ix. Cited in Jansson 14. Jansson provides a helpful overview of the field, including those who focus more on historical specificity. See also the wider Palgrave Macmillan series, Mental Health in Historical Perspective.

60 Clark Lawlor, 'Introduction'. *From Melancholia to Prozac: A History of Depression*. Oxford: OUP, 2012. See also Allan Ingram et al. *Literature of the Long Eighteenth Century: Before Depression, 1660–1800*. Basingstoke: Palgrave, 2011, which considers depression before it became a standardised medical concept in the nineteenth century.

61 'Religious melancholy, generally speaking, seems to be nothing else but a disordered imagination, owing to some ill disposition of the blood, or some distemper in the nerves, or in the brain ... Here seems to be nothing in all this, but a bodily indisposition, which is indeed a misfortune, but no fault of the person suffering under it.' Daniel Waterland, *The Works of The Rev. Daniel Waterland, D. D.* Ed. William Van Mildert. 6 vols. Oxford: OUP, 1843, V 555.

a degree. Jocelyn was thus able to receive some relief through her Anglican faith, identifying the fault as being beyond her capacity.[62]

In addition to melancholy, the more widespread ungovernability of one's emotions is another cause for concern that is recorded in these diaries in the pursuit of good mental health. Jocelyn frequently regretted that her passions were not under her control, and her diary notes the difficulties arising from this: 'I have comfort in thinking I recovered my calmness in a very painful situation; but it is strongly impressed upon my mind, how dreadful it is to be under the dominion of violent, ungovernable passion' (23/1/1799). She also refers to being in 'a state of great agitation' and anxiety (30/4/1801). Jocelyn interprets herself as frequently being ruled by her emotions rather than having dominance over them, but the diary supplied her with a tool to better modulate this behaviour, highlight the challenges, and, as in this instance, recognise her success in recovering a state of calm under difficult circumstances, identifying a positive element amidst her struggles. The diary therefore enabled the recording of success and positive mental health experiences, as well as being a method of achieving it. Jocelyn frequently tried to chart positive aspects of her life and include recognition of her feats and her achievement of calm, alongside the more painful aspects, antici- pating the modern practice of 'Positive Affect Journaling'.[63] Her diary is full of consideration of various small mercies and comforts, and notes how she wanted to appear cheerful in order to make others happy (2/8/1799). Her constant recognition of positive aspects and mercies becomes particularly striking during the Rebellion of 1798, when she was persuaded by her daughter Harriet to leave the family estate in Co. Down in order to seek refuge in Belfast and then Scotland:

> let me deeply impress upon my mind the wonderful mercies that attended us from the beginning of our flight [...] We never suffered half what our dearest concerns in Ireland did. Our spirits were not broken by the continual view of horrors which has nearly overcome some of those dear objects, and none of us have lost anything essential to our happiness or comfort (12/9/1798)

---

62 Crawford Gribben has suggested that the possibility of such relief for those from Anglican faiths might be in opposition to the experience of women from Calvin- ist-oriented denominations, who also worried about salvation in a way that Methodists or Quakers did not. See Crawford Gribben and Graeme Murdock, eds., *Cultures of Calvinism in Early Modern Europe*. Oxford: OUP, 2019. See also John Stachniewski, *The Persecutory Imagination: English Puritanism and the Literature of Religious Despair*. Oxford: Clarendon Press, 1991, which argues that Calvinism drove its adherents to despair. With thanks to Crawford Gribben for his insights.
63 For example, 3/7/1799.

Here, she praises God for his protection of her family, especially her son whom she portrays as 'brave' in the face of the 'unfortunate rebels', as she strives to produce a positive account of her own experience of a violent and traumatic period. Extending this to her larger family, she repeatedly draws on inclusive plural pronouns, using 'our' and 'us' to signify shared familial good fortune and the communal graces they experienced.

Throughout Jocelyn's diary, however, we get the sense of a woman struggling with the experience of being alone following her husband's death. There are repeated references to her deep love for Robert Jocelyn and the affectionate bonds and partnership established between the pair. She frequently juxtaposes her current circumstances with her previous married state: 'it was not riches or worldly grandeur that gave that supreme happiness. Of that latter there was then enough; I have now both, but not to share, I am alone.'[64] A sense of loneliness is remarked upon in similar style by Theodosia Blachford, the mother of Mary Tighe, whose widowhood, in May 1773 after only three years of marriage to Rev. William Blachford, prompted the composition of a short diary that engages with her feelings of loss and charts her total lack of preparation for her current, overwhelming emotions.[65] Her monthly diary entries chart 'the painfull sensibility of my unhappy state' (24/9/1773); track her struggles with accepting William's death; her reflections upon visiting her husband's grave; and record her deep, consuming grief (14/7/1773).[66] Blachford's first entry in her diary compares her present state with the couple's previous felicity, which has now vanished. She writes that without her 'friend and lover', 'I am left to struggle with loneliness sorrow and difficulties' (14/7/1773). Both widows' experience of loneliness following bereavement is very much connected to a physical state of being alone, as it is defined in Johnson's *Dictionary* (1755), and bound up in earlier concepts of 'oneliness', 'the fact or condition of being alone'.[67] We see the descriptor applied similarly in

---

64 We should of course bear in mind that throughout her life Anne Jocelyn was a very wealthy woman of high social standing, the daughter of the Earl of Clanbrassil, whose husband, the 2nd Viscount, was created Earl of Roden in 1771. On the death of Jocelyn's brother James, 2nd Earl of Clanbrassil, in 1798, she became her father's heir and inherited a large fortune.

65 NLI MS 38,639/1/7. Maria Luddy, 'Theodosia Blachford, née Tighe', *ODNB*. Her entries make clear that she had imagined she would be resigned upon the death of her husband, following his illness, as she could then devote herself to God, but she discovered this was not at all the case, and instead she struggled greatly.

66 Separately to the short diary, Blachford later wrote 'Some memorandums relative to the death of my ever dear Husband', NLI MS 38,639/1/8.

67 Fay Bound Alberti, 'When "Oneliness" Becomes Loneliness: The Birth of a Modern Emotion'. *A Biography of Loneliness: The History of an Emotion*. Oxford: OUP, 2009, 18.

the diary of Elinor Goddard upon the death of a neighbour's mother – 'Coll Medows came to tell me he had disclosed to Mrs Medows the melancholy event of her mothers death, I could not pluck up resolution to go to her directly, as soon as I could I did and found her just as I expected lonely afflicted God almighty comfort her' (15/2/1780). In the same fashion as the widows' loss of their husbands, this woman's loneliness is conveyed as being a direct result of the loss of her mother.

The diary of the younger Anne Jocelyn is also full of references to being alone, but in the more modern sense of an emotional state, which Fay Bound Alberti argues developed around 1800 as 'a conscious, cognitive feeling of estrangement or social separation; an emotional lack that concerns a person's place in the world':[68]

> Had an unkind letter today from poor Mama [Anne's stepmother], which made me feel wretched indeed, looking all around me I feel standing alone in the world (21/6/1822)

> This place brought so many sad thoughts to my mind, then Mr. P and all the sisters being together, and I only a poor lone, solitary branch in the midst of them, this filled me with envy and jealousy (8/7/1822)[69]

In her early 20s, the younger Anne Jocelyn suffered from a sensation of loneliness most keenly when finding herself surrounded by others, rather than when on her own physically. The younger Anne's sense of herself as a branch off a more solid tree is underscored with the triple descriptor of poor, lone, and solitary. She is connected to these others physically, but only tangentially. Although surrounded by other men and women she does not experience a sense of belonging, nor feel part of the rituals of her peers. Alongside her recognition of this negative emotion, she notes the resulting related feelings of wretchedness in the month of June and envy and jealousy in July. On both occasions, her feelings of loneliness are prompted by others, whether by their actions or their presence, which supports the more modern idea that 'sharing a physical space is not the same as sharing an emotional space', drawing parallels with Dorothea Herbert's description of herself in her diary as 'devoutly lonesome en famille' (25/1/1807).[70] The modern

68 Fay Bound Alberti, 'This "Modern Epidemic": Loneliness as an Emotion Cluster and a Neglected Subject in the History of Emotions'. *Emotion Review* 10.3 (July 2018): 243.

69 Quoted by Janice Holmes, 'The Century of Religious Zeal, 1800–74'. *The Field Day Anthology of Irish Writing, Volumes 4 and 5, Irish Women's Writing and Traditions*. Eds. Angela Bourke. et. al. Cork: Cork UP, 2002, IV 546.

70 Olivia Laing, *The Lonely City: Adventures in the Art of Being Alone*. New York:

interpretation of the condition as being one of 'emotional distress that arises when a person feels estranged from, misunderstood, or rejected by others' seems particularly fitting here and more pertinent than a sense of being alone subsequent to the removal of the affectionate bonds and companionship offered by relationships severed upon death, which we can observe in the earlier diaries of Jocelyn, Goddard, and Blachford.[71]

A sense of disconnection from the larger world is notable in the diary of Elizabeth Stirum, née Richards. There are intermittent references throughout Elizabeth's diary to ill health and low spirits, as well as repeated attempts to extricate herself from such moods. Stirum notes her own difficulties in fully accepting a quiet domestic life, particularly after her return to her childhood home of Rathaspeck in Co. Wexford with her children and her Dutch husband Count Frederik Willem van Limburg Stirum, a move undertaken for financial reasons:

> I am out of conceit with myself, I used to think I could be perfectly happy in the performance of my domestic duties, and without any society but that of my husband and children. But alas, I begin to suspect, that though I am happy, both as a wife and a mother, I should be *happier* if there were sometimes witnesses of my happiness. Never to mix in society, that is disagreeable. (3/5/1810)[72]

An entry from 31 May 1810 mentions that date as the first time Stirum had drunk tea away from her home in seven months, and her frustrations at remaining exclusively within the home, away from society, offer an additional perspective on female loneliness within the domestic sphere and the human need to interact with others. The editor of the modern edition of the diary describes Elizabeth as 'an overly-anxious mother', but the combination of entries makes it clear that she cared deeply for her children and was attempting to be the best mother she felt she could be, including by educating, breastfeeding, and vaccinating her offspring, while using the diary form to openly acknowledge her frustrations at the limitations of her circumstances in a strikingly modern way.[73]

Picador, 2016. Dorothea Herbert, 1806–1807 Diary, on deposit at TCD.

71 L. Andersson, 'Loneliness Research and Interventions: A Review of the Literature'. *Aging and Mental Health* 4.2 (1998): 264–74.

72 Elizabeth Richards, *The Diary of Elizabeth Richards (1798– 1825): From the Wexford Rebellion to Family Life in the Netherlands*. Ed. Marie de Jong-Ijsselstein. Intro. Kevin Whelan. Hilversum: Verloren, 1999. The family would eventually move to the Netherlands in 1821.

73 Marie de Jong-Ijsselstein, 'Elizabeth Richards, Family Life in the Netherlands' in Richards, 18.

The diary of Anne Weldon functions almost as a reversal of Anne Jocelyn and Theodosia Blachford's responses to bereavement in that Weldon's abruptly ends four days *before* her husband's death, at age 49, on 23 August 1773.[74] The diary's composition was initially prompted by a journey from Ireland to England in June 1761, during which time Anne met her future husband, Walter, whom she would marry the following year.[75] As with Jocelyn and Blachford, the diary entries communicate a deep love for her husband, whom she seems to have adored. Anne was Walter's second wife. He had previously been married to Mary Steuart, with whom he begot his heir, Stewart Weldon. Despite its repeated assertions of her love for him, Anne's diary makes clear that the couple spent extremely little time together, much to the diarist's regret. The diary is not particularly reflective, but those passages that do pause to consider the diarist's spirit or temperament mostly do so in order to record her low moods when separated from Walter, such as the following entry from 1768:

> Aug 31 I far from well, & very low speret to be left alown, for I had alass thought I might have had the happiness of Mr. W. staying with me, but how great my disappointment that the very day I got to Bath he mead an appointment to go to London ye Monday fortnight after I got ther, so that he stad with me but a fortnight & one day after I went to Bath by his order to me and on his return but from Thursday evening tel ye Wensday after.[76]

This becomes a recurrent pattern whereby the diarist juxtaposes the possible happiness that could be achieved with her current situation, thereby amplifying the disappointment experienced. The coincidence of her husband's planned departure being scheduled on the 'very day' of her arrival heightens Anne's displeasure. She is keen to note the consequences of the decisions made, rather than her dissatisfaction or disapproval, describing herself as 'far from well' and noting her low spirits. The extent of Walter's absences becomes apparent in a sentence conveying her joy at his extended presence the year before his passing: 'I have not known so much happiness in ever particuler, and comfort and ease this eight years, as I have done since I came here, nor have I ever had ye comfort and happiness of haveing him ever before 15 weeks together with me, and so much happiness' (1/9/1772). The word 'happiness' is repeated thrice within this one sentence as the diarist attempts to express her satisfaction at having her husband with her for almost four consecutive months. This period is of short duration, however,

---

74 Anne Cooke Weldon, 'Anne Cooke Diary'. *Journal of the County Kildare Archaeological Society* VIII (1915–1917): 104–32; 205–19; 447–63.

75 Walter Weldon held the office of MP for Athy, Co. Kildare, in 1745.

76 Weldon 119.

with the diary tracking Walter's descent into ill health, and listing the failed medical treatments sought for his recovery.

Anne Weldon's diary records not only the ill health of her husband from 1770 onwards but the deteriorating health and subsequent death of the diarist's mother in 1770: 'she dide this Evening about 9 a Clock quite easy, and in pace with God and man. May my latter end be like unto her! She is happy, and I will not repine' (25/11/1770). The day following she describes as 'A Blank to me' (26/11/1770). Weldon records that she had her mother laid to rest the next day, beside the diarist's father in St James' Church. By the following day she notes, 'Thursday 29 Still my Heart Bleeds but I must hid my sorrow' (29/11/1770). While the diaries still retain a performative dimension and are to be considered as potentially public documents with an audience,[77] they also offered some writers the opportunity to record emotions that they were frequently forced to dissimulate off the page. Anne here uses the diary as a platform to record her grief, while acknowledging that she must hide this emotion publicly, only four days after her mother's demise. Writing contemporaneously, Mary Mathew also explores the connections between the experience of grief and both its performance and concealment in her diary. In an era of sensibility, Mathew still notes the trend for repression of emotion by her peers, recognising the behaviour in herself and others on several occasions, particularly following the sudden death of Catherine White, Lady Westmeath, where several family members, including White's young son, struggled to suppress or 'put off' their emotions, with the diarist lamenting, 'I think it is a false shame we are all liable to in striving to conceal our feelings of that sort and at the same time should be very sorry to be thought insensible, but perhaps it is polite to do so' (19/9/1772). This conflict is apparent at various times throughout the diary, including in Mathew's own attempts to distract from the 'great agitation' of another by engaging them in conversation on 'indifferent subjects' rather than discuss the cause of this person's distress, thus participating fully in this culture of repression despite her distaste for it (12/10/1772). As with Weldon, the diary form, conversely, afforded Mathew an opportunity to fully acknowledge her own deep sorrow, as again and again she returns to the subject of Lady Westmeath's passing and her own difficulty in dealing with this loss.[78]

We are frequently confronted by a conflict between experienced emotion and expressed emotion throughout the diaries. The diary form offered a space for the recording of one's feelings as well as one's opinions on ideas often not thought proper for women to vocalise. It enabled them to acknowledge painful events that they might not be able to express elsewhere,

77 See Chapter 1.
78 Luddy in Mathew x.

assisting their mental health as well as the process of recovery, particularly in relation to the loss of a child. The experience of pregnancy, miscarriage, and infant loss in an eighteenth-century context has received earnest scholarly attention over the past two decades, particularly from social historians.[79] Diaries can offer the historian a useful source for data acquisition, as well as closer access to the individual emotional effect, though still very much mediated. In addition to the individual entries and records, it should be noted that evidence of pregnancy complications and loss is present too through the silences and gaps within multiple women's diaries. Anne Cooke, for example, married her beloved Walter Weldon in February 1762 and gave birth to her first son in October of the following year, followed by two daughters Mary and Jane by January 1766. However, references to later preparations for her lying in, in January 1767 and December 1768, are not followed by the mention of any subsequent children.[80] There is a complete silence in the diary regarding Anne's feelings on these presumed stillbirths.

Then as now, discussion of miscarriage and stillbirth existed across a spectrum from open discussion to total silence, and many of the diaries implicitly hint at the experience of miscarriage and stillbirth in the gaps in entries, the illnesses, and the low spirits reported.[81] Others at this time were more forthright in their allusion to such loss. Published contemporaneously, in 1766, for example, the celebrated correspondence of Elizabeth

79 Paige Donaghy, 'Miscarriage, False Conceptions, and Other Lumps: Women's Pregnancy Loss in Seventeenth- and Eighteenth-Century England'. *Social History of Medicine* (2021): 1–23; Sarah Anne Buckley, 'Women, Men and the Family, *c.*1730–*c.*1880'. *The Cambridge History of Ireland, Volume 3, 1730–1880*. Ed. James Kelly. Cambridge: CUP, 2018, 231–54; Rosemary Raughter, '"A time of trial being near at hand": Pregnancy, Childbirth and Parenting in the Spiritual Journal of Elizabeth Bennis, 1749–79'. *'She said she was in the family way': Pregnancy and Infancy in Modern Ireland*. Ed. Elaine Farrell. London: Institute of Historical Research/University of London Press, 2012, 75–90 ; Gabrielle Ashford, 'Childhood: Studies in the History of Children in Eighteenth-Century Ireland'. PhD Thesis, St. Patrick's College, DCU, 2012.

80 'Mr Weldon & Steuart & I left Rahen for St Catherine's in my way to Town to Lyin; kept ye 3 Children behind me at Rahen' (8/1/767); 'From this till I lyin I only went out in ye morning either to visit or take ye air, except one evening' (7/12/1768).

81 Many of the diaries reference the stillbirths experienced by other women, including Frances Jocelyn's which records that 'The first thing I heard this morning was that poor Harriet Foster was safely brought to bed on Thursday, but her Baby is dead'. Frances Theodosia Jocelyn, Diary, 1810–1812. NLI MS 18,430 (7/11/1811). See also Elizabeth Stirum's mention of her sister Martha's stillbirth, 'My sister writes to me that she has lain in of a dead son and has been extremely ill' (24/8/1810); and Mary Anne Dawson's 'News of poor Lady Lanesborough's being brought to Bed of a Dead Child' (25/7/1782), TCD MSS 7270.

and Richard Griffith features several mentions of the fear and dread of pregnancy loss, as well as the experience of miscarriage and the subsequent attribution of blame.[82] Mother of at least nine surviving children by early 1820, who were born between 1803 and 1817, Elizabeth Stirum's affection for her family and the joy she receives from her children is clear in her lament for what she believes to be a recent, unconfirmed pregnancy loss: 'I have not been well, I believe, I am almost sure, I have had a *fausse couche*, and I am not glad of it, Fredda gives me so much pleasure! And now I shall have no little one to supply her place when she grows too old for a plaything' (29/2/1820). Frederica Johana (b. 1817) was in fact followed by one final sibling, Albertina Catherine, in 1820, but this entry makes clear the regret provoked by a suspected miscarriage and the affectionate bonds between mothers and children that clearly existed in the early nineteenth century.

The diary of Mary Anne Fortescue, née McClintock, of Co. Louth, by then mother of three children, includes reference to her own devastation after a stillbirth that occurred in 1798, 11 years after her marriage to her husband, John. After a silence of several weeks, her diary resumes in Dublin's Merrion Street, where she had arrived on 31 March:

> I was brought to bed on Easter Sunday the 8th of this month, the poor child was dead & it was a boy. I kept tolerably well until the Saturday following & then felt ill & was as low as possible [...] The loss of my poor child made my confinement very lonely. I have borne it better than I should have supposed I coud. The weather is uncommonly fine & I hope to recover now very fast. (21/4/1798).[83]

After delivery, the period referred to as confinement, in which an elite woman could stay in bed to recover from labour, generally lasted up to one month.[84] Here we see that Mary Anne found this recovery period without

82 Elizabeth and Richard Griffith, *A Series of Genuine Letters Between Henry and Frances. Volume 3*. London, 1766, 6; 15; 56–57. See also Letter 375, 'This has been an unlucky Province to me: The first Time I came to it, was on Account of your Miscarriage; and I had hardly sat down in Roscommon, in the same Place, before I received a Letter from you, to the same Purpose. I declare I will manage you my own Way, the very next Time you get yourself with Child: for I will not be always playing Shakespear's *Love's Labour lost*, at this Rate', 60.

83 Mary Anne Fortescue, 'The Diary of Marianne Fortescue, 1797–1800'. Ed. Noel Ross. *Journal of the County Louth Archaeological Society* 24.2–3 (1998): 222–48.

84 Of course, this practice was not possible for most eighteenth-century women. Angela Joy Muir, 'Midwifery and Maternity Care for Single Mothers in Eighteenth Century Wales'. *Social History of Medicine* 33.2 (2020): 408. Frances Jocelyn records her stepmother going out in the carriage 'for the first time since her confinement' on 25/1/1811, one month after the birth of a son on 26/12/1810.

the accompanying child to be difficult and lonely. One week after the above note regarding her determination to recover quickly, she records that 'I have not ventur'd out yet'; that her head is still 'sometimes bad'; and that she does not go down to dinner or supper (27/4 and 29/4/1798). Mary Anne's sorrow at this stillbirth is very much integrated into the diary as a whole and forms but one part even of the above entry, which communicates her physical loneliness and low spirits alongside comments on the weather. Other diarists allowed themselves greater space to grieve, or indeed dedicated entire diaries to the commemoration of a lost infant.

Melesina Trench was left distraught upon the death of her two-and-a-half-year-old son Frederick in June 1806.[85] A mourning journal was written in consequence, to simultaneously commemorate his short life and provide an exercise in healing for his bereft mother. Katherine Kittredge, who discovered the diary in the early twenty-first century, describes how 'for fifty-eight pages and just under 8,000 words, Trench uses original prose, quotations from published works, lists, and broken exclamations to record her son's death, create a memoir of his life, and cope with her grief and guilt'.[86] Though intensely personal, these feelings of loss and heartache solidified the friendship formed in 1802 between Trench and Mary Leadbeater, who had lost her four-year old daughter Jane as a result of a fire in 1798. Leadbeater's diary also records feelings of self-reproach: 'Just then my sweet Jane told me she wanted to go upstairs and I most unfortunately, stupidly and carelessly trusted the wax taper with her' (29/11/1798).[87] This triplet of contrition and regret later mingles with descriptions of overpowering sorrow wherein 'my dear Jane's idea pours on me and sinks me exceedingly low' (7/12/1798). Barbara Hughes interprets the fact that Leadbeater continues writing in her

85 Trench was beset with personal tragedy, having been widowed in 1790, aged just 21, following the birth of two children. Her second-born child, a son, died aged just 9 days old in 1788, and a daughter from her second marriage (m. 1803) died aged only 2 weeks in 1805. Similarly, the diary of Elizabeth Clibborn contains very affecting entries on the death of her six-year-old son, her first-born child, John. This section of the diary is composed in retrospect, after his death.

86 Katherine Kittredge, 'A Long-Forgotten Sorrow: The Mourning Journal of Melesina Trench'. *Eighteenth-Century Fiction* 21.1 (2008): 158. See also Katherine Kittredge, '"It spoke directly to the heart": Discovering the Mourning Journal of Melesina Trench'. *Tulsa Studies in Women's Literature* 25.2 (2006): 335–45.

87 Cited in Barbara Hughes, *Between Literature and History: The Diaries and Memoirs of Dorothea Herbert and Mary Leadbeater*. Bern: Peter Lang, 2010, 143. Trench was later to lose her youngest child and only daughter, Elizabeth (Bessy), in November 1816. For the developing friendship between Trench and Leadbeater, see Stephen Behrendt, '"There is no second crop of summer flowers": Mary Leadbeater and Melesina Trench in Correspondence'. *Forum for Modern Language Studies* 52.2 (2016): 130–43.

diary as 'indicative of how habitual, almost addictive, diary-keeping has become for her'.[88] Though Hughes does accept that the diary is also used to record and analyse Leadbeater's feelings of anguish, providing the historian with an account of the 'course that grief can take', it seems to me that both Trench and Leadbeater used these mourning diary entries primarily to process their feelings and provide a necessary outlet for their grief, affording space to their emotions.

Those writing within the spiritual tradition also recorded the difficulty of arriving at resignation and acceptance when confronted with infant and child mortality. Elizabeth Bennis's pain at losing six of her ten children is noted within her diary wherein she struggles to 'achieve the resignation to which she aspired': 'It is my desire that the Lord should deal with me according to his own good pleasure, yet find I have not strength to bear the worst ... find nature shrink at the thought of losing my only child. Indeed, I find a continual struggle between nature and grace' (13/5/1753).[89] Similar patterns are followed across all the diaries considered in this chapter as each of the writers in turn expresses their struggle to give thanks and count one's blessings in the face of myriad challenges and tragedies. Following the seventeenth-century tradition of recording all one ought to be thankful for alongside a list of sins and misdemeanours, each of the women tried to incorporate these elements of thankfulness and wrongdoing into their diaries in a bid both to improve the self and to achieve a more positive mental state. This eighteenth-century version of 'Positive Affect Journaling' sees Anne Jocelyn, the Dowager Countess, outline the positives in her life, for example – namely 'ten of the best and most affectionate children', her brother, friends, grandchildren, and 'health and sight more than at <u>my age</u> I might expect' – while perennially struggling with low spirits.

Jocelyn was one of the oldest of the diarists in Ireland to be tempted to commence diary writing, beginning her first entry at 67 years of age and engaging with the diary as an account of her life as she was preparing for its closure.[90] Her entries are marked by specific references to her advanced age and how it impacted upon her writing and her daily life, as well as on

---

88 Hughes 143.

89 Bennis 91–92. In another example, when faced with the potentially fatal illness of her daughter, the diarist 'Harriet' Kiernan exclaims, 'I have just heard that my dear Maria is ill – if it is to be thy will – preserve her precious life – but make us Submissive to all thy wise dispensations'. 'Harriet' Kiernan, Diary of Harriet Kiernan. 1799–1808. PRONI D1728/28/1 (15/12/1799). The child Harriet and her 5 siblings were born in the 1790s. This is clearly not the diary of such a young girl, in which the diarist mentions her children.

90 Harriet Blodgett, in *Centuries of Female Days: Englishwomen's Private Diaries*. New Brunswick: Rutgers UP, 1988, identified Louisa Bain and Amelia Opie as being of a

her overall project of improvement. She cites both the 'languor, so natural to my time of life' and a 'want of firmness' that has been increased by 'the weakness of age' as preventing her from always completing her entries and as contributing significantly to her neglect of retrospection (30/4/1801; 20/4/1799). As well as offering reflection on her current low spirits, many entries draw conclusions from her life as a whole, recognising her relatively advanced age and assessing her state of mind. Jocelyn views her key duties and role as having been bound up in her position as wife: 'that my importance was totally derived from one beloved object is no mortification' (12/7/1799). Deprived of this status, she presents herself as unmoored and without a strong, defined purpose, instead turning to diary writing as an outlet and a guide, aiming for both improvement and for a more positive state of mind.

The diaries discussed here are fragmentary and sequential by nature, with individual entries accumulating over time to produce the final, completed documents. Mathew introduced clear margins into her diary, by which the date is divorced from the main body of the entries, alongside a summary of the day's weather, drawing attention to the daily nature of her exercise. This is in contrast with the earlier sections of her manuscript wherein she chose underlining, spacing, and titles to indicate separate topics, whether in relation to planting, health, or recipes. Mathew's diary lasted precisely 12 months, while Blachford's brief engagement with the diary form took place over a few short months, and Anne Jocelyn's diary writing spanned five years, until her death. The diary projects of Leadbeater and Trench were the work of several decades, with Mary Shackleton Leadbeater producing 54 diary volumes in total. Built upon autonomous though interconnected entries, the diary form facilitated all these women's schemes of gradual and cumulative personal development, regardless of project length, regularity of entry, or presentation style. By mapping the formal aspects of genre onto improvement, we can see how the latter could become accessible to these women via their engagement with the process of diary writing.

All the diaries considered in this chapter demonstrate the inherent agency of the women writers in question. Their engagement with the diary form as a tool for improving the self upholds interpretations of improvement as a strategic, active undertaking rather than a passive gesture.[91] The diarists were responding to their present situations and actively inserting themselves into a larger cultural conversation, using the instruments at their disposal. They were striving for autonomous self-improvement to achieve better public and private outcomes, and their diaries show the intersections that

relatively advanced age at the time of their diary commencement, at 54 and 58 respectively, 11.
91 Tarlow 19.

existed across spiritual, emotional, moral, and intellectual dimensions of improvement of the self. All the women considered in this chapter were also, in various guises, engaging with an earlier form of self-care, with some using their diaries as treatment for grief or anxiety, as with Weldon, Blachford, Leadbeater, and Trench, and as a mental health tool for symptom management and health maintenance. Including the diaries of Jocelyn and Mathew in this consideration of improvement discourse places women at the centre of improvement projects rather than as peripheral actors and transforms our understanding of their participation in improvement culture. All these Irish diaries offer us an insight into the lived experience of mental health struggles in the long eighteenth century, as well as into women's active attempts to overcome these and to better position themselves as agents of improvement, using their situations to contribute to what they saw as positive change at both an individual and societal level.

CHAPTER FIVE

Creating and Curating the Diary Environment

Place and Identity

Irish diaries from the long eighteenth century were written from within many different physical environments, encompassing urban and rural settings, composed both from within Ireland and abroad. Almost all the diaries include some form of domestic travel, and a circulation of people across space, frequently from Dublin town houses to country estates and family demesnes. The environments depicted shift from marine and coastal landscapes, boglands, and mountain ranges, to townscapes and sculpted demesnes. This chapter explores and dissects aspects of the physical landscapes the different women inhabited, as well as the curated landscapes and abstract homelands they created within their diaries, reflecting on questions of place, community, and identity, and considering how these diarists both responded to and shaped their environments. The relationship between literature and the physical environment is to the fore throughout, as the chapter poses questions concerning the representation of nature in the diary and what role the physical setting in which the diary was composed plays in the diarist's narrative and writing style. Ecocriticism explores how literature affects and is affected by the physical world, and it is clear that the diarists' relationships with both their built and natural environment impacted on their immediate employment of language, including narration, pacing, syntax, the density of figurative language, and tone.[1] We see dramatic shifts in tone take place in

---

1 Cheryll Glotfelty, *The Ecocriticism Reader*. Athens: University of Georgia Press, 1996, remains one of the field's foundational texts. Greg Garrard, *Ecocriticism*. London: Routledge, 2012, offers a helpful synthesis. For an overview of how the critical field of literary ecocriticism has diversified and to gain a sense of ecocriticism in a global context, see Jessica Maufort, 'Multiple Convergences: Ecocriticism and Comparative Literary Studies'. *Recherche littéraire/Literary Research* (2019): 101–25, and Elizabeth DeLoughrey and George B. Handley, *Postcolonial Ecologies: Literatures of the Environment*. Oxford: OUP, 2011.

certain diaries as the diarist moved through geographical space, particularly from town to countryside, with diarists drawing on the language and traditions of the sublime, the classical pastoral, and topographical poetry to convey the landscape unfolding before them.

Many of the diaries were composed within demesne settings, and what is most often communicated in the daily entries from the countryside is the diarists' sensual and intellectual experience of life behind solid demesne walls. Agricultural improvement is championed and interventions into the landscape frequently held up for praise. So that alongside mountainous terrain and sea views, what we encounter is an 'improved' demesne landscape of *cottages ornés* and *fermes ornées*, dairies, orchards, manicured walks, and gardens. The social privilege of many of this study's diarists is apparent throughout this chapter, as is the direct correlation between those men and women belonging to the Established Church and those in possession of the majority of Ireland's land following centuries of confiscation.[2] Toby Barnard has associated the idea of improvement itself with 'schemes to transform Ireland into a prosperous, peaceful and *English* place', and adherence to such perspectives is often discernible in the diaries of the Anglican elite.[3]

There is almost no allusion to poverty, distress, or unhappiness in the local population in most of the diaries by women that survive from this period in Ireland, though the diaries of female international visitors to Ireland are frequently full of such descriptions. Are these women insulated and isolated from such distresses or are they ignoring reality? I propose that a combination of lack of comprehension and misinterpretation frequently coexists with the construction of a paternalistic, self-aggrandising narrative. Andrew Carpenter details how English-language poets in eighteenth-century Ireland often 'closed their eyes to the plight of those forced off the land', maintaining that the countryside was peaceful, for example.[4] One suspects echoes of this in women's diary writing from late eighteenth- and early nineteenth-century Ireland. Indeed, it is generally only in those diaries charting the Rebellion of 1798 and its immediate fallout that we

---

2 See Introduction.

3 Toby Barnard, *Improving Ireland? Projectors, Prophets and Profiteers, 1641–1786*. Dublin: Four Courts Press, 2008. For a detailed study of landscapes in the earlier period in Ireland and attempts by landlords to emulate and reproduce the garden designs of England, see Vandra Costello, *Irish Demesne Landscapes, 1660–1740*. Dublin: Four Courts Press, 2015.

4 Andrew Carpenter, 'Land and Landscape in Irish Poetry in English, 1700–1780'. *Irish Literature in Transition, 1700–1780*. Ed. Moyra Haslett. Cambridge: CUP, 2020, 151.

get a *sustained* engagement with political issues, agitation, and a sense of those people living their lives beyond the demesnes.[5] Finola O'Kane has documented how the perception of Ireland as a picturesque location was created, painted, and manipulated during the mid-eighteenth century.[6] Similarly, by selecting and rejecting aspects of the surrounding landscape to depict within their diaries, the diarists manipulate their environment, privileging certain elements in order to produce a curated vision of the world around them, often obscuring the social deprivation that formed part of the landscape.

Equally, one must acknowledge the silences within the diaries regarding enslavement. Many commodities generated by the labour of enslaved people are brought into the intimate and sociable environments described in the diaries. Research has shown how enslavement became mobilised, embedded, and normalised in eighteenth-century Britain through the consumption of sugar, tea, tobacco, and the wearing of cottons.[7] Ireland's own connections to the broader slave economy have been made more explicit by the recent efforts of historians.[8] We must be alert to all types of invisible presences within life writings, being conscious of diarists' silences regarding marginalised communities, domestic servants, impoverished people, and enslaved labour connections.

Demesne landscapes play a role in the majority of the extant Anglican diaries, with intermittent mentions throughout the diaries of Elinor Goddard and Mary Anne Fortescue, for example.[9] The 1809–1810 and 1810–1812 diaries of Letitia Galloway and Frances Jocelyn are particularly

5 See John D. Beatty, ed., *Protestant Women's Narratives of the Irish Rebellion of 1798*. Dublin: Four Courts Press, 2001.

6 Finola O'Kane, *Ireland and the Picturesque: Design, Landscape Painting and Tourism in Ireland, 1700–1840*. New Haven: Yale, 2013. O'Kane's extensive body of research, including *Landscape Design in Eighteenth-Century Ireland*. Cork: Cork UP, 2004, represents the key work on landscapes in Ireland during the period under question.

7 Joanna de Groot, 'Metropolitan Desires and Colonial Connections: Reflections on Consumption and Empire'. *At Home with the Empire*. Eds. Catherine Hall and Sonya O. Rose. Cambridge: CUP, 2006, 166–90. I am also grateful to have taken part in discussions on the topics of silence, power, and agency, led by de Groot and Karen Lipsedge, at the Jane Ewbank conference, 'Science, Gender, and Sociability in a Northern City, c. 1775–1820', CECS, University of York, June 2023.

8 Ciaran O'Neill and Finola O'Kane, *Ireland, Slavery and the Caribbean; Interdisciplinary Perspectives*. Manchester: MUP, 2022; Nini Rodgers, *Ireland, Slavery, and Anti-Slavery 1612–1865*. Basingstoke: Palgrave, 2007. See also Mobeen Hussain, Ciaran O'Neill, and Patrick Walsh, 'Working Paper on George Berkeley's Legacies at Trinity,' TARA, 2023. http://hdl.handle.net/2262/104216.

9 Elinor Goddard, An anonymous lady's journal (possibly that of Mrs Lucy Goddard). Wicklow Papers, NLI MS 3573; and Mary Anne Fortescue, 'The Diary of Marianne

useful documents from which to pursue an examination of landscape that explores identity, with both young women travelling with members of their immediate families to the Co. Wicklow countryside from Dublin city within one year of each other.[10] Writing almost a decade after the Act of Union, which saw many members of the elite relocate to Britain, both Jocelyn and Galloway sought to chart their own experiences and impressions of the Irish environment within their diaries, evoking a bucolic setting for their daily narratives, one that was not simply a backdrop but a presence that informed the structure of their day, their emotions, and their sense of self and of community.

The vast majority of diarists in the corpus explored throughout this book do not explicitly reference either Ireland or Irishness. Those diarists who do invoke the national do so once they leave the country, where their sense of national identity then becomes something to be negotiated and considered. The 1796–1797 diary of Charity Lecky is exceptional in providing sustained exploration of national identity during Lecky's winter spent in Bath with her mother, seeking out examples of Irishness and perennially reinforcing that aspect of her identity.[11] The manuscript diaries of Melesina Chenevix St. George Trench, beginning in the 1790s and continuing for several decades, detail a multi-layered sense of identity, common within the Huguenot tradition, whereby Trench navigates a broader European sense of self, informed by an identification with England. Engagement with Ireland and her Irish background do feature more than the published *Remains of the Late Mrs. Richard Trench* (1862) suggests, and the MS diary written in Ireland brings into greater relief issues of land and its possession and dispossession, so central to life in early nineteenth-century Ireland.[12]

The space the diarists carved out for themselves within Ireland during this period was in fact frequently informed by the local more than the national. We see the diarists creating their own environment on the written page, echoing that built by their peers as they strengthened their concept of community through writing. The significance and impact of an overriding

Fortescue, 1797–1800'. Ed. Noel Ross. *Journal of the County Louth Archaeological Society* 24.2–3 (1998): 222–48; (1999): 357–79.

10 Letitia Galloway, Diary of Letitia Galloway, NLI MS 32,517; and Frances Theodosia Jocelyn, Diary of Frances Theodosia Jocelyn, 1810–1812. NLI MS 18,430.

11 Anon. [Charity Lecky], Diary of a Winter in Bath, 1796–97. James Marshall and Marie-Louise Osborn Collection, Beinecke Rare Book and Manuscript Library, Yale University, Osborn c446. See also Chapter 2.

12 Melesina Chenevix St. George Trench, *The Remains of the Late Mrs. Richard Trench. Being Selections from her Journals, Letters, & Other Papers.* Ed. Dean of Westminster. London, 1862, and Diary kept by Melesina St. George, later Trench, 1801–1802. HRO, 23M93/1/5.

sense of communal, collective identity is considered here alongside the more traditional sense of individual identity within diary writing. A defined community was further strengthened through the rituals of visiting and the women's embeddedness in the various Protestant communities they formed part of, which is to the fore throughout these diaries. A large network of people was also incorporated through intermarriage, with the same men and women appearing as major or minor characters in multiple diaries. This is apparent across the elite diaries of the Church of Ireland women, but also conspicuous in the diaries of those from the Society of Friends. The Irish Quaker diaries are centred around several hubs, including Clonmel in Co. Tipperary, but none more obvious than that of Ballitore, Co. Kildare, immortalised by Mary Shackleton Leadbeater in her posthumously published *The Leadbeater Papers. The Annals of Ballitore* (1862) and threaded throughout her many diary volumes, which portray the bonds of religious community established and maintained in that Quaker settlement, reinforced by those men and women's commitment to life writing.[13]

Benedict Anderson famously wrote about nations in terms of communities drawn together through communication, especially newspapers.[14] Here, we also find communities reinforced through the exchange of life writing. Place and community are in dialogue throughout the diaries as the diarists reflect on their evolving sense of belonging to different communities or local areas, as well as countries, pausing on how best to signal this belonging in writing and in life. The diaries document visual markers of Irishness, through the donning of shamrock, for instance, as well as recording clothing being used to indicate membership of a religious group, with the clear example of the Quaker community's adherence to plain dress. Charity Lecky's diary presents an awareness of the correlation between identity and language on her journey across England and Wales, while the choice of language embraced by the diarists themselves offers a clear signal of belonging, whether to a broader Huguenot diaspora or a European elite, or by displaying an antiquarian awareness of Irish traditions. Signifiers of belonging are threaded throughout these diaries, as the women both respond to the environment in which they find themselves and create new spaces within the pages of their diaries, combining evocations of place with a sense of community and communal identity.

13 See Michael Ahern, 'The Quakers of County Tipperary 1655–1924'. PhD Thesis, NUI Maynooth, 2003; Mary Leadbeater, *The Leadbeater Papers. The Annals of Ballitore...* [Ed. Elizabeth Shackleton.] 2 vols. London, 1862; Mary Leadbeater, Diaries covering the years 1769–1789 in 22 volumes. NLI MSS 9292–9314. NLI MS 9297.

14 Benedict Anderson, *Imagined Communities: Reflections on the Origin and Spread of Nationalism*. 1983. Revised edition, New York: Verso, 2006.

The Ideological Import of Landscape Description

Within one year of each other, during the summers of 1809 and 1810, two young diarists set out from Dublin to the Wicklow countryside. The diary of Letitia Galloway opens on Midsummer's Day 1809 as she leaves North Cumberland Street, in the centre of Dublin, for Crone, Co. Wicklow, where the diarist resided with the Evans family for exactly three months, until 24 September, afterwards remaining in Dublin for almost the entirety of the diary, apart from the final three days; she returned to Wicklow on 2 June 1810, before concluding her diary with 'to be continued' on 4 June 1810. Galloway is described as an actress in the National Library of Ireland catalogue overview, which seems unlikely, but there are no further details extant for the young woman, who appears to have died unmarried. Much more information survives for Lady Frances Theodosia Jocelyn, 16 years old at the time of her diary's commencement, and at the apex of elite Irish society, substantially higher in status than Galloway. The granddaughter of the devout Church of Ireland diarist Anne Jocelyn, and Robert, 1st Earl of Roden, she was the daughter of his successor, also Robert, who inherited the Roden estate in Dundalk, Co. Louth, and Frances Theodosia Bligh of Elphin, Co. Roscommon, who died young, before the composition of her daughter's diary. The Dundalk demesne was laid out in 1746, and by 1752 had an artificial serpentine river and a Chinese Bridge, as well as 'some fine plantations and walks with elm hedges on each side'.[15] The geographical range of Jocelyn's diary encompasses various estates, notably her own family's Tollymore demesne in Co. Down, as well as that of family friends, the Shaws' Bushy Park House in Terenure; the Parnells' Avondale House; and the Powerscourt estate of her future husband Richard Wingfield (whom she married in 1813) in Co. Wicklow. For the duration of the diary's three years, Jocelyn is more frequently in Co. Wicklow than counties Louth or Down, interspersed with her time spent in Dublin.

Co. Wicklow had become well established as a 'thrilling' tourist destination by 1809, alongside settings such as the Giant's Causeway, Killarney, and Connemara, all of which provided 'wild and uncultivated landscapes with romantic scenery, picturesque peasants and exotic Gaelic customs'.[16] By the late 1820s, a distinctive subculture of Evangelical Protestants that included Richard Wingfield would use the landscape of the county to impose order,

15 Harold O'Sullivan, 'Introduction'. *Dundalk*, Irish Historic Towns Atlas, No. 16. Dublin: Royal Irish Academy, 2006, 5; 22.

16 O'Kane, *Landscape Design*, 172. See eighteenth-century Irish landscape paintings of Wicklow scenery, including George Barret, 'A View of Powerscourt Waterfall' (*c.* 1760). National Gallery of Ireland, Dublin.

so that Co. Wicklow became further connected to both the sublime and cultures of improvement.[17] The impact of the Wicklow environment upon the composition of the diaries of Galloway and Jocelyn is immediately apparent. Galloway's first full day in Wicklow shows evidence of agency and several expressions of ownership, with an active voice very much to the fore:

> – in the Eveng took a walk up the mountain and were delighted with the extended prospect, every place I bring Mary to see she is more & more Charmed with it, – Several laughable adventures on the mountain such as Mary sitting down on a heap of furz imagining it to be a nice seat. An invitation from Miss Arthur to tea, which however we declined having already walked so much. Went to my favourite cascade with our books where we sat on a nook reading till the sun sett behind the neighbouring hills – I read one book of Orlando Furioso, Mary has Rural Tales (25/6/1809)[18]

The diarist is careful to highlight her prior relationship with the landscape. Galloway establishes herself as the knowledgeable party, setting the itinerary, and taking her sister to locations she herself was familiar with, in order for her to share in the appreciation of the sites. It is Letitia's favourite cascade that the sisters visit and where they read their books together. She wholeheartedly embraced her role as both tour guide and recorder of events, shaping the days and the manner in which the activities are then framed. As so often occurs across the diaries, the full entry opens and closes with weather details, with the day's activities then centre stage.[19] There is a narrative quality to the entry, and interjections and anecdotes are intermingled rather than the reader being presented with a rote listing of activities.

Frances Jocelyn also connects her reading to waterfall locations, in her case finishing Walter Scott's recently published *The Lady of the Lake* (1810) and praising the last canto in particular, reflecting that 'What I like so much in poetry is it refines one's ideas & gives one a power of seeing the beauties

17 With thanks to Seán Connolly and Crawford Gribben for their comments on the Plymouth Brethren at Powerscourt. See Andrew Holmes and Crawford Gribben, eds., *Protestant Millennialism, Evangelicalism and Irish Society, 1790–2005*. Basingstoke: Palgrave, 2006.

18 *Orlando Furioso*, the sixteenth-century Italian epic poem by Ludovico Ariosto. Possibly Robert Bloomfield, *Rural Tales, Ballads, and Songs*. London, 1802.

19 Weather had a tremendous impact on the daily lives of men and women in the long eighteenth century, facilitating or prohibiting a whole range of leisure activities and transport options, in addition to its role in agriculture. See Alan J. Smyth, 'Studying the Seasons: Weather Recording in Ireland in the Mid-Eighteenth Century'. MPhil Thesis, TCD, 2008. See also Alexandra Harris, *Weatherland, Writers and Artists under English Skies*. London: Thames and Hudson, 2015.

& faults of prose & teaches one a fluency & softness of arranging one's sentences in speaking' (20/9/1810). Her descriptions of the waterfall itself borrow from such poetry and adhere perfectly to the tenets of the sublime, praising it 'as grand & majestic' and noting how the waterfall 'naturally raises one's mind to nature's God – what bounties he has bestowed on his miserable creatures'.[20] A month later, in Co. Wicklow, she describes the waterfall viewed there as 'the most beautiful thing I ever saw'. The sublime theme continues in the surrounding landscape, with Jocelyn's commentary that 'the woods are so very luxuriant, & in such a mass. There are rocks & everything that could add to the magnificence of the scene' (24/10/1810). Throughout this entry and others Jocelyn tries to capture her sense of awe in her prose writing and to transmit her appreciation of the divine sublime, infusing her writing with references to the tremendous and to grandeur, and demonstrating how diarists could also participate in the Romantic tradition.[21] Galloway too continues this emphasis on the Burkean sublime, seeing it within other aspects of nature, such as the contrasting extremes of light and dark: 'It was dark except what light we had from a wonder of fine stars' (10/9/1809).[22] In her work on Irish Gothic literature, Christina Morin has argued that the Gothic's 'representation of the country [Ireland] as part of the sublime geographical fringes of the British nation' rejects, interrogates and deconstructs 'prevailing English understandings of Ireland as a marginal zone of incomprehensible strangeness'.[23] Ireland's uncivilised, barbarous wildness is repurposed as one element of the sublime, forming part of a wider post-Union landscape that was still in the process of being transformed by the 'improving' methods of those at the apex of Irish society and within the country estates.[24] The diaries of both Jocelyn and Galloway

20 Edmund Burke, *An Enquiry into the Origins of our Ideas of the Sublime and Beautiful*. London, 1757.

21 For a useful discussion of Ireland and Romanticism see Jim Kelly, ed., *Ireland and Romanticism: Publics, Nations and Scenes of Cultural Production*. Basingstoke: Palgrave, 2011.

22 Carole Fabricant, 'Colonial Sublimities and Sublimations: Swift, Burke, and Ireland'. *ELH* 72.2 (2005): 309–37; Luke Gibbons, *Edmund Burke and Ireland: Aesthetics, Politics and the Colonial Sublime*. Cambridge: CUP, 2003.

23 Christina Morin, *The Gothic Novel in Ireland c.1760–1829*. Manchester: MUP, 2018, 118; 120. See also Eoin Magennis, '"A land of milk and honey": The Physico-Historical Society, Improvement and the Surveys of Mid-Eighteenth Century Ireland'. *Proceedings of the Royal Irish Academy* 102C.6 (2002): 199–217, which examines the attitudes of the Society's almost exclusively Church of Ireland members, who sought to 'rebut the continuing association of Irishness with barbarism … and to show the potential for further improvement', 200.

24 Helen O'Connell, 'The Nature of Improvement in Ireland'. *Nature and the*

echo such assertions, making it clear to anyone who might read their diaries that the sublime was readily accessible in a safe, improved, and welcoming Ireland, and that they had the skills necessary to discern it.[25]

In Galloway's diary there is a sense that walks in the countryside are taken, not just for exercise, as in earlier diaries, but to appreciate nature – 'after dinner took a delightful walk up the mountain from whence we had a most delightful view' (4/7/1809) or, 'I read one book of Orlando Furioso – set out then on a long & beautiful Walk to the Military Road' (7/7/1809).[26] Alongside the many entries on waterfalls, there are also references to bathing in a nearby 'chrystal stream' (22/7/1809) or visiting the meetings of the Rivers Avon and Owen (8/10/1810) between Avondale and Castle Howard, which Jocelyn had described as 'the most lovely spot I can imagine' (1/7/1811). Animals play a role in her diary, with Galloway concerned at the poor health of cows, as well as being careful to remark upon the shearing of sheep and the swarming of bees. Elinor Goddard was fond of birds and gardening, and her diaries combine the planting of flowers and sowing of seeds with the raising of birds: 'bought a canary bird, set ranunculas anemones and sowed mignonette' (8/2/1778). Goddard's diaries include multiple records of her attempts to raise birds, from their emergence out of 'their shells' (19/4/1779), to their accompanying her to Co. Kilkenny (26/7/1779) and their laying eggs (4/9/1799), to her lament the following year that 'my bird Pinky flew away and I spent the whole morning in looking for it to no purpose' (4/9/1800). Galloway's encounter with bees is noted as 'a hive of bees swarmed to day, quite a new sight to me' (8/7/1809). This recording is typical of the nature journals of the period, which were dedicated exclusively to charting the environment. Mary Ellen Bellanca describes 'the declaration of encounter with the "never seen" or

Environment in Nineteenth-Century Ireland. Ed. Matthew Kelly. Liverpool: LUP, 2019, 16–34.

25 Kathryn Carter's work on women diarists in Canada demonstrates multiple parallels regarding the use of the sublime. See, for example, the diary of Elizabeth Simcoe, who arrived in Quebec in 1791 and described the country in terms of the sublime, producing illustrations to visually show the grandeur of the country. Other Canadian diarists who overtly used the sublime to explain their entrance into Canadian life include Frances Stewart and Susanna Moodie. See Kathryn Carter, *The Small Details of Life: 20 Diaries by Women in Canada, 1830–1996*. Toronto: University of Toronto Press, 2002, and *Diaries in English by Women in Canada, 1755–1795: An Annotated Bibliography*. Ottawa: CRIAW/ICREF, 1997. I am grateful to Kathryn Carter for drawing my attention to all these examples.

26 See the diary of Mary Anne Dawson as an example of an earlier diary. Galloway makes an obvious distinction between the activity as it occurs in the town and countryside: 'After my visit I walked for exercise in Mt. Joy Square' (1/2/1810).

"never heard" thing' as a widespread pattern in such works, commenting that 'Exclaiming over the first-time exposure is an expression of wonder, a basic response to discovery that serves the diarists in exploring new territories of knowledge.'[27] This directly correlates with Galloway's quest for better understanding of her environment and her attempts to obtain information about particular aspects of her surroundings, which gain her a certain degree of power over what it is she observes.

Letitia Galloway returned to Dublin on 24 September 1809. From that point on we witness a stylistic departure, with entries of an entirely different texture from those composed in the countryside. The pace shifts, and the lengthy reflections and commentary cease. The diary written in town allows no space for poetic expressions or description and becomes simply a record of which people visit the family and which people were visited. Galloway also takes meticulous notes regarding whoever they missed while they themselves were out visiting. Her whole life now revolves around this circuit of visits, whether missed, early, planned, or promised. The Romantic inflections are gone, as is the omnipresent sublime. Despite their decidedly clichéd view of rural life, the countryside entries evoke and convey a sense of freedom, of autonomy, joy, youth, adventure, and of shared experiences. Interestingly, Galloway notes that visits to and from others while she was in the countryside were actively declined rather than sought out. Upon her return to an urban setting, we no longer encounter either enthusiasm or verve in the diary, just iterative, rote evenings passed pleasantly, but without hyperbole or excitement.

Thursday 21 December 1809 sees a typical urban entry where Galloway's whole day is divided into periods of visiting. The diarist's life was structured around the pattern of these visits, including those not directly involving the diarist herself. The diary entries build upon one another to create a sense of days filled with limitations, on both personal movement and creative freedoms, as entire entries, such as the following, contain no reflection nor any attempts at creative expression:

> Fanny came down soon after breakfast this Morng & early in the day Captain Cartere who is in town called here to see Fanny and sat about 2 hours – Godfrey Fetherstone dined here again this day he leaves town in the Morng. Miss Hill dines at Mrs Lawrences and after tea My Father & Mother went to see Mrs. Mansell and left Godfrey John & I at home, after they came home we had supper.

---

27 Mary Ellen Bellanca, *Daybooks of Discovery: Nature Diaries in Britain, 1770–1870*. Charlottesville: University of Virginia Press, 2007, 32–33.

There are no ruminations on adventurous interludes or personal activities, no playful comments or sense of agency, instead the power to shape her days is rendered unto others. In similar fashion, Jocelyn's time in Dublin was made up of a great many visits and some shopping. She herself remarks upon the juxtaposition between town and country, between the urban and rural environments at her disposal: 'I have never spent a stupider evening in my life. What the reason is I do not know. How different to the evenings in dear Bushy' (22/11/1810), and 'The country is charming after the odious town' (9/9/1811).[28] Such privileging of the countryside is reflective of the gendered discourse that began to emerge in the latter eighteenth century whereby the educational and fertility needs of women were declared as being better met in the countryside, which became characterised as containing points of refuge and retirement, described as 'green retreats'.[29] These retreats centred around the demesne, which is the core landscape illustrated across the surviving diaries.

The 1797–1800 diary of Mary Anne Fortescue describes multiple visits from her husband's estate at Stephenstown, Co. Louth, to nearby Clermont Park, as well as to the house of her father, John McClintock, at Drumcar, northeast of Dunleer, also in Co. Louth. Her excursions frequently took her beyond Co. Louth to Co. Dublin. During the Rebellion of 1798, and amidst her comments that there is 'Still sad work going on with the United' (25/5/1798) and her mentions of young men hung or lying dead, the family visited Rathfarnham in South County Dublin. At Rathfarnham, Fortescue praises the building and its contents, the latter of which incorporated a collection of birds including a golden pheasant: 'We went yesterday to Rathfarnham & saw a number of beautiful birds […] the place is beautifull, the house has some fine rooms & fine paintings' (24/5/1798). Mary Anne and her fellow diarists present themselves as passing effortlessly from one demesne landscape to another, commending the beauties to be observed, appreciated, and imbibed.

---

28 Trench is particularly vociferous in her dislike of London: 'London, as usual, agitates and disquiets me. It appears to me a gulf of splendid misery and attractive wickedness.' *Remains*, 27.

29 Finola O'Kane, 'Design and Rule: Women in the Irish Countryside, 1715–1831'. *Eighteenth-Century Ireland* (2004): 67–69; Stephen Bending, *Green Retreats: Women, Gardens and Eighteenth-Century Culture*. Cambridge: CUP, 2013. The opposition between the town and country is remarked upon by various members of the Bluestockings. A clear preference for the countryside is declared by most, particularly by Elizabeth Vesey while in Lucan, Co. Dublin, and Elizabeth Montagu, during her time in Sandleford. It should be acknowledged that Jocelyn's diary also includes references to enjoyable periods spent shopping in town and visiting others.

There is particular emphasis in both Jocelyn's and Galloway's diaries on the consumption of food as part of their appreciation of their environment:

Newtown Barry, and dined there upon cold meat, and in the evening we all set out to Col. Barry's place which is a most beautiful thing indeed, the garden and shrubbery are charming we went to a waterfall there is there, a sweet thing. (Jocelyn, 13/7/1810)

Walk'd to Powerscourt Cherry Orchard, had our Book passd a delightful ^Mary^ reading under the Shade of a beautiful tree beside a murmuring river eating cherrys and reading Grandison (Galloway, 14/7/1809)

These encounters with the rural demesne provoke a multi-sensory experience whereby the aural qualities of the waters complement the local fruits and meats being tasted, and the visual gardenscapes being enjoyed. The pleasure of immersing oneself into the waters and the enjoyment of river bathing is commented upon by Galloway: 'I went & bathed, the walk to the river and back again is one of the most beautiful about here and as it is all Mr Evans' ground we may go in any dress we never meet a Creature. In the evening we took a walk a beautiful Moon light Night' (24/7/1809). Galloway here celebrates her freedoms and rejoices in being able to partake of such liberating rituals, attired informally beneath the moonlight, safe in the knowledge that no undesirable strangers will be encountered.

However, this freedom for Galloway and other diarists meant exclusion for others. Beyond the high walls of the demesne, the majority of the population found themselves entirely cut off from partaking in such landscape appreciation. The erasure of the presence of any Irish-speaking Catholic 'neighbours' and the espousal of an exclusively colonial perspective seems to have been fully internalised by many diarists. These diary entries echo poetry from earlier in the century, such as William Balfour Madden's *Bellisle: a poem, Inscribed to Sir Ralph Gore, Bart* (1761), which explicitly compares the Co. Fermanagh estate, Bellisle, to Arcadia's plains, and celebrates 'the Joys the sportive Country yields'.[30] It has been argued that a degree of detachment, such as we find in the diaries, means that those living within such settings 'are able to sanction a worldview devoid of wilderness, work and hardship so that colonial order (in miniature, the demesne) might serve as iconic representation; among other things, might minimize indigenous presence along with any native categories pertaining to Ireland's ecological/ natural space'.[31] The 'improving' traditions in place since the seventeenth

30 Andrew Carpenter and Lucy Collins, *The Irish Poet and the Natural World*. Cork: Cork UP, 2014, 258. See also Carpenter and Collins, 'Introduction', 1–48.
31 James McElroy, 'Ecocriticism & Irish Poetry A Preliminary Outline'. *Estudios*

century continued apace in this post-Union landscape, wherein the Protestant descendants of earlier generations of English and Scottish men and women still sought to neutralise the Irish countryside, maximising the resources that could be exploited, while ostensibly civilising the population and enforcing change. The targeting of the enclosure of the Munster countryside by gangs of Whiteboys in the 1760s, for instance, demonstrates the existence of many smallholders who were 'actively hostile to improvement because it collided with traditional ways'.[32] Andrew Carpenter and Lucy Collins also recognise the complex cultural and political dynamics at play, and their anthology of English-language poetry from Ireland communicates the multiplicity of attitudes towards the natural world in Ireland, not only during the early nineteenth century, but for centuries previous, owing to the 'differing intellectual, religious or ethical traditions and lived experience'.[33]

When natural, untamed, or unconquerable Irish landscapes are described by those subscribing to the discourses of improvement in the long eighteenth century, it is primarily in order to regret their presence.[34] For all their enjoyment in the thrill of the natural sublime, this is equally true for the diaries from this period. Finding herself almost at the top of a mountain with her mother, Letitia Galloway laments that 'our progress was stopped by an immense turf bog' (31/8/1809). Here, it is unequivocally the natural, untamed bog that is identified as obstructing their passage. The multiple connotations of that word 'progress' chosen by Galloway to describe their climb, connected as it is with ideas of improvement, suggests a historical current of amelioration – one in which the Galloways participated.[35] The bogs of the Irish midlands were frequently bemoaned as impassable, unmanageable, and unsightly, and evoked as evidence of Ireland's backwardness, from the seventeenth century onwards.[36] In Maria Edgeworth's novel *Castle Rackrent: An Hibernian Tale* (1800), one of the Rackrent wives famously

Irlandeses 6 (2011): 56, McElroy here engages with ideas proposed by Eamon Slater in *Irish Journal of Sociology* 3 (1993): 23–55.

32 James Kelly, 'Introduction'. *The Cambridge History of Ireland, Volume 3*. Cambridge: CUP, 2018, 4.

33 Carpenter and Collins 2.

34 See Chapter 4 on diaries and individual improvement.

35 Sarah Tarlow, *The Archaeology of Improvement in Britain, 1750–1850*. Cambridge: CUP, 2007, 18–20.

36 See for example, Arthur Young, *A Tour in Ireland: with General Observations on the Present State of that Kingdom*. Dublin, 1780 and Thomas Blenerhasset, *A Direction for the Plantation in Ulster*. London, 1610. Discussed in Ian Campbell Ross, 'Maria Edgeworth and the Culture of Improvement'. *Still Blundering into Sense: Maria Edgeworth, Her Context, Her Legacy*. Eds. Fiorenzo Fantaccini and Rafaella Leproni. Florence: Firenze UP, 2019, 29–48.

describes the bog before her as 'a very ugly prospect', while an epistolary account following the Battle of Ballinamuck describes Edgeworth and her family as having 'turned away from the bog' strewn with bodies, with critical speculation suggesting Maria Edgeworth 'cannot allow herself to see those aspects of reality that invalidate her progressive vision'.[37] Progress and progressive visions can supposedly be impeded by many of Ireland's ecological spaces and the people who inhabit them (we need only think of the insulting phrase 'bog-trotter', applied to rural Irish people during the seventeenth and eighteenth centuries).[38] Conversely, ostensible interventions and improvements to the surrounding terrain are celebrated throughout many of the diaries, with landscapes, both built and natural, functioning to provide protection for the country's landowning elite.[39]

The demesne walls provided security for those women bathing in the property's rivers, while shelter from inclement weather could also be sought from the structures and trees within those walls, as Galloway comments:

> Proceeded toward the Dargle carrying a basket of provisions [...] we were obliged to shelter from very heavy rain in ^the^ Cottage in Powerscourt [...] We then all returned home did not get much rain the fine old trees of Powerscourt afforded us shelter (31/7/1809)

The word 'shelter' is twice invoked here, as both noun and verb, and it is clear that the members of the party were protected from either becoming wet or being accosted by others by the demesne's boundaries. The cottage mentioned here is one of many *cottages ornés* that appear across the diaries and indeed that were constructed across the Irish landscape in the latter half of the eighteenth century.[40] O'Kane has shown how these *cottages ornés*, which were associated with France's Queen Marie Antoinette, demonstrated human interference with the landscape, taming it, while simultaneously celebrating the surrounding wildness then in vogue – 'the cottage was the archetypal rural dwelling, and no other building proclaimed so effectively its disengagement from the urban environment'; 'the ultimate picturesque

---

37 Anthony Mortimer, 'Castle Rackrent and Its Historical Context'. *Études Irlandaises* (1984): 110.

38 The *OED* gives the first instance as 1682, with 'an idle flam of shabby Irish Bogtrotters' from 'Philanax Misopappas', *A Tory Plot*.

39 Within the diary of English woman, Jane Ewbank (1778–1824), interventions are portrayed in a very different manner, with landscapes described as having 'suffer'd a little from the improvements of Mr Curwin', for example. Jane Ewbank, Journal of Miss Ewbank of York, 1803–5. NLS MS 9481 (9/9/1803).

40 Elinor Goddard's diary frequently references cottages too.

constructions, cottages were carefully designed to appear artless and naïve'.[41] The location of the proposed cottage was of seminal importance, intended to be integrated into the landscape as though belonging to it, appearing entirely natural, though an elite, manmade intervention, as Galloway's diary entries make clear:

> We joined our party at the cottage, where we all breakfasted. It was delightful. The cottage is the most charming spot I ever was in, situated by the river with an immense thick wood on the other side, & every here & there a fine bold rock is seen among the trees. It is the most romantic place I ever was in. (8/10/1810)

Employing the markers of youth with her repeated use of superlatives, Galloway is at pains to convey both the beauty and the appropriateness of the cottage and its location. The wild landscape is celebrated, but now feels tamed and controlled by this human intervention into it, whereby the bold rocks and thick woods are made to support the cottage.

This sense of altering, idealising, and indeed fetishising aspects of the Irish countryside and its vernacular for the delight and amusement of the elite was not confined to the construction of cottages and follies. The diaries note multiple socially unrealistic simulacra of country pursuits, buildings, and customs, and echo the earlier eighteenth-century English tradition of relocating the Arcadian pastoral from the classical period to the present time, wherein the English country estates came to represent a contemporary idyll, with 'representations of nature that strategically omit any sense of elements that might be counter to this positive image'.[42] Frances Jocelyn's diary entries document her involvement in such activities as churning butter before reading (1/7/1811); strawberry picking before playing the lute (3/7/1811); and studying animals on various farms, such as Dr McMurray's farm at Avondale (9/10/1810), and that at Trimsillin, where they observed pigs, horses, and poultry (12/6/1811). As ever, the diarists' diet was in keeping with the environs in which they found themselves, and there are frequent references to potatoes, butter, and milk. This suggests perhaps a fleeting engagement with what we now consider as ideas of bioregionalism and being a 'locavore', through the consumption of foods grown or produced locally as alternatives to exotic luxuries, though

---

41 Finola O'Kane, 'Design and Rule', 64, 65; See also O'Kane, *Landscape Design*, 72–79.

42 Terry Gifford, 'Pastoral, Anti-Pastoral and Post-Pastoral as Reading Strategies'. *Critical Insights Series: Nature and the Environment*. Ed. Scott Slovic. Ipswich: Salam Press, 2012, 42–61; 8.

here this substitutionalism seems to be limited to the time spent in the countryside.[43]

The diarists' lives of escapist, pastoral leisure are encapsulated in the following entry by Frances Jocelyn, written from Avondale Garden in October 1810, evoking the apples and pears of Theocritus's *Idylls* as well as the Irish landscape poetry of Co. Cavan-born Wetenhall Wilkes (1705/6–1751):

> After breakfast as usually we went into the garden, as F is making a new one. We stood there sunning ourselves & talking, & sometimes walking about the garden & running after the pheasants. The apples & pears are excellent. F & I took a walk down to the cottage to copy some riddles that are upon a screen there, but we could not get in, & came home to dinner. Spent a very pleasant evening looking over prints of flowers. (10/10/1810)[44]

There is a strong sense of an appreciation of the ecological environs. Again, the fruits are plucked from within arms' reach; different species of flowers are studied; many pleasant walks are taken; and the autumnal sun shines down upon them all. The 'complex social and environmental impact of agricultural improvement', so prevalent in Ulster-Scots poetry from the period, is entirely absent from such considerations, with exclusively complimentary references to the pleasures afforded by the countryside and no hint of the possibility of agrarian unrest.[45] There are a few brief glimpses into genuine agricultural life, as well as to the customs of the Irish peasantry in the wider corpus of diaries. Elinor Goddard's diary mentions both the Catholic observation of the feast day of the patron saint of the parish and the playing of Ireland's indigenous games, for instance, noting patterns and hurling respectively (5/7/1778). There are fleeting references to a pattern (30/7/1809) and a wake (29/6/1809) in Galloway's diary, while she also refers to the beliefs of others, noting that 'this cow doctor is considered by

43 See Mathew Simpson's discussion of Robert Ferguson's bioregionalism in '"Hame Content": Globalization and a Scottish Poet of the Eighteenth Century'. *Eighteenth-Century Life* 27.1 (2003): 107–29.

44 'We lay stretched out in plenty, pears at our feet, / Apples at our sides and plumtrees reaching down.' Theocritus, *The Idylls*. London: Penguin Books, 1989, 86. Cited in Terry Gifford, *Pastoral*. London: Routledge, 1999, 10; 'A Circle where all kinds of Fruit-Tress grow / Fair to the Eye, delicious to the Taste, / With pleasant Walks, and neat Divisions grac'd.' Wetenhall Wilkes, 'Belville, a poem'. *An Essay on the Pleasures ad Advantages of Female Literature … To this are subjoin'd A Prosaic Essay on Poetry, … The Chace, a poem, and three Poetic Landscapes*. London, 1741. Carpenter and Collins 196–97.

45 David Gray, 'An Ecocritical Reading of Ulster-Scots Poetry c. 1790–1850'. PhD Thesis, Ulster University, 2014.

the common people to be a fairy' (12/6/1809). These 'common people' also become part of the studied landscape, as Carpenter has argued: 'This side of country life became a form of tourist spectacle designed to enhance the pleasure experienced by city dwellers who went, in increasing numbers as the century progressed, to the wild places of Ireland to look at the people who lived there as well as to admire the landscape.'[46] There is an anthropological dimension to Galloway's comments on these people, with investigative tools mentioned in her pursuit of knowledge; for example, 'at last a favourable day thank God, all hands busy at the hay, we walked up the mountain with our book & the telescope' (15/8/1809). The main outcome of such empirical research is not simply knowledge acquisition or advancement but the women's own amusement, as Galloway notes, 'A most delightful morng, sheep shearing commenced, with which Mary & I were highly amused' and 'amused ourselves looking at the sheep shearing, branding, cows milking and all such country occupations which are quite new to me' (26/6/1809).

Rural labourers feature in the diary of the wealthy Eleanor Butler (who removed from Co. Kilkenny to Wales with her partner Sarah Ponsonby), as seen in her particularly striking evocation of the Welsh landscape – 'Light airy Clouds, purple mountains, lilac and silver rocks, hum of Bees, rush of Waters, Goat, Sheep. Cattle. Melody of Hay-makers. What weather. What a Country' (7/8/1789).[47] The haymakers' work adds to the cacophony of sounds and images that collide to produce a vibrant, exhilarating landscape. Much of the English labouring-class poetry of the eighteenth century attempted to counter such rich, but idealised visions of agricultural labour. Stephen Duck's 'The Thresher's Labour' (1730) responds to and anticipates sanitised pastoral portraits through the poet's series of negations: 'No Fountains murmur here, no Lambkins play, / No Linnets warble, and no Fields look gay; / 'Tis all a gloomy, melancholy Scene, / Fit only to provoke the Muse's Spleen.'[48] Duck's heroic couplets reference 'The Sweat, the Dust, and suffocating Smoak', and explicitly address those who enjoyed lives of

---

46 Carpenter, 'Land and Landscape' 161; William H. A. Williams, *Creating Irish Tourism: The First Century, 1750–1850*. London: Anthem Press, 2010, Chapters 4 and 5. In an English context, Jane Ewbank of York could participate in excursions to sites such as flint mills and aluminium works as a legitimate form of cultural tourism for women. Ewbank's observations at such industrial sites focus on the scientific processes involved rather than the labour expended, with the reader gaining no sense of the workers' living and working conditions. Papers offered by John Christie and Rachel Feldberg, at the Jane Ewbank conference, CECS, University of York, June 2023.

47 Eleanor Butler, Butler's Journal 1788–91. NLW MS 22971C / NLI POS 9614. Cited in G. H. Bell, *The Hamwood Papers of the Ladies of Llangollen and Caroline Hamilton*. London: Macmillan, 1930, 219.

48 Stephen Duck, *Poems on Several Occasions...* London, 1736.

ease, unaware of, or happy to ignore, the hardship involved in the production of their meals: 'LET those who feast at Ease on dainty Fare, / Pity the Reapers, who their Feasts prepare'. This appeal to wealthier readers brings the various classes together, recognising their co-existence and offering them a reminder of their co-dependency, as Mary Collier also endeavoured to do in her response, 'The Woman's Labour: To Mr Stephen Duck' (1739), wherein she evokes the toil and physical pain involved in the cleaning of the 'cambricks and muslins which our ladies wear'.[49]

There are almost no explicit references to the relationship between the landowning classes and the peasantry in the Irish diaries, with the exception of several comments lamenting the death of Richard Wingfield, 4th Viscount Powerscourt, the father of Frances Jocelyn's future husband, in which connections are drawn between his life and those in the surrounding area. Upon his death Galloway writes, 'Sorry to hear of the death of Ld Powerscourt, he was a charitable good man, & will be an unspeakable loss to the poor of the neighbourhood' (21/7/1809); and 'well may they mourn for he was a kind landlord' (23/7/1809). That Powerscourt was kind could imply an acknowledgement by the diarist that all landlords were not necessarily so. However, there is clearly an ideological import to the manner in which the landscape is described in the diaries under scrutiny, with the power dynamic of the land possessor to the fore. A paternalistic tone is apparent here as the poor are aided from above by the ostensibly 'kind' local landlord who offers them protection. From both an ecocritical and ecofeminist viewpoint – the latter of which 'challenges all relations of domination' – we see how the diarists engaged with nature in order to observe it, to treasure and celebrate it, and to provide them too with a degree of power and agency.[50] Kathryn Carter has suggested parallels with the Canadian context, where it was frequently the colonial enterprise itself that gave many of the women diarists agency and a framework from which to write, while drawing attention to the absences within their diaries and explaining how much was hidden from them, particularly regarding extra-marital interactions between the members of the Hudson Bay Company and local women.[51] In an Irish context, the

---

49 Mary Collier, *Poems on Several Occasions...* Winchester, 1762. See also Dominick Kelly, 'The Battle of the Chaunters' Sequence from *Fugitive Pieces* (1770)'. Eds. Ian Campbell Ross and Anne Markey. *Eighteenth-Century Ireland* 33 (2018): 133–54.

50 Starhawk, 'Power, Authority, and Mystery: Ecofeminism and Earth-Based Spirituality'. *Reweaving the World: The Emergence of Ecofeminism.* Eds. Irene Diamond and Gloria Feman Orenstein. San Francisco: Sierra Club Books, 1990, 76. For work on ecofeminism in an Irish context see, Annalise Torcson, 'Ecocriticism and Ecofeminism in the Works of Contemporary Irish Poets Vona Groarke and Sinéad Morrissey'. MPhil Thesis, TCD, 2018.

51 See, for example, the diary of 18-year-old Frances Simpson, married to the

omission of certain realities cannot be ignored. That the Catholic poor were not visible from the demesne walls is not a feasible excuse, their omission becoming particularly obvious when one examines diaries of those travelling to Ireland from abroad during the same period.

The diaries of Galloway and Jocelyn, and indeed Fortescue and Goddard, can be compared and contrasted with the extant diaries of three visitors to Ireland: Anna Walker (1763–1816), wife of the Colonel commanding the 50th Regiment of Foot, who travelled to Belfast from Portsmouth, via Cork and then Dublin, from April to June 1802; Elizabeth Quincy Guild (1757–1825) of Massachusetts, United States of America, wife of Benjamin Guild, a bookseller in Boston, who also ran a circulating library; and Margaret Boyle Harvey (1786–1832) of Philadelphia, USA, daughter of Martha Williams, 'a heroine of the Revolution', and the Irish-born Captain James Boyle, and married to Irish Quaker Edward Harvey.[52] Walker's diary in particular makes several references to the 'wretched situation of the poor' in her itinerary.[53] Kilworth, Co. Cork, for example, is described thus: 'a Miserable Place, exhibiting only a continuance of Mud Cabins without Window or Chimney – & the Wretched Inhabitants covered with vermin & clothed in Rags' (17/5/1802). What is particularly striking in Walker's entries is that the demesne landscapes of the Irish countryside are placed side by side with this destitution, which is thereby rendered more acute due to this juxtaposition. In Leighton Bridge (Leighlinbridge), Co. Carlow, for instance, Walker notes: 'The Face of the Country certainly improves. Hedges are seen to divide the Lands, & here & there Plantations. The Road very Good & Several Gentlemen's Houses embellished the Scene – but the Cottages of the poor continue equally Miserable' (22/5/1802). Improvement methods are noted and recognised, including the interventions into the physical landscape through hedgerow division and road developments, but the homes of the poor remain just as miserable. The ostensible improving touch does not seem to have encompassed their cottages.

From her position on board the *Perri-Auger* approaching Cork Harbour, Margaret Boyle Harvey observed the abundance of vernacular buildings scattered across the landscape: 'The coast of Ireland is very high and has a very grand and powerful look on approaching it [...] Gardens and potato

Governor of the Hudson's Bay Company. Carter, *Small Details*, 33–39. Again, I am indebted to Kathryn Carter for sharing these thoughts with me.

52 Finding Aid for the Guild Family and Eliot Family Papers, Houghton Library, Harvard University, MS AM 2922.

53 Anna Walker, Typescript edition of the diary kept by Anna Walker, 1802–1807. PRONI T1565/1.

fields interspersed with cabins' (8/6/1809).[54] Her fellow American, Elizabeth Quincy Guild, writing in 1790, remarked upon the juxtaposition of wealth and poverty to be found in the area during her visit to Dublin:

> We from the Shop took an Hack & rode seven miles round the City, thro the Phenix park, over island Bridge & c & round. The prospect in every direction pleasant, except the mud walled Cottages which forcibly exhibit the extream of poverty. (11/8/1790)[55]

These cabins and the 'extremes of poverty' are absent from the demesne landscapes of crystal streams, thick woods, beautiful birds, and murmuring rivers, depicted by Galloway and Jocelyn, Goddard and Fortescue. These women's diaries evince patterns of similarities in their engagement with their environments and suggest shared perspectives, ideals, and values. As ever, diary audience and motivation must be considered when engaging with the travel journals. Boyle Harvey acknowledges her own prejudices and her expectation that she will be met with 'the brogue, and the wild appearance of the Irish', reflecting that 'Americans in general despise Ireland and its inhabitants – and I did myself once' (8/6/1809).[56] Walker in particular does not seem favourably inclined towards Ireland, and it is likely she was content, or in fact predisposed, to continue the then prevalent English tradition of criticising the country, its people, and its lands.[57]

While one would not expect to find our diarists detailing examples of human exploitation, or writing forms of anti-pastoral such as is evident in, for example, James Porter's *Billy Bluff and Squire Firebrand* (1796), 'a thinly disguised political allegory on landlordism in County Down', it remains striking that Galloway and Jocelyn give no glimpse at all of the endemic

---

54 Margaret Boyle Harvey, *A Journal of a Voyage from Philadelphia to Cork in the Year of our Lord, 1809; Together With a Description of a Sojourn in Ireland*. Philadelphia, 1915, 23. Boyle Harvey, Margaret. Journal 1809–1812. RSFIHL P10.

55 Elizabeth Quincy Guild, Journal in Ireland and England. Guild Family and Eliot Family Papers, Houghton Library, Harvard University, MS AM 2922/38.

56 Boyle Harvey 24.

57 Walker does praise Dublin, however: 'Dublin Seems very pleasant & the Town a good One; the beauty & even Cleanliness, wonderfully Surpassed my Expectations [...] Many of the Streets & Squares are excellent' (27/5/1802). The tradition of hostile accounts of the country includes Edmund Spenser's infamous account *A View of the State of Ireland* (1599; pub. 1633) where he imagines the natives being exterminated. James Kelly has explored commentary by male visitors to Ireland, including the travel accounts of James Hall and John Trotter, which praise the contentment of the peasantry, offering a 'counter-perspective to the normative focus on poverty and the potato'. Kelly, *The Cambridge History of Ireland*, 5.

poverty of the rural Irish or of the disaffection so obvious in the 1790s.[58] Their diary entries gesture instead to the long tradition of country house poems, which praise patrons and in doing so elide conditions of agricultural labour and servitude. Here, it is a case of the diaries conforming to more conservative literary genres and traditions rather than more subversive voices and views, such as in Porter's allegory; Mary Leapor's 'Crumble Hall' (1751); and Ann Yearsley's prospect poem 'Clifton Hill, Written in January 1785', which serve to challenge those traditions.[59] Ellen Taylor's 'Written by the Barrow side, where she was sent to wash Linen' (c. 1792) draws on the country house poetry and modes of sensibility to lament her 'servitude' in Co. Kilkenny, evoking the banks of the river Barrow – 'the Muses' choicest haunt' – only to be reminded of her 'misery', 'condemned to move beneath the servile weight'.[60] *Poems by Ellen Taylor, the Irish Cottager* (Dublin, 1792) also includes a verse, 'Written to a Fellow Servant, who went to Dublin to get a place, or to visit her Friends', which contrasts 'our grand metropolis' with her employer's 'mansion', which now seems 'lonely quite to me'.[61] Moving unobserved in the same demesne environments as our diarists, servants generally did not have the opportunity to compose such written records, with Taylor one of the few examples of an Irish labouring-class female poet from the time, with no diaries as yet discovered.[62]

Servants themselves make a few fleeting appearances in the diary of the adolescent Marianne ffolliott of Hollybrook House, though they are often introduced only to be dismissed: 'there has been a great fight amongst the servants but one must not mind such things' (23/12/1809) or to have their beliefs ridiculed or their competencies questioned.[63] In contrast, the diary of Quaker woman Elizabeth Clibborn includes extensive thanks to Dinah Close, who took charge of Clibborn's three-month-old baby after the death of Elizabeth's first-born child John, from scarlet fever. In a state of extreme grief and agitation, and herself feverous and vomiting, Elizabeth

---

58 David Gray, '"Stemmed from the Scots"? The Ulster-Scots Literary *Braird* and the Pastoral Tradition'. *Eighteenth-Century Ireland* 32 (2017): 30.

59 Ann Yearsley, *Poems, on several occasions. By Ann Yearsley, a milkwoman of Bristol.* 2nd edition. London, 1785. See also Sharon Young, 'Visiting the Country House: Generic Innovation in Mary Leapor's "Crumble Hall"'. *Tulsa Studies in Women's Literature* 34.1 (Spring 2015): 51–64.

60 Poem included in Andrew Carpenter, *Verse in English from Eighteenth-Century Ireland.* Cork: Cork UP, 1998.

61 Ellen Taylor, *Poems by Ellen Taylor, the Irish Cottager.* Dublin, 1792, 13.

62 Andrew Carpenter, 'Working-Class Writing in Ireland before 1800'. *A History of Irish Working-Class Writing.* Ed. Michael Pierse. Cambridge: CUP, 2017, 72–88.

63 Marianne ffolliott, Diary of Mary Anne Ffolliott, Boyle Co. Roscommon, 1809–1827. PRONI D1995/1.

was advised by her doctor 'not to suckle the child that night but I dreaded a lodgement of milk and my nerves were so agitated that I longed for the baby' (26/5/1808). A later diary entry states, 'I have paid Dinah Close £11:7:6 for ten months nursing, she took excellent care of our child & I shall always think myself indebted for her good nature & nobility which money cannot purchase' (23/3/1809).[64] There are a few glimpses into the lives of others in the diary of Elizabeth Stirum, née Richards, more commonly known for its substantial entries devoted to the unfolding of the 1798 Rebellion and the Richards family's role in this.[65] There is very little sustained engagement on issues of unrest, poverty, or the lives of the surrounding populace from the period post 1798 in the published diary, but an entry on the celebration of St. Peter's Eve in 1811 offers a glimpse into the composition of the neighbourhood surrounding Rathaspeck, the Richards' family home in Co. Wexford:

> Summer has begun, this day we have left off fires. It is St. Peters eve, which according to an old Irish custom is celebrated throughout the country by bonfires... We went with the children to see one that had been lighted at our avenue-gate [...] The moon arose in a clear sky, and shining through the old ash at the avenue-gate, encreased the beauty of the scene. The breadth of the road was filled up with decent dressed farmers and their wives, sellers of ballads, of gingerbread, beggars and their barefooted children. The fiddler was seated on a chair, overcanopied with evergreens intermixed with garden flowers. (28/6/1811)[66]

Here we see the demesne landscape to the fore again, with its long avenue and the avenue gate marking a boundary and further underscoring possession, alongside the established old ash tree, Ireland's most common native tree.[67]

---

64 Elizabeth Clibborn, Journal of Elizabeth (Grubb) Clibborn (1780–1861). RSFIHL P9. Michael Ahern has noted that by the nineteenth century, Tipperary's Quaker community had 'for the most part, become comfortable and successful members of the middle classes ... wealthy Quakers lived in large houses, were tended by numerous servants', 392.

65 Susan B. Egenolf, '"Our fellow creatures": Women Narrating Political Violence in the 1798 Irish Rebellion'. *Eighteenth-Century Studies* 42.2 (2009): 217–34; Elizabeth Richards, *The Diary of Elizabeth Richards (1798– 1825): From the Wexford Rebellion to Family Life in the Netherlands*. Ed. Marie de Jong-Ijsselstein. Intro. Kevin Whelan. Hilversum: Verloren, 1999.

66 Such bonfires are more commonly associated with St. John's Eve (23 June), known as Bonfire Night in many parts of Ireland. This is a tradition that continues today, in the west of Ireland in particular.

67 After the 'almost total eradication of the woodland cover for both economic and strategic purposes' in the sixteenth and seventeenth centuries, the planting of trees

The bonfire is lit in this peripheral spot, on the edge of the demesne's perimeter. The people present are described by the diarist as existing across a spectrum, from respectable to visibly impoverished, signalled through their clothing, whether 'decent dressed' or 'barefooted'. Clearly there is no interrogation regarding the reasons for this poverty, but its acknowledgement within the diary is itself noteworthy. Elizabeth's awareness of Irish customs finds echoes in her employment of the Anglicised Irish word 'knock' within the diary, 'walked on the knock' (*cnoc* being the Irish for hill) (25/4/1807). The presence of such nouns within Stirum's diary hints at the cultural intersections between the different communities coexisting in Ireland during this period and at how women identified with different elements of their immediate and larger environment in life and in their diaries.

Creating Communities: Signifiers of Belonging in the Diaries

Reading these particular diaries in relation to ideas of landscape and the natural world strengthens our understanding of these Anglican women's sense of identity, which was bound up with their recognition of their belonging to a landowning elite devoted to ideas of agricultural and estate improvement, and complementary civilising endeavours. Alongside those factors explored in other chapters (particularly regarding gender and age) nationality, religion, and class are shown here to play a key part in the intersectional development of these diarists' personal identities. What is particularly to the fore in this respect, is the communal, collective ethos that emerges. Pastoral literature's emphasis on 'rural plenty and generous community' has long been recognised, understood as 'a literature of place, of community, or of ethos'.[68] While such sense of community is traditionally associated with the pastoral's omnipresent shepherds, this focus on invitation and country entertainment was enthusiastically espoused by the occasional residents of the country demesnes, who wished to partake of the 'rustic feast, country entertainments, or simply a homely cottage' enjoyed by the fictional shepherds, transposing these elements into an elite setting, but retaining the focus on community and belonging.[69] Frances Jocelyn's diary in particular

---

'became a central symbol of this new civilisation' for improving landlords by the eighteenth. William J. Smyth, 'The Greening of Ireland: Tenant Tree-Planting in the Eighteenth and Nineteenth Centuries'. *Irish Forestry* 54.1 (1997): 55.

68 Katy Shaw and Kate Aughterson, *Jim Crace: Into the Wilderness*. Basingstoke: Palgrave, 2018; Kimberly Huth, 'Come Live with Me and Feed My Sheep: Invitation, Ownership, and Belonging in Early Modern Pastoral Literature'. *Studies in Philology* 108.1 (2011): 44–69.

69 Huth 44.

mentions multiple 'country dances' (24/4/1811) and detailed preparations for a ball (5/11/1811), but all of the diarists discussed here support a system of visiting wherein the network of extended family and friends was reinforced and upheld through such exchanges.[70]

This creation of rural networks of communities, echoing the urban exchanges in Dublin town houses, finds formal parallels in the content and composition of the diaries. The front of Letitia Galloway's diary shows it was originally intended as an account of her brother John Galloway's expenses.[71] Letitia Galloway's repeated use of plural pronouns, and the collaborative composition of her diary, evoke a clear sense of belonging. Her focus is repeatedly on communal rather than individual experience, as she often speaks for both her sister and herself in such expressions as 'we are charmed with the many beauties of this Country' (24/6/1809). Certainly, the first-person plural is more frequently employed than the first-person singular. A particularly remarkable element of her diary's composition history is the fact that it is the product of more than one hand and one voice, being added to during an extended interval by the diarist's mother:

> I resume my journal which I find my mother has made good use of during my absence. I yesterday returned from Mrs E Shannons sweet little Cottage where I passed three delightful days. Mrs ES & the two dear girls mentioned by My Mother come home with me. (29/6/1809)

Discovering this literary intrusion, Galloway displays no annoyance at these interjections, instead echoing and supporting her mother's comments. Such fluent communal, collaborative writing practices serve to reinforce the family and the community's ethos and values, merging the different voices to produce one text and presenting life writing more as 'a dynamic expression of relationship within social networks of writers and readers, rather than exclusively the consecration of individual identity'.[72] These shared values and the sense of 'collective endeavour' could then serve to guide the group's actions and behaviours, as part of the wider ruling class's civic and patriotic

70 Frances Jocelyn, Diary of Frances Theodosia Jocelyn. 1810–1812. NLI MS 18430.

71 Most probably John Galloway, 'secretary, commissions of the consolidated fund, 37 North Cumberland Street, Dublin'. CSO/RP/1824/266. National Archives, Dublin. There are references to Letitia's brother John, or Johnny, throughout the diary.

72 Felicity James and Julian North, 'Special Issue: Writing Lives Together: Romantic and Victorian Auto/Biography'. *Life Writing* 14.2 (2017): 134. The diary of Henry McClintock (1783–1843), brother of Mary Anne Fortescue, was continued for five years after his death by his widow, Elizabeth, née Fleury. Henry McClintock, *Journal of Henry McClintock*. Ed. Padraig O'Neill. Co. Louth Archaeological and Historical Society, 2002.

commitment to ostensibly improving Ireland, its people and its lands, which had become such a well-established narrative by the early nineteenth century.[73]

While the focus of this chapter is primarily on those diarists from an elite, Church of Ireland background, the diaries of women from the Society of Friends are also grounded in a commitment to community, reinforced through their sharing and exchange of life writing.[74] Place was again central to these women's sense of self. The village of Ballitore, Co. Kildare, played a fundamental role within the life of Mary Shackleton Leadbeater. Described in 1792 as 'a colony of Quakers' where 'industry reigns', Ballitore had been set up in the late seventeenth century by two Friends, John Barcroft and Abel Strettel, with the village subsequently becoming a vibrant Quaker hub. The village and its inhabitants are central to the Leadbeater diaries throughout Mary's writing career. After her father gifted her a pocketbook for her eighteenth birthday, Mary began to write with an awareness that her diary would be more widely read, and her diary shifted to function more explicitly as a space in which to chronicle the life stages of the members of the Irish Quaker community.[75] This 1777 diary begins with references to the women's meeting and the select meeting, more reminiscent of the diary kept by Mary's mother, Elizabeth.[76] There is a notable shift in emphasis here to incorporate members of the community beyond Mary's peer group and immediate family. Unlike in her earlier ten diaries, we now get information regarding, for example, a couple married on 22/1/1777 in Mountmellick, Co. Laois, or the death of Mary Haughton on 8/2/1777, with an obituary for her in preparation.[77]

The later diaries are a community chronicle, but the adolescent diaries also include multiple references to Ballitore and celebrate the village and Mary's environs:

> here I must observe the beauty of the landscape before us. Ballitore certainly beats any other part of Ireland. Dear, sweet native village

73 O'Connell 16–34. Lynn M. Linder, ed., 'Co-Constructed Selves: Nineteenth-Century Collaborative Life Writing'. Special Issue of *Forum for Modern Language Studies* 52.2 (2016): 121–29.

74 See Introduction.

75 See Chapter 1.

76 Elizabeth Shackleton, Elizabeth Shackleton Diary (holograph, signed) 1753–63. Beinecke Rare Book and Manuscript Library, Yale University, Ballitore Papers, OSB MSS 50, Box 4.

77 Mary Leadbeater, Diaries covering the years 1769–1826, 54 vols. NLI MSS 9292–9346. NLI MS 9303.

surrounded by high hills which smile upon the vale below, the River, the Groves, the Bridge, the near houses, [...] charming Ballitore! (2/1/1776)[78]

Ballitore is held up as the best village in Ireland, its natural landscape lauded and its leading features itemised and praised. In 1790 the diary's title page was still showcasing the centrality of location to Mary's diary project: 'The Journal and Diary of Mary Shackleton 1790 / Ballitore'.[79] Inside the fly leaf, and echoing the writings of Galloway and Butler, there is mention of hay making and bees swarming, alongside information on the diarist's weight. These diary entries were later drawn upon by the diarist in creating her *Annals*, praised by her friend and fellow diarist Melesina Trench thus: 'Your prose *Ballitore* resembles a highly finished Dutch painting [...] As a faithful portrait of the manners of a small but interesting circle, it is really curious, and will become more so every day' (Letter to Leadbeater, n.d., 1802).[80] The posthumously published *The Leadbeater Papers. The Annals of Ballitore* (1862), a work of social and cultural history, opens with descriptions of Ballitore in verse and prose, selected by the editor Elizabeth Shackleton, examples from the former evoking the village's 'neat houses' and 'cultured fields'.[81] Personal betterment through education is celebrated in the poem 'Ballitore', written by Mary in 1778, wherein the school holds a privileged position at the centre of the village. Leadbeater's evocation of the village's etymology again casts the Irish bog in negative light while demonstrating the author's knowledge of the Irish language – 'Ballitore derives its name from its former marshy condition ("bally" in Irish signifying a town or village, and "togher" a bog) from which it was reclaimed by drainage and careful cultivation'.[82] However, while this careful reclamation is praised, not all such agricultural improvements are positively depicted in the *Annals*, which reminds us of the social and denominational distinctions between the diarists. The verse sketch of childhood in Co. Kildare is at times reminiscent of the environmental strains discernible in Oliver Goldsmith's *The Deserted Village* (1770). The village plain of Ballitore is lovely, 'But lovelier once, all gaily drest, / The cowslip gliding o'er her breast, / The ruthless plough her bosom tore; / The golden cowslip charms no more.'[83] The human propellor of the plough is absent, however, and instead the people there are presented as happy and virtuous. Behind everything of course is these villagers'

78 NLI MS 9301.
79 NLI MS 9315.
80 Trench, *Remains*, 134.
81 Leadbeater, *Annals*, I 17.
82 Leadbeater, *Annals*, I 15.
83 Leadbeater, *Annals*, I 18.

religion, uniting them all and binding them together in faith, friendship, and community: 'our friendships formed by thee [Religion] endure'.[84] The emphasis throughout the diaries of Mary Shackleton Leadbeater is on the local and a sense of belonging to this immediate local community, rather than a focus on a wider, national identity.

Indeed, it is often only when they left Ireland that women articulated their awareness of their place within not only a local, but a larger, national community, and a sense of Ireland and Irishness. The following letter from author Maria Edgeworth to Charlotte Rawdon, daughter of salon hostess, Elizabeth Rawdon, Lady Moira, captures this sense of needing a degree of distance from Ireland to appreciate it in her comment that

> I love Ireland as a patriot ought – that is to say as much as I can (Just as Parson Adams forgave as a Christian should that is to say as much as he could) But I dare say I should love my country as people sometimes love their best friends a great deal the better for being absent from it a little while. (Edgeworthstown, 28 April 1811)[85]

The diary of Charity Lecky, from Co. Derry, narrates the young diarist's journey to and from Bath and includes multiple references to questions of nationality and markers of place. The diary provides us with a young person's observations on a variety of people and places, frequently considered through the lens of national affiliation, as well as the opportunity to assess the self within a national framework.

During her travels across Britain, Charity Lecky remarked upon the customs and differences that she was presented with – and found those people she encountered also sought to determine the diarist's origins.[86] A fellow coach traveller who engaged her, for example, asked 'if I was not a Scot, to which I answered in the affirmative, at the same time shewing the ribbons by which my scissors & pin cushion were fastened as a proof that what I said was not quite out of the way (they both Plaid)' (28/10/1796). Charity Lecky's family were of Scottish origin, descendants of Captain Alexander Leckie (1631–1717), son of the 11th Laird of Leckie, who moved to Ireland from Leckie, near Stirling, in Scotland. Captain Leckie acted as commissioner on behalf of the city of Derry during the siege of 1689.[87]

84 Leadbeater, *Annals*, I 26.
85 Maria Edgeworth to Charlotte Rawdon. Letters from members of the Edgeworth family, National Records of Scotland, Anderson Collection, GD 297/3/2.
86 Lecky travelled from Parkgate Harbour to Bath via towns and cities including Neston, Chester, Derbyshire, Wrexham, Ellsemere, Burlton, Shrewsbury, Coalbrookdale, Bridgnorth, Kidderminster, Worcester, and Gloucester.
87 John Graham, *A History of the Siege of Londonderry and Defence of Enniskillen, in*

This siege was explicitly commemorated one hundred years later, during the election campaign of 1790, in which the diarist's own father was elected to serve as Member of Parliament for Derry in the House of Commons in Dublin, a role he filled until 1797:

> After the mayor had declared Lecky elected, reformers had carried their new MP from the town hall in a chair made from one of the gates that had stood the Siege. They placed the chair on a square pedestal, from which rose four green pillars … supporting a circular canopy … The city arms and the words 'The Relief of Derry 1790' appeared on the front of the canopy and, on the top there was a green silk flag, displaying the Irish Harp, a wreath of shamrocks, and the inscription *Pro Patria Semper* [Always for my country].[88]

As N. C. Fleming and others have noted, the shamrock held an appeal 'not just for catholics but for the state, members of the establishment in general, and for protestants of "enlightened" views'.[89] In the embracing of Irish symbols here, we can see a rejection of the exclusive association of such symbols with those subscribing to Gaelic ethnicity and Catholicism.[90] Used to commemorate an incident of Protestant success, these symbols were here promoted by Ulster MPs to highlight their commitment to an explicitly Irish identity. While the public symbolisms inherent in the election campaign and the written recording of speeches were the preserve of men, the donning of Irish symbols and the commitment of such adornment to paper was clearly an avenue open to Charity Lecky, whose diary also features symbols of Irishness: 'Friday March 17th being Patrick's Day I mounted a large Shamrock in my hat' (17/3/1797). Thus, the diarist is careful to adorn herself with a visual signifier of her connection with Ireland as well as to note and explore this facet of her identity at length within her diary.[91]

1688. Dublin, 1829, 21; 29.

88 Breandán Mac Suibhne, 'Spirit, Spectre, Shade'. *Field Day Review* 9 (2013): 178.

89 N. C. Fleming, *Ireland and Anglo-Irish Relations since 1800: Critical Essays, Volume 1*. Aldershot: Ashgate, 2008.

90 See also Padhraig Higgins, *A Nation of Politicians: Gender, Patriotism, and Political Culture in Late Eighteenth-Century Ireland*. Wisconsin: University of Wisconsin Press, 2010; and Joep Leerssen, *Mere Irish and Fíor-Ghael*. Amsterdam: John Benjamins, 1986.

91 The diarist recognises the symbolism of the harp too on another occasion and declares, 'to be sure if I was worth £20,000 I'd learn to play on the harp & buy a very good one'. For women's commitment to promoting Irish manufacture in the late 1770s and early 1780s in a show of solidarity with those advocating for parliamentary and legislative independence for Ireland, see Padhraig Higgins, 'Consumption, Gender, and the Politics of "Free Trade" in Eighteenth-Century Ireland'. *Eighteenth-Century Studies* 41 (2007): 87–105; and Mary O'Dowd, 'Politics, Patriotism and the Public Sphere:

We also see Charity Lecky explicitly acknowledging and indeed celebrating and embracing these Irish elements of her identity. The diary form offered her a platform for exploring her Irishness and the opportunity to conceptualise an Irish identity that is bound up with its composition: Lecky frequently places Irishness at the forefront of her sense of self. Throughout the work, there is a clear sense of Lecky's pride in Ireland and the people from there. This echoes a general trend from the late eighteenth century, with the promotion of Irish language, culture, and customs being celebrated in the salons at Moira House on Ussher's Island in Dublin and in the work of those connected to that salon, such as Joseph Cooper Walker and Charlotte Brooke.[92] Those from different backgrounds are shown as embracing markers of Irishness and incorporating them into their work and their own sense of identity, a tradition that continued into the early nineteenth century when 'the Union led to more self-consciousness about what it was to be Irish'.[93] In Lecky's diary, her pride in Irish successes is explicitly signalled on numerous occasions, including her mention of seeing 'curious pieces of mechanism which seemed to have rational powers, & I gloried they were all made by an Irishman' (22/11/1796). Again and again, the reader encounters the diarist's approval of Irish achievements and Irish people, and indeed her praising of those who compliment them, for example: 'liked the young Mrs Chapman very much for her liking the Irish people & their & my country, where she had spent some years' (15/12/1796).[94]

While in Bath, Lecky acknowledges that she is unable to speak French, and her diary French is limited to a smattering of expressions, such as 'le jeune Mr J' and 'I was the only fille on deck'. Her inadequacy with the language limits her opportunities for conversing with potential suitors, although rather than overly lamenting this loss, the diarist emphasises the pleasures of

Women and Politics, 1692–1800'. *A History of Women in Ireland, 1500–1800*. Harlow: Longman, 2004.

92 Amy Prendergast, *Literary Salons Across Britain and Ireland in the Long Eighteenth Century*. Basingstoke: Palgrave, 2015.

93 Carpenter and Collins 45. Ian Campbell Ross's survey of literature from 1700 to 1780 through the prism of national identity demonstrates that as early as the 1720s 'those who had referred to themselves thirty years earlier as the "Protestants of Ireland" or "the English gentlemen" of this kingdom" might call themselves "Irish gentlemen", while remaining firmly attached to Protestant values'. Ian Campbell Ross, '"We Irish": Writing and National Identity'. *Irish Literature in Transition, 1700–1780*. Ed. Moyra Haslett. Cambridge: CUP, 2020, 53.

94 Equally, one finds examples where Lecky reflects on her disappointment at the behaviour of some Irish people, for example: '[at tea] a great number of young people & such a riotous set I had not before seen in England, & hardly so in Ireland, but, alas, they were all Irish' (23/1/1797).

conversing in English – and specifically in conversing with Irishmen at the balls and not their English counterparts. Both knowledge of French and its employment could be used to signal belonging to a broader European world, as well as to the Republic of Letters, incorporating this dimension into an Irish identity. The cosmopolitan European aspirations and achievements of numerous figures from Ireland is evidenced in the life writing that survives from the eighteenth century, as well as in literary writing, particularly the novel.[95] Knowledge of the French language was a competency generally shared by many elite women in eighteenth-century Ireland, as attested to by the numerous instances of the language's employment across surviving letters from the period, as well as by the numbers of women engaged in the process of translation.[96]

While fluency in a second language such as French or German might have increased the opportunity of gaining a partner in a multilingual environment and secured access to certain elite circles, the use of French could also be used to erase markers of difference. The German Frederick Kielmansegge also notes this tendency of the Irish during his 1761 visit to Bath: 'they are aided by their French, which they speak more frequently and better than most Englishmen'.[97] Other Irish diaries from the same period as Lecky's record the tendency of Irish men and women to speak French rather than English in order to disguise their Irish origins. For example, Elizabeth Sheridan relates in her letter-journal, 'Our Irish Doctor is very civil and talks french in Public, as he says "to *hide* his Brogue" I talk'd little but French the Whole Eveng' (5/1/1790).[98] James Caulfeild, the 1st Earl of Charlemont, goes further in his comment that 'the Irishman in London, long before he has lost his brogue, loses or casts away all Irish ideas, and, from a natural wish to obtain the goodwill of those with whom he associates, becomes, in effect, a partial Englishman. Perhaps more partial than the

95 Susan Manly and Joanna Wharton, eds. Special Issue: 'Worlds of Maria Edgeworth'. *European Romantic Review* 31.6 (2020): 655–786.

96 Amy Prendergast, 'Elizabeth Griffith, Translation, Transmission, and Cultural Transfer'. *Women's Writing* 27.2 (2020): 184–202. In addition to these elite women, Catholics educated abroad and the descendants of Huguenot refugees also embraced the language.

97 Frederick Kielmansegge, *Diary of a Journey to England*, cited in Peter Borsay, 'Georgian Bath; A Transnational Culture'. *Leisure Cultures in Urban Europe c. 1700–1870: A Transnational Perspective*. Eds. Peter Borsay and Jan Hein Furnée. Manchester: MUP, 2015, 110.

98 Sheridan herself had been accused of speaking in Irish-accented English during her time in London, much to her father's disgust, who dismissed any such suggestions. Elizabeth Sheridan, *Betsy Sheridan's Journal*. Ed. William Le Fanu. Oxford: OUP, 1986, 92.

English themselves'.[99] Such manoeuvres, however, are entirely absent from the diary of Charity Lecky, who instead actively seeks out communities of Irish people abroad and opportunities to celebrate this facet of her identity.

Lecky's immediate observations on place and nation position language as being of central importance in allowing for markers of difference and as a guide to establishing geographical location. On her way to Bath, having passed through Ellesmere, the diarist admits, 'whether this is a Welsh or an English town I know not, but I believe it to be the former for I heard people speaking Welsh' (28/10/1796). Language as a marker of identity and as a signifier of belonging is in evidence through the repeated use of French in the diary of Melesina Trench. Trench converses in French throughout her writing, and her diary is peppered with French expressions, in addition to numerous Latin phrases. Her bilingual competence is apparent in sentences such as 'I scarcely think je reve au lieu de penser' (21/1/1802). As the diary progresses, there are entire paragraphs exclusively in French. She also describes speaking in 'bad German', but it is the French language that connects her with the greater Huguenot diaspora of which she is a part.[100] Trench's diary also evokes a sense of the wider, transnational networks of elite figures from various European countries, all adhering to 'an elite horizontal sense of solidarity'.[101] This network was sustained through transnational association and exchange, including Trench's involvement in diplomatic sociability and her travels across cities such as Prague and Vienna. One gets a sense of the privileging of an encompassing European identity in her diary. The diarist frequently casts herself in the role of 'English traveller', and her references to England and Englishness (rather than Britishness) suggest a sense of connection, affiliation, and assimilation with English culture and traditions.[102]

Ireland is largely absent from Trench's published *Remains*. However, this is a distortion of the original diary. The manuscript entries show awareness of various Irish estates, Irish tenants, and the difficulties suffered during and after the 1798 Rebellion.[103] Trench was an heiress through both her

99 James Caulfeild, Lord Charlement, *The Manuscripts and Correspondence of James, first Earl of Charlemont, Volume 1, 1745–1783*. London: HMC, 1891, 14.
100 Trench, *Remains*, 98.
101 Stephen Conway, *Britain, Ireland, and Continental Europe in the Eighteenth Century: Similarities, Connections, Identities*. Oxford: OUP, 2011, 213.
102 Trench, *Remains*, 51. See also examples on pages 38; 42; 54; 55; 86. It is Englishness rather than Britishness that is highlighted throughout, with the first reference to Britishness not arising until 1817, simply in reference to the heiress of the British Empire, with the following, in 1820, lauding the successes of a show that was 'all that Oriental pomp, feudal ceremonial, and British wealth could unite', 451.
103 Melesina Chenevix St. George Trench, Diary kept by Melesina St. George,

maternal and paternal grandfathers (Archdeacon Gervais and Dr Richard Chenevix, Bishop of Waterford) and was at the apex of Irish society. Her diary volume written during her time in Ireland (1801–1802) portrays her moving freely between demesnes and notes how her time 'Passed happily between Bellevue, Sonna, Dublin':

> I am now ^at Belview^ enjoying tranquillity, fine air, beautiful scenery, and the spectacle of active goodness, ^grounded in religion^ blessed with great wealth, & attended with 'honor, love, audience, troops of friends' and all that makes life desirable (8/6/1801)

Bellevue, near Delgany, Co. Wicklow, was originally the Ballydonagh estate, purchased in 1753 by another Huguenot, the banker David La Touche.[104] His second wife, Elizabeth, née Vicars, had helped establish a girls' orphanage and a school at Bellevue.[105] Trench's next diary entry, on the verso and partially torn out, references 'Mrs La Touche's charitable establishments'. Trench's diary explicitly connects such philanthropic displays of 'active goodness' and her own enjoyment of the demesne with the families' religion and wealth. There are no allusions in the diary to the family's connections with enslavement, though the La Touche property portfolio has been described as 'one of the most extensive to have connections to Irish slave-ownership'.[106] As with Galloway and Jocelyn, Trench's entries instead see the values of countryside living held up for praise, wherein that environment connotes virtue, retirement, and domesticity: 'The latter part of this month, I have passed with Mr and Mrs Congreve – [...] they have always lived in the Country, a situation most favourable to characters such as theirs. Their grounds are most beautifully situated on the Suir, & laid out with taste' (31/10/1801). The Congreves and others are praised for being in tune with their surrounding environs, being shaped by and

---

later Trench, 1801–1802. HRO, 23M93/1/5. Motivations for editorial omissions are discussed in Chapter 1. Subsequent quotations from Trench's diary are taken from this manuscript source, unless otherwise stated.

104 Turlough O'Riordan, 'David La Touche'. *DIB*.

105 This echoes the practices of elite English women such as Sarah Dawes and Mary Cotterel, with Briony McDonagh showing how 'alongside enclosing their fields, landowners invested new cottages and schools…'. Briony McDonagh, *Elite Women and the Agricultural Landscape, 1700–1830*. London: Routledge, 2018, 94.

106 Ciaran O'Neill, 'The Public History of Slavery in Dublin'. *The 24th Annual Sir John T. Gilbert Commemorative Lecture Delivered on 26th January, 2021*. Dublin City Libraries, 2022, 13. O'Neill draws attention to the continuation of such silences, noting that the family's slave ownership and their extensive Jamaican estates are 'almost never remarked upon in the various glowing accounts of their private banking past'. Ibid.

shaping their environment. Their property is described as benefitting from its natural proximity to the River Suir, but it has also been 'improved', with the demesne grounds 'laid out with taste'.

In addition to her time spent in these 'maison[s] de plaisance', Trench documents in her diary her involvement with the operation of her farm in Co. Wexford and her interactions with those of a lower class: 'Went to visit my farm near Gorey...' (13/8/1801).[107] The mental health of these tenants is referenced in the diary: she declares that the wife of Mr Boyne, her principal tenant, 'like most of the lower or middling Irish' seems 'possessed oppressed by a real or affected melancholy' (13/8/1801). Use of the verb 'oppress' is chosen by Trench as more fitting, with her previous choice, 'possessed', struck out. Thus, she owns that some of her tenants do suffer from melancholy in a manner recalling the experiences of diarists such as Anne Jocelyn. The reasons that lead to her estimation that this emotion was sometimes only an affectation also reveal much regarding the landlord system in Ireland, bringing to mind, though not explicitly referencing, the late eighteenth- and early nineteenth-century agitations over tenant rights:

> That it is sometimes the last, particularly in the presence of those they consider their superiors, my own observation has convinced me. A variety of causes operate to produce this effect. The chief of these seems to be an idea that the higher class have a sort of jealousy of the prosperity of their inferiors, and a fear, in some cases too well founded, that the increasing opulence and happiness of the tenant will excite unreasonable and dispro-portioned exactions on the part of the landlord. (13/8/1801)[108]

With this entry and her recognition of the 'disproportioned exactions', the sufferings and difficulties of the Irish tenant population are at least acknowledged.

Rather than reflections on land ownership *per se*, it is the middleman system that is held up for scrutiny and condemnation by Trench:

> it is ^often^ as hurtful to the landlord as the tenant, to admit of a middle man, – this cruel system has [illegibile] hitherto kept the industrious occupier of the ground in a wretched state of misery & dependence. Never

---

107 'La maison de plaisance est une Ecole de Vertue' (1/3/1802). 'Maison de plaisance' is defined by *The Concise Oxford Dictionary of Art Terms* as 'A term used during the 18th and 19th centuries to describe rural and suburban houses designed as retreats for the wealthy and the nobility.'

108 This passage appears in the *Remains* too, with the tenants' surname redacted. See S. J. Connolly, 'Jacobites, Whiteboys and Republicans: Varieties of Disaffection in Eighteenth-Century Ireland'. *Eighteenth-Century Ireland* 18 (2003): 63–79.

will I suffer any pecuniary advantage to seduce me to act on a principle which literally defrauds 'the labourer of his hire.' (12/11/1801)

The full line from Ecclesiasticus from which Trench quotes, and the quotation marks are hers, is, 'He that taketh away from his neighbour's living slayeth him; and he that defraudeth the labourer of his hire is a bloodshedder.'[109] One assumes Trench's son and editor deemed the quotation too censorious to be included in her *Remains* and the publication omits it in its entirety. Such criticisms of the 'cruel system' were further explored in the novels emanating from Ireland during this time. The paratext of Edgeworth's *Castle Rackrent* (1800) glosses the middleman system thus, for instance: 'The agent was one of your middle men*, who grind the face of the poor… *The characteristics of a middle man were, servility to his superiors, and tyranny towards his inferiors – The poor detested this race of beings.'[110] Both Edgeworth and Trench aligned themselves and their families with paternalistic landlords, whether in imaginative literature, or in the diary form, offering justification for their privileged positions within Irish society.

These issues of possession and dispossession of land are difficult to divorce from considerations of nature in an Irish context, where 'nature was not only the backdrop of events [in Ireland] but an active part of agential relations with social and judicial factors'.[111] Landlords, middlemen, agents, and tenants all feature in Trench's diary and inform its composition and her own perspective on her environment. The ideological import of both the actions chosen and the descriptions recorded by the Irish elite is apparent throughout the diaries of Trench as well as those of Galloway, Jocelyn, Goddard, ffolliott, and Fortescue. These diaries offer a new source for considerations of place and identity within a local, national, and international context. The diarists' perception of their surroundings, their crafting of environments both within the demesnes and upon the pages of the diaries, allows us to better understand the self in a national framework, as well as within a communal context, whereby the diaries serve to endorse

---

109 Ecclesiasticus 34:22. King James Bible.

110 Maria Edgeworth, *Castle Rackrent. An Hibernian Tale*. London, 1800, 28. Following on from her satirical examination of landlords throughout *Castle Rackrent*, Maria Edgeworth's *The Absentee* (1812), as the name suggests, teases out issues of absenteeism and the disastrous consequences of abandoning estates to middlemen. The rackrenting practises of Edgeworth's earlier novel are here multiplied as Lord Colambre goes undercover to explore first-hand the exploitation being meted out to his family's tenants, encountering examples of poverty and cruelty committed by villainous agents.

111 Marie Mianowski, 'Review: Nature and the Environment in Nineteenth-Century Ireland'. *Estudios Irlandeses* 16 (2021): 269.

and reinforce the core values of the members of the individual diarist's community.

Many of these diaries also highlight the paradoxes inherent in the simultaneous celebration of the majesty of waterfalls and rivers, the consumption of locally grown produce, and pursuit of botanical studies, alongside the steadfast commitment to an ethos of improvement that sought to maximise existing Irish resources and tame and civilise evidence of wildness and the so-called 'excess of naturalness', in order to ultimately *lessen* Irish difference.[112] Such homogenising projects find a counter-narrative in the espousal by some diarists of a distinctly Irish identity and signifiers of Irishness, as in the explicit celebration of Irish difference in the diary of Charity Lecky. While the diaries often concentrate on reinforcing one particular facet of the diarist's sense of national identity, Trench's reminds us of the multi-faceted nature of both religious and national identity, with her sense of self informed by European, Irish, British, Anglican, and Huguenot contexts.

All the diarists considered here sought to convey a sense of place and often focus on the settings for their individual entries, though this chapter has shown that these diary portraits have multiple omissions and peculiarities. Particularly held up for praise in several of these constructed environments are the agricultural dimensions of rural life, which are communicated in laudatory language, often actively embraced and even fetishised by diarists such as Galloway and Jocelyn in almost parodic fashion, producing a very constructed and peculiar environment within the diary. These two diaries in particular display continuities with the 'politically conservative function of English Pastoral literature through its distortions and omission' and its ignoring of the actual agrarian processes of cultivation.[113] These diaries are also very much part of the Romantic tradition, with entries steeped in the language of the sublime, broadening our sense of that movement's writings.

The impact of place upon all these diarists is apparent throughout, affecting every element of the diaries' form, content, and register, exemplifying the impressions left by the myriad encounters and dialogues between people and landscape, with each shaped and influenced by the other, for better or worse. These women's representations of their environments, of the natural and manmade worlds around them, add to our current appreciation of the natural world, providing a literary and historical tradition. The diaries reveal a sense of belonging and the symbiotic relationship between people and place, with the diarists and their surroundings in constant dialogue.

---

112 O'Connell 16–34.
113 Gifford 21.

Afterword

Throughout this book we have observed individual diarists' prejudices and shortcomings and acknowledged the collective involvement of many of the writers in a system that perpetuated social divisions and upheld religious persecution, all of which can make for a difficult relationship with the protagonists. I have, however, frequently felt a deep sense of privilege to have had the opportunity to read these women's handwritten accounts of their struggles with grief and loss, with pregnancy, with their mental health, and with personal autonomy. Though we have established that these diaries were almost always written with an audience in mind, I hope the foregoing chapters have offered a respectful exploration of these women's writings and of their responses to difficult, often traumatic, personal experiences, including abusive incidents and family bereavements.

The extant diaries showcase the depth of literary talent in existence in Ireland during the long eighteenth century and the efforts of many diarists to exhibit their creativity and literary prowess, as well as the writers' individual attempts to craft a voice with which to communicate with posterity. I sincerely hope that the corpus presented here is supplemented by future archival discoveries, whether of diaries by Catholics, Irish speakers, and Presbyterians, or by the unearthing of additional Quaker and elite examples. These can only enhance a body of life writing that strengthens our appreciation of Irish literature and of literature of the long eighteenth century, contributing to our understanding of the value and diversity of the writing produced at this time, as well as extending new avenues concerning authorship and female agency, as we continue to re-evaluate our understanding of women's contributions to literature and to cultural life.

Bibliography

Manuscript Sources

Ireland

Ballinamore Library, Co. Leitrim
Slack, Angel Anna. The Diary of Angel Anna Slack, June 1785–July 1796. File 275.

Muniment Room, Castle Forbes, Newtownforbes, Co. Longford
Rawdon and Hastings Correspondence. Granard Papers T3765/M/3.

National Library of Ireland, Dublin
Adlercron, Meliora. Adlercron account books. Household expenses and wages book of Mrs Meliora Adlercron of Dawson St., Dublin, including some notes on births and deaths of members of her family, and references to smallpox epidemics in Dublin, 1782–1794. NLI MS 4481.
Balfour, Letitia Townley. Codicil to will of Letitia Townley Balfour, 23 May 1837. Townley Hall Papers. NLI D15,133–D15,178.
Blachford, Theodosia. Journal of Theodosia Blachford (née Tighe), covering the years 1773–1774. NLI MS 38,639/1/7.
Blachford, Theodosia. 'Some memorandums relative to the death of my ever dear Husband'. NLI MS 38,639/1/8.
Edgeworth, Elizabeth. Diary of Elizabeth Edgeworth, sister of Maria, with occasional entries for period December 1797–February 1800. NLI MS 18,756.
Edgeworth, Elizabeth. Bessie Edgeworth letter to Mrs Frances Edgeworth. NLI POS 9027 231.
Edgeworth, Elizabeth. Bessie Edgeworth letters to Harriet Beaufort. NLI POS 9027 204; 217–218; 220; 234–237.

Edgeworth, 'Maria'. Diary of Maria Edgeworth, with references to political affairs; June–December 1803. NLI MS 18,752 / POS 9038. [Attribution queried.]

Edgeworth, Maria. Maria Edgeworth's notes on Paris 1803. Edgeworth Papers. NLI POS 9028 366A.

Edgeworth, Maria. Maria Edgeworth letter to Charlotte Sneyd. Edgeworth Papers. NLI POS 9027 224.

Galloway, Letitia. Diary of Letitia Galloway. NLI MS 32,517.

Goddard, Elinor. An anonymous lady's journal (possibly that of Mrs Lucy Goddard). Wicklow Papers. NLI MS 3573.

Jocelyn, Anne. Diary of Anne Jocelyn. 1822. NLI MS 18,430.

Jocelyn, Frances Theodosia. Diary of Frances Theodosia Jocelyn. 1810–1812. NLI MS 18,430.

Leadbeater, Mary. Diaries covering the years 1769–1789 in 22 volumes. NLI MSS 9292–9314.

Leadbeater, Mary. Diaries covering the years 1790–1809 in 15 volumes. NLI MSS 9315–9329.

Leadbeater, Mary. Diaries covering the years 1810–1826 in 17 volumes. NLI MSS 9330–9346.

Mathew, Mary. Cookery recipes, household accounts and diary by Mary Mathew, 1741– 1777. NLI MS 5102.

Tighe, Mary. Letters from Mary Tighe to her cousin Caroline Hamilton (née Tighe). NLI MS 38,639/1/14–20.

Religious Society of Friends in Ireland Historical Library, Dublin

Ashbridge, Elizabeth. Account by herself of the early part of the life of Elizabeth Ashbridge (1713–1755) (copy; printed). P2. [This is a beautifully presented memoir, with an index.]

Boyle Harvey, Margaret. Journal 1809–1812. P10.

Clibborn, Elizabeth. Journal of Elizabeth (Grubb) Clibborn (1780–1861) (original and typescript copy). P9.

Shackleton, Hannah. Ballitore Journal 1766–1772, P25 & Second Volume 1772–1784, P26. [This is a manuscript copy of *The Annals of Ballitore*.]

Trinity College Dublin

Beaufort, Louisa Catherine. Tour Journal of Louisa Catherine Beaufort, 1808. TCD MS 4034.

Beaufort, Mary. Tour Journal of Mary Beaufort, 1808. TCD MS 4035.

Beaufort, Mary. Tour Journal of Mary Beaufort, 1810. TCD MS 4036.

Beaufort, Mary. Travel Journal of Mary Beaufort, 1779–1[7]80. TCD MS 4025.

Dawson, Mary Anne. Diary of Mary Anne Dawson, 1782–84. Clements Papers, TCD MSS 7270–7270a.

Herbert, Dorothea. Dorothea Herbert 1806–1807 Diary. On deposit at TCD.
Herbert, Dorothea. Retrospections. On deposit at TCD.

United Kingdom

Bodleian Library, University of Oxford, England
Frances Edgeworth, Fanny's journal of a tour of England, 1819–20. MS Eng.
Lett. c744, fols. 129–72.
Sophia Edgeworth, Sophy's journal of a tour of Scotland, 1823. MS Eng. Lett.
c746, fols. 166–92.

Hampshire Record Office, England
Trench, Melesina Chenevix St. George. Diaries of Melesina St. George, later
Trench, from 1791 to 1802. 23M93/1.
Trench, Melesina Chenevix St. George. Diary kept by Melesina St. George,
later Trench, 1801–1802 [while in Ireland]. 23M93/1/5.
Trench, Melesina Chenevix St. George. Copies of extracts from Melesina's
diaries, mainly in the hand of Richard Chenevix Trench, undated. 23M93/1/6.

John Rylands Research Institute and Library, University of
Manchester, England
Hamilton, Mary. Diary of Mary Hamilton. The Mary Hamilton Papers.
HAM/2/1–16.

National Library of Scotland, Edinburgh
Ewbank, Jane. Journal of Miss Ewbank of York, 1803–5. NLS MS 9481.

National Records of Scotland, Edinburgh
Edgeworth family. Letters from members of the Edgeworth family. Anderson
Collection, GD 297/3.

National Library of Wales, Aberystwyth [Microfilm reels available in NLI]
Butler, Eleanor. Butler's Pocket book, 1784. NLW MS 22968A / NLI POS
9613.
Butler, Eleanor. Butler's Journal 1788–91. NLW MS 22971C / NLI POS 9614.
Butler, Eleanor. Butler's Incomplete Journals (1791; 1799; 1802; 1807). NLW
MS 22972C; 22973A; 22974A; 22975A / NLI POS 9615.
Goddard, Elinor. Mrs Elinor Goddard: Journal (1774–1778). NLW
22993A. Consulted on microfilm, NLI POS 9617.
Ponsonby, Sarah. Account of a Journey in Wales, 1778. NLW 22967C / NLI
POS 9613.

Public Record Office of Northern Ireland, Belfast

Clibborn, Elizabeth. MS copy of the personal diary of Elizabeth Clibborn of Anner Mills, Clonmel, Co. Tipperary. 1807–1813. T2983/2. [Missing from PRONI.]

ffolliott, Frances. Typescript copy of a few pages of the diary of Mrs John Ffolliott, mother of Maryanne Young. 1808. D3045/6/1.

ffolliott, Marianne. Diary of Mary Anne Ffolliott, Boyle Co. Roscommon, 1809–1827. D1995/1.

Hancock, Mary. Diary of Mary Hancock, Sister of Isabella Steele-Nicholson. 1788. D3513/3/1.

Kiernan, 'Harriet'. Diary of Harriet Kiernan. 1799–1808. D1728/28/1. [Attribution queried; MS copy.]

Walker, Anna. Typescript edition of the diary kept by Anna Walker, 1802–1807. T1565/1.

Ward, Arabella. Extract from the diary of Lady Arabella Ward, 1804. D2092/1/10. MIC.

Queen's University Belfast, Northern Ireland

Skeffington, Harriet. Diary, 5–25 June 1798. MS1/206.

West Yorkshire Archive Service, Calderdale, England

Lister, Anne. Diary of Anne Lister of Shibden Hall, 1806–1814. SH:7/ML/E/26/1.

Lister, Anne. Diary of Anne Lister of Shibden Hall, 11 April 1819 to 22 November 1819. SH:7/ML/E/3.

United States of America

Beinecke Rare Book and Manuscript Library, Yale University, Connecticut

Anon. [Charity Lecky]. Diary of a Winter in Bath, 1796–97. James Marshall and Marie-Louise Osborn Collection. Osborn c446.

Shackleton, Elizabeth. Elizabeth Shackleton Diary (holograph, signed) 1753–63. Ballitore Papers, OSB MSS 50, Box 4.

Davidson Library, University of California, Santa Barbara

Shackleton, Sarah. Sarah Shackleton's Journal in 4 volumes, 1787–1821. Department of Special Collections. Ballitore Collection. Box 13, F.1. [Microfilm reels available in NLI: n.1009–10, p.1091–2.]

Houghton Library, Harvard University, Massachusetts

Guild, Elizabeth Quincy. Journal in Ireland and England. Guild Family and Eliot Family Papers, MS AM 2922/38.

Huntington Library, California

Larpent, Anna. Mrs Anna Margaretta Larpent's 'Methodized Journal', 1773–1780. HM 31201.

Larpent, Anna. Mrs Larpent's Diary. Vols. 1–16. 1790–1830. HM 31201.

Thrale Piozzi, Hester Lynch. Thraliana, 1776–1809. HM 12183.

Printed Primary Diaries

Beatty, John D. ed. *Protestant Women's Narratives of the Irish Rebellion of 1798*. Dublin: Four Courts Press, 2001.

Beaufort, Louisa. 'Louisa Beaufort's Diary of Her Travels in South-West Munster and Leinster in 1842 and 1843'. Eds. Magda Loeber and Rolf Loeber. *Analecta Hibernica* 46 (2015): 123–205.

Bell, Mrs G. H. *The Hamwood Papers of the Ladies of Llangollen and Caroline Hamilton*. London: Macmillan, 1930.

Bennis, Elizabeth. *The Journal of Elizabeth Bennis 1749–1779*. Ed. Rosemary Raughter. Dublin: Columba Press, Blackrock, 2007.

Berry, H. F. 'Notes from the Diary of a Dublin Lady [Katharine Bayly] in the Reign of George II'. *The Journal of the Royal Society of Antiquaries of Ireland* 8.2 (1898): 141–54.

Blachford, Theodosia, 'Observations on the foregoing journal by her mother, Mrs Blachford'. Mary Tighe, *The Collected Poems and Journals of Mary Tighe*. Ed. Harriet Kramer Linkin. Lexington: University Press of Kentucky, 2005.

Blackburne, E. Owens. *Illustrious Irishwomen. Being Memoirs of some of the Most Noted Irishwomen from the Earliest Ages to the Present Century*. 2 vols. London, 1877. [Volume II contains extracts from Elinor Goddard's diary.]

Bouhéreau, Élie. *The Diary and Accounts of Élie Bouhéreau*. Eds. Marie Léoutre, Jean-Paul Pittion, Jane McKee, and Amy Prendergast. Dublin: Irish Manuscripts Commission, 2019.

Boyle Harvey, Margaret. *A Journal of a Voyage from Philadelphia to Cork in the Year of our Lord, 1809; Together With a Description of a Sojourn in Ireland*. Philadelphia, 1915.

Burney, Frances. *The Early Journals and Letters of Fanny Burney, Volume 1, 1768–1773*. Ed. Lars E. Troide. Oxford: Clarendon Press, 1988.

Burney, Frances. *A Known Scribbler: Frances Burney on Literary Life*. Ed. Justine Crump. Toronto: Broadview, 2002.

Bury, S. *An Account of the Life and Death of Mrs. Elizabeth Bury*. Bristol, 1720.

Campbell, Thomas. *Dr Campbell's Diary of a Visit to England in 1775*. Ed. James L. Clifford. Cambridge: CUP, 1947.

Caulfeild, James. *The Manuscripts and Correspondence of James, first Earl of Charlemont, Volume 1, 1745–1783*. London, 1891.

Cooper, Austin. *An Eighteenth-Century Antiquary; the sketches, notes and diaries of Austin Cooper (1759–1830)*. Ed. Liam Price. Dublin: Falconer, 1942.

Day, Robert. *Mr. Justice Robert Day (1746–1841): The Diaries and the Addresses to Grand Juries 1793–1829*. Ed. Gerald O'Carroll. Tralee, Co. Kerry: Polymath Press, 2004.

Drinker, Elizabeth. *The Diary of Elizabeth Drinker, the Life Cycle of an Eighteenth-Century Woman*. Ed. Elaine Forman Crane. Pennsylvania: University of Pennsylvania Press, 2010.

Fortescue, Mary Anne. 'The Diary of Marianne Fortescue, 1797–1800'. Ed. Noel Ross. *Journal of the County Louth Archaeological Society* 24.2–3 (1998): 222–48; (1999): 357–79.

Grubb, Sarah. *Some account of the life and religious labours of Sarah Grubb…* Dublin, 1792.

Hamilton, Mary. *Mary Hamilton, Afterwards Mrs John Dickenson, at Court and at Home. From Letters and Diaries, 1756 to 1816*. Eds. Elizabeth and Florence Anson. London: John Murray, 1925.

Hardy, Mary. *The Diary* of *Mary Hardy 1773–1809*. Ed. Margaret Bird. Kingston upon Thames: Burnham Press, 2013.

Herbert, Dorothea. *Introspections: The Poetry & Private World of Dorothea Herbert*. Ed. Frances Finnegan. Kilkenny: Congrave Press, 2011.

Herbert, Dorothea. *Retrospections of Dorothea Herbert*, with an Introduction by L. M. Cullen. Dublin: Town House, 1988, 2004.

Hurst, Sarah. *The Diaries of Sarah Hurst, 1759–1762: Life and Love in Eighteenth-Century Horsham*. Ed. Susan C. Djabri. Stroud: Amberley Publishing, 2009.

Jocelyn, Anne. *The Diary of Anne, Countess Dowager of Roden, 1797–1802*. Dublin, 1870.

Johnson, Dorothea. *The memoirs of Mrs. Dorothea Johnson, late of Lisburn: extracted from her journals and other papers*. Ed. Adam Averell. Cavan, 1818.

Mathew, Mary. *The Diary of Mary Mathew*. Ed. Maria Luddy. Thurles: Co. Tipperary Historical Society, 1991.

McClintock, Henry. *Journal of Henry McClintock*. Ed. Padraig O'Neill. Co. Louth Archaeological and Historical Society, 2002.

Mordaunt, Elizabeth, Viscountess. *The Private Diarie of Elizabeth, Viscountess Mordaunt*. [d. 1678]. Ed. Robert Jocelyn Roden. Duncairn, 1856.

Ponsonby, Sarah. 'Account of a Journey in Wales; Performed in May 1778 by Two Fugitive Ladies'. Ed. Elizabeth Edwards. *Curious Travellers Digital Editions*. editions.curioustravellers.ac.uk/doc/0004.

Powys, Caroline. *Passages from the Diaries of Mrs Philip Lybbe Powys, of Hardwick House, Oxon, AD 1756 to 1808*. Ed. Emily J Climenson. London, 1899.

Rich, Mary, Countess of Warwick. *Memoir of Lady Warwick, Also Her Diary from AD 1666 to 1672…* London, 1847.

Richards, Elizabeth. *The Diary of Elizabeth Richards (1798– 1825): From the Wexford Rebellion to Family Life in the Netherlands*. Ed. Marie de Jong-Ijsselstein. Intro. Kevin Whelan. Hilversum: Verloren, 1999.

Scully, Denys. *The Irish Catholic Petition of 1805: The Diary of Denys Scully*. Dublin: Irish Academic Press, 1992.

Sheridan, Elizabeth. *Betsy Sheridan's Journal*. Ed. William Le Fanu. Oxford: OUP, 1986.

Stacpoole, William. 'The Diary of an Eighteenth-Century Clare Gentleman'. Ed. Leo F. McNamara. *North Munster Antiquarian Journal* 23 (1981): 25–65.

Tennent, John. 'The Journal of John Tennent, 1786–90'. Ed. Leanne Calvert. *Analecta Hibernica* 43 (2012): 69–128.

Thrale, Hester Lynch. *Thraliana, The Diary of Hester Lynch Thrale (Later Mrs Piozzi) 1776–1809*. Ed. Katherine C. Balderston. Oxford: Clarendon Press, 1951. 2nd ed. 2014.

Tighe, Mary. *The Collected Poems and Journals of Mary Tighe*. Ed. Harriet Kramer Linkin. Lexington: University Press of Kentucky, 2005.

Tone, Theobald Wolfe. *Life of Theobald Wolfe Tone... Written by himself, and continued by his Son; with his Political writings, and Fragments of his Diary...* Ed. William Theobald Wolfe Tone. Washington, 1826.

Trench, Melesina Chenevix St. George. *Journal Kept During a Visit to Germany in 1799, 1800*. Ed. Dean of Westminster. Privately, 1861.

Trench, Melesina Chenevix St. George. *The Remains of the Late Mrs. Richard Trench. Being Selections from her Journals, Letters, & Other Papers*. Ed. Dean of Westminster. London, 1862.

Weldon, Anne Cooke. 'Anne Cooke Diary'. *Journal of the County Kildare Archaeological Society* VIII (1915–1917): 104–32; 205–19; 447–63.

General Printed Primary

Anon. *Vertue Rewarded; Or, The Irish Princess*. Eds. Ian Campbell Ross and Anne Markey. Dublin: Four Courts Press, 2010.

Astell, Mary. *A Serious Proposal to the Ladies, by Mary Astell*. Ed. Patricia Springborg. Peterborough: Broadview Press, 2002.

Austen, Jane. *Northanger Abbey, Lady Susan, The Watsons, Sandition*. Oxford: OUP, 2008.

Beadle, John. *A Journal or Diary of a Thankful Christian*. London, 1656.

Burke, Edmund. *An Enquiry into the Origins of our Ideas of the Sublime and Beautiful*. London, 1757.

Burney, Frances. *Evelina*. Ed. Edward A. Bloom. Oxford: OUP, 2008.

Burney, Frances. *The Memoirs of Doctor Burney*. London, 1832.

Collier, Mary. *Poems on Several Occasions...* Winchester, 1762.

Defoe, Daniel. *The Fortunes and Misfortunes of the Famous Moll Flanders...* Eds. G. A. Starr and Linda Bree. Oxford: OUP, 2011.

Denny, Arabella. '"My dear Lady C": Letters of Lady Arabella Denny to Lady Caldwell, 1754–1777'. Ed. Rosemary Raughter. *Analecta Hibernica* 41 (2009): 133–200.

Drennan, William, and Martha McTier. *The Drennan-McTier Letters 1776–1819*. Eds. Jean Agnew and Maria Luddy. 3 vols. Dublin: IMC, 1998–2000.

Duck, Stephen. *Poems on Several Occasions…* London, 1736.

Edgeworth, Maria. *The Absentee*. Ed. Heidi Thomson. London: Penguin Books, 2007.

Edgeworth, Maria. *Belinda*. Ed. Kathryn Kirkpatrick. Oxford: OUP, 2009.

Edgeworth, Maria. *Castle Rackrent. An Hibernian Tale*. London, 1800.

Edgeworth, Maria. *An Essay on Irish Bulls*. Eds. Marilyn Butler, Jane Demarias, and Tim McLoughlin. London: Pickering & Chatto, 1999.

Edgeworth, Maria. *Maria Edgeworth's Letters from Ireland*. Ed. Valerie Pakenham. Dublin: Lilliput Press, 2018.

Edgeworth, Maria, and Richard Lovell Edgeworth. *Memoirs of Richard Lovell Edgeworth, Esq.* 2 vols. London, 1820.

Edgeworth, Maria, and Richard Lovell Edgeworth. *Practical Education*. Ed. Mitzy Myers. London: Pickering & Chatto, 1996.

Elder, Olivia. *The Poems of Olivia Elder*. Ed. Andrew Carpenter. Dublin: IMC, 2020.

Goff, Dinah. *Divine Protection Through Extraordinary Dangers During the Irish Rebellion in 1798*. Philadelphia, 1890.

Goldsmith, Oliver. *The Vicar of Wakefield*. Ed. Arthur Friedman. Oxford: OUP, 2008.

Graves, Richard. 'The Heroines: or, Modern Memoirs'. *A Collection of Poems in Six Volumes. By Several Hands*. London, 1763.

Griffith, Elizabeth and Richard Griffith, *A Series of Genuine Letters Between Henry and Frances*. London, 1766.

Haywood, Eliza. *The City Jilt*. London, 1764.

Haywood, Eliza. *The History of Miss Betsy Thoughtless*. 4th ed. London, 1768.

Hogg, James. *Private Memoirs and Confessions of a Justified Sinner*. Ed. Ian Duncan. Oxford: OUP, 2010.

Kelly, Dominick. '"The Battle of the Chaunters" Sequence from *Fugitive Pieces* (1770)'. Eds. Ian Campbell Ross and Anne Markey. *Eighteenth-Century Ireland* 33 (2018): 133–54.

Kelly, Gary, ed. *Bluestocking Feminism: Writings of the Bluestocking Circle 1738–1790*. London: Pickering & Chatto, 1999.

Leadbeater, Mary. *Cottage Dialogues. Vol. 1*. Dublin and London, 1811.

Leadbeater, Mary. [Anon.] *Extracts and Original Anecdotes for the Improvement of Youth*. Dublin, 1794.

Leadbeater, Mary. *The Leadbeater Papers. The Annals of Ballitore… And the Correspondence of Mrs. R. Trench and Rev. George Crabbe with Mary Leadbeater*. [Ed. Elizabeth Shackleton.] 2 vols. London and Dublin, 1862.

Leadbeater, Mary. *Memoirs and Letters of Richard and Elizabeth Shackleton, Late of Ballitore, Ireland; Compiled by their Daughter, Mary Leadbeater…* London, 1822.

Leadbeater, Mary. *Poems, by Mary Leadbeater, (Late Shackleton)...* London, 1808.

Leeson, Margaret. *The Memoirs of Mrs Margaret Leeson. Written by herself...* Dublin, 1795–1797.

Opie, Amelia. *The Father and Daughter.* London, 1801.

Pilkington, Laetitia. *The Memoirs of Laetitia Pilkington.* Ed. A. C. Elias, Jr. 2 vols. Athens: University of Georgia Press, 1997.

Pilkington, Laetitia. *Memoirs of Mrs Laetitia Pilkington, Wife to the Reverend Mr Mathew Pilkington, Written by Herself. Wherein are occasionally interspersed, All Her Poems.* 2 vols. Dublin, 1748.

Radcliffe, Ann. *A Sicilian Romance.* Ed. Alison Milbank. Oxford: OUP, 2008.

Radcliffe, Ann. *The Mysteries of Udolpho.* Ed. Bonamy Dobrée. Oxford: OUP, 2008.

Richardson, Samuel. *Clarissa: Or, The History of a Young Lady.* Eds. John Richetti and Toni Bowers. Toronto: Broadview, 2010.

Richardson, Samuel. *Pamela.* Eds. Thomas Keymer and Alice Wakely. Oxford: OUP, 2008.

Sheridan, Frances. *The Memoirs of Miss Sidney Bidulph.* Ed. Heidi Hutner and Nicole Garret. Toronto: Broadview, 2011.

Smollett, Tobias. *The Expedition of Humphry Clinker.* Ed. Lewis M Knapp. Oxford: OUP, 2009.

Sterne, Laurence. *The Life and Opinions of Tristram Shandy, Gentleman.* Ed. Ian Campbell Ross. Oxford: OUP, 2009.

Taylor, Ellen. *Poems by Ellen Taylor, the Irish Cottager.* Dublin, 1792.

Tighe, Mary. *Selena.* Ed. Harriet Kramer Linkin. Farnham: Ashgate, 2012.

Trench, Melesina Chenevix St. George. [Published anon.] *Campaspe, an Historical Tale; And Other Poems.* Southampton, 1815.

Trench, Melesina Chenevix St. George. [Published anon.] *Ellen, a Ballad. Founded on a Recent Fact. And Other Poems. Sold for the Benefit of the House of Protection.* Bath, 1815.

Trench, Melesina Chenevix St. George. [Published anon.] *Lady Mary Queen of Scots, an Historical Ballad; with Other Poems. By a lady.* London: Stockdale, 1800.

Trench, Melesina Chenevix St. George. [Published anon.] *Laura's Dream; Or The Moonlanders.* London, 1816.

Waterland, Daniel. *The Works of The Rev. Daniel Waterland, D. D.* Ed. William Van Mildert. 6 vols. Oxford: OUP, 1843.

Wollstonecraft, Mary. *Mary and The Wrongs of Woman.* Ed. Gary Kelly. Oxford: OUP, 2009.

Wollstonecraft, Mary. *A Vindication of the Rights of Woman.* Ed. Janet Todd. Oxford: OUP, 2008.

Wood, John. *A Description of Bath.* 2 vols. London, 1765.

Yearsley, Ann. *Poems, on several occasions. By Ann Yearsley, a milkwoman of Bristol*. 2nd ed. London, 1785.

Young, Arthur. *A Tour in Ireland: with General Observations on the Present State of that Kingdom. Made in the Years 1776, 1777, and 1778*. Dublin, 1780.

Secondary Sources

Aalders, Cynthia. '"Your journal, my love": Constructing Personal and Religious Bonds in Eighteenth-Century Women's Diaries'. *Journal of Religious History*, 39.3 (2015): 386–98.

Ahern, Michael. 'The Quakers of County Tipperary 1655–1924'. PhD Thesis, NUI Maynooth, 2003.

Aikin, Síobhra. *Spiritual Wounds: Trauma, Testimony and the Irish Civil War*. Dublin: Irish Academic Press, 2022.

Alberti, Fay Bound. 'This "Modern Epidemic": Loneliness as an Emotion Cluster and a Neglected Subject in the History of Emotions'. *Emotion Review* 10.3 (July 2018): 242–54.

Alberti, Fay Bound. 'When "Oneliness" Becomes Loneliness: The Birth of a Modern Emotion'. *A Biography of Loneliness: The History of an Emotion*. Oxford: OUP, 2009.

Allen, Robert C. *The British Industrial Revolution in Global Perspective*. Cambridge: CUP, 2009.

Anderson, Benedict. *Imagined Communities: Reflections on the Origin and Spread of Nationalism*. 1983. Revised ed. New York: Verso, 2006.

Andersson, L. 'Loneliness Research and Interventions: A Review of the Literature'. *Aging and Mental Health* 4.2 (1998): 264–74.

Ashford, Gabrielle. 'Childhood: Studies in the History of Children in Eighteenth-Century Ireland'. PhD Thesis, St. Patrick's College, DCU, 2012.

Ballaster, Ros. *Seductive Forms: Women's Amatory Fiction from 1684 to 1740*. Oxford: Clarendon Press, 1992.

Barclay, Katie. 'From Rape to Marriage: Questions of Consent in Eighteenth-Century Britain'. *Interpreting Sexual Violence, 1660–1800*. Ed. Anne Leah Greenfield. London: Pickering & Chatto, 2014, 35–44.

Barclay, Katie. *Love, Intimacy and Power: Marriage and Patriarchy in Scotland, 1650–1850*. Manchester: MUP, 2011.

Barclay, Katie, and Sarah Richardson. 'Introduction. Performing the Self: Women's Lives in Historical Perspective'. *Women's History Review*. Special issue: 22.2 (2013): 177–81.

Barnard, Toby. *The Abduction of a Limerick Heiress*. Dublin: Irish Academic Press, 1998.

Barnard, Toby. 'The Hartlib Circle and the Cult and Culture of Improvement in Ireland'. *Samuel Hartlib and Universal Reformation: Studies in Intellectual*

Communication. Eds. Mark Greengrass, Leslie Michael, and Timothy Raylor. Cambridge: CUP, 1994.

Barnard, Toby. *Improving Ireland? Projectors, Prophets and Profiteers, 1641–1786*. Dublin: Four Courts Press, 2008.

Barnard, Toby. 'Libraries and Collectors, 1700–1800'. *The Oxford History of the Irish Book, Volume 3*. Eds. Raymond Gillespie and Andrew Hadfield. Oxford: OUP, 2006, 111–34.

Barnard, Toby. *Making the Grand Figure: Lives and Possessions in Ireland, 1641–1770*. New Haven and London: Yale UP, 2004.

Barnard, Toby. *A New Anatomy of Ireland: The Irish Protestants, 1649–1770*. New Haven and London: Yale UP, 2004.

Bartlett, Thomas. 'Ireland During the Revolutionary and Napoleonic Wars, 1791–1815'. *The Cambridge History of Ireland, Volume 3, 1730–1880*. Ed. James Kelly. Cambridge: CUP, 2018, 74–101.

Batchelor, Jennie. 'Fashion and Frugality: Eighteenth-Century Pocket Books for Women'. *Studies in Eighteenth-Century Culture* 32 (2003): 1–18.

Beattie, Heather. 'Where Narratives Meet: Archival Description, Provenance, and Women's Diaries'. *Libraries & the Cultural Record* 44.1 (2009): 82–100.

Beatty, John D., ed. *Protestant Women's Narratives of the Irish Rebellion of 1798*. Dublin: Four Courts Press, 2001.

Behrendt, Stephen. '"There is no second crop of summer flowers": Mary Leadbeater and Melesina Trench in Correspondence'. *Forum for Modern Language Studies* 52.2 (2016): 130–43.

Bellanca, Mary Ellen. *Daybooks of Discovery: Nature Diaries in Britain, 1770–1870*. Charlottesville: University of Virginia Press, 2007.

Bending, Stephen. *Green Retreats: Women, Gardens and Eighteenth-Century Culture*. Cambridge: CUP, 2013.

Bergin, John, Eoin Magennis, Lesa Ní Mhunghaile, and Patrick Walsh. *New Perspectives on the Penal Laws*, *Eighteenth-Century Ireland* Special Issue 1 (2011): 1–290.

Berndt, Thomas J. 'The Features and Effects of Friendship in Early Adolescence'. *Child Development* 53.6 (1982): 1447–60.

Bigold, Melanie. *Women of Letters, Manuscript Circulation and Print Afterlives in the Eighteenth Century*. Basingstoke: Palgrave, 2013.

Blackstock, Allan F. '"A dangerous species of ally": Orangeism and the Irish Yeomanry'. *Irish Historical Studies* 30.119 (1997): 393–407.

Blodgett, Harriet. *Centuries of Female Days: Englishwomen's Private Diaries*. New Brunswick: Rutgers UP, 1988.

Bloom, Lynn Z. '"I write for Myself and Strangers": Private Diaries as Public Document'. *Inscribing the Daily: Critical Essays on Women's Diaries*. Eds. Suzanne Bunkers and Cynthia Huff. Amherst: University of Massachusetts Press, 1996, 171–85.

Boldrini, Lucia, and Julia Novak, eds. *Experiments in Life Writing*. Basingstoke: Palgrave, 2017.

Borsay, Peter. *The English Urban Renaissance: Culture and Society in the Provincial Town*. Oxford: Clarendon Press, 1989.

Borsay, Peter, and Jan Hein Furnée, eds. *Leisure Cultures in Urban Europe c. 1700–1870: A Transnational Perspective*. Manchester: MUP, 2015.

Botonaki, Effie. 'Seventeenth-Century Englishwomen's Spiritual Diaries: Self-Examination, Covenanting, and Account Keeping'. *The Sixteenth Century Journal* 30.1 (1999): 3–21.

Bourke, Angela, Maria Luddy, Siobhán Kilfeather, Margaret MacCurtain, Gerardine Meaney, Máirín Ní Dhonnchadha, Mary O'Dowd, and Clair Wills, eds. *The Field Day Anthology of Irish Writing, vols. 4 and 5, Irish Women's Writing and Traditions*. Cork: Cork UP, 2002.

Brant, Clare. *Eighteenth-Century Letters and British Culture*. Basingstoke: Palgrave, 2006.

Breen, Catherine Mary. 'The Making and Unmaking of an Irish Woman of Letters'. PhD Thesis, University of Oxford, 2012.

Brewer, John. *The Pleasures of the Imagination*. London: Routledge, 2013.

Brown, Michael. *The Irish Enlightenment*. Cambridge, MA: Harvard UP, 2016.

Brown, Michael, and Lesa Ní Mhunghaile, 'Enlightenment and Antiquarianism in the Eighteenth Century'. *Cambridge History of Ireland, Volume 3*. Cambridge: CUP, 2018, 380–405.

Buchanan, Averill. *Mary Blachford Tighe: The Irish Psyche*. Cambridge: Cambridge Scholars Publishing, 2011.

Buckley, Sarah Anne. 'Women, Men and the Family, *c*.1730–*c*.1880'. *The Cambridge History of Ireland, Volume 3, 1730–1880*. Ed. James Kelly. CUP, 2018, 231–54.

Byrne, Angela. 'Life Lines: Agency and Autobiography in Sarah Curran's Poetry'. *Women's History Review* 32.1 (2023): 126–41.

Byrne, Angela. 'Supplementing the Autobiography of Princess Ekaterina Romanovna Dashkova: The Russian Diaries of Martha and Katherine Wilmot'. *Irish Slavonic Studies* 23 (2011): 25–34.

Calvert, Leanne. '"From a woman's point of view': The Presbyterian Archive as a Source for Women's and Gender History in Eighteenth and Nineteenth-Century Ireland'. *Irish Historical Studies. Special Issue: A New Agenda for Women's and Gender History in Ireland* 46 (2022): 301–18.

Calvert, Leanne. '"He came to her bed pretending courtship": Sex, Courtship and the Making of Marriage in Ulster, 1750–1844'. *Irish Historical Studies* (2018): 244–64.

Carpenter, Andrew. 'Land and Landscape in Irish Poetry in English, 1700–1780'. *Irish Literature in Transition, 1700–1780*. Ed. Moyra Haslett. Cambridge: CUP, 2020, 151–70.

Carpenter, Andrew. *Verse in English from Eighteenth-Century Ireland*. Cork: Cork UP, 1998.

Carpenter, Andrew. 'Working-Class Writing in Ireland before 1800'. *A History of Irish Working-Class Writing*. Ed. Michael Pierse. Cambridge: CUP, 2017, 72–88.

Carpenter, Andrew, and Lucy Collins. *The Irish Poet and the Natural World*. Cork: Cork UP, 2014.

Carter, Kathryn. *Diaries in English by Women in Canada, 1755–1795: An Annotated Bibliography*. Ottawa: CRIAW/ICREF, 1997.

Carter, Kathryn. *The Small Details of Life: 20 Diaries by Women in Canada, 1830–1996*. Toronto: University of Toronto Press, 2002.

Clark, Anna. *Women's Silence, Men's Violence: Sexual Assault in England, 1770–1845*. London: Pandora, 1987.

Clark, Lorna J. 'The Diarist as Novelist: Narrative Strategies in the Journals and Letters of Frances Burney'. *English Studies in Canada* 27.3 (2001): 283–302.

Clarke, Norma. 'Bluestocking Fictions: Devotional Writings, Didactic Literature and the Imperative of Female Improvement'. *Women, Gender and Enlightenment*. Eds. Sarah Knott and Barbara Taylor. Basingstoke: Palgrave, 2007, 460–73.

Clarke, Odette. 'Caroline Wyndham-Quin, Countess of Dunraven (1790–1870): An Analysis of Her Discursive and Material Legacy'. PhD Thesis, University of Limerick, 2010.

Cogan, Lucy. 'Fountains of Wine: The Drunken Excesses of Georgian Ireland and the End of an Era'. *Irish Times* (21 September 2021).

Cohen, Jere. *Protestantism and Capitalism: The Mechanisms of Influence*. London: Routledge, 2002.

Colley, Linda. *Britons: Forging the Nation, 1707–1837*. New Haven: Yale UP, 1992.

Colombo, Claire Miller. '"This pen of mine will say too much": Public Performance in the Journals of Anna Larpent'. *Texas Studies in Literature and Language* 38.3/4 (1996): 286.

Connolly, Claire. 'Irish Romanticism, 1800–1830'. *The Cambridge History of Irish Literature, Volume 1, to 1890*. Eds. Margaret Kelleher and P. O'Leary. Cambridge: CUP, 2006, 407–48.

Connolly, S. J. 'Family, Love and Marriage: Some Evidence from the Early 18th Century'. *Women in Early Modern Ireland*. Eds. Margaret MacCurtain and Mary O'Dowd. Dublin: Wolfhound Press, 1991, 276–90.

Connolly, S. J. 'Jacobites, Whiteboys and Republicans: Varieties of Disaffection in Eighteenth-Century Ireland'. *Eighteenth-Century Ireland* 18 (2003): 63–79.

Connolly, S. J. *Religion, Law, and Power: The Making of Protestant Ireland 1660–1760*. Oxford: Clarendon Press, 1995.

Connolly, S. J. 'A Woman's Life in Mid-Eighteenth-Century Ireland: The Case of Letitia Bushe'. *The Historical Journal* 43.2 (2000): 433–51.

Conway, Stephen. *Britain, Ireland, and Continental Europe in the Eighteenth Century: Similarities, Connections, Identities*. Oxford: OUP, 2011.

Coolahan, Marie-Louise. '"It is with pleasure I lay hold of evry occasion of wrightin": Female Domestic Servants, *The Bordeaux-Dublin Letters*, and the Epistolary Novel'. *Ireland, France and the Atlantic in a Time of War: Reflections on the Bordeaux-Dublin Letters, 1757*. London: Routledge, 2017.

Costello, Vandra. *Irish Demesne Landscapes, 1660–1740*. Dublin: Four Courts Press, 2015.

Craciun, Adriana. 'Eliza Mary Hamilton'. *Irish Women Poets of the Romantic Period*. Alexandria, VA: Alexander Street Press, 2008.

Crookshank, C. H. *Memorable women of Irish Methodism in the last century*. London, 1882.

Crowell, Ellen. 'Ghosting the Ladies of Llangollen: Female Intimacies, Ascendancy Exiles, and the Anglo-Irish Novel'. *Eire-Ireland* 39.3–4 (2004): 202–27.

Culley, Amy. *British Women's Life Writing, 1760–1840, Friendship, Community and Collaboration*. Basingstoke: Palgrave, 2014.

Culley, Amy, and Daniel Cook, eds. *Women's Life Writing, 1700–1850: Gender, Genre and Authorship*. Basingstoke: Palgrave, 2012.

Curtin, Nancy J. *The United Irishmen: Popular Politics in Ulster and Dublin, 1791–1798*. Oxford: OUP, 1998.

Darcy, Ailbhe, and David Wheatley, eds. *A History of Irish Women's Poetry*. Cambridge: CUP, 2021.

de Groot, Joanna. 'Metropolitan Desires and Colonial Connections: Reflections on Consumption and Empire'. *At Home with the Empire*. Eds. Catherine Hall and Sonya O. Rose. Cambridge: CUP, 2006, 166–90.

DeLoughrey, Elizabeth, and George B. Handley. *Postcolonial Ecologies: Literatures of the Environment*. Oxford: OUP, 2011.

Desiderio, Jennifer. 'The Life Itself: Quaker Women's Diaries and the Secular Impulse'. *Early American Literature* 49.1 (2014): 185–99.

Doll, Dan, and Jessica Munns. *Recording and Reordering: Essays on the Seventeenth- and Eighteenth-Century Diary and Journal*. Lewisburg: Bucknell UP, 2006.

Donaghy, Paige. 'Miscarriage, False Conceptions, and Other Lumps: Women's Pregnancy Loss in Seventeenth- and Eighteenth-Century England'. *Social History of Medicine* (2021): 1–23.

Dooley, Terence, and Christopher Ridgway, eds. *The Irish Country House: Its Past, Present and Future*. Dublin: Four Courts Press, 2011.

Douglas, Aileen. *Uneasy Sensations: Smollett and the Body*. Chicago: University of Chicago Press, 1995.

Douglas, Aileen. *Work in Hand: Script, Print, and Writing, 1690–1840*. Oxford: OUP, 2017.

Dowd, Michelle M., and Julie A. Eckerle. *Genre and Women's Life Writing in Early Modern England*. London: Routledge, 2007.

Dowd-Arrow, Emily J. and Sarah R. Creel, '"I know you want it": Teaching the Blurred Lines of Eighteenth-Century Rape Culture'. *ABO: Interactive Journal for Women in the Arts, 1640–1830*. 6.2.2 (2016): n.p.

Duffy, Patrick. 'Landed Estates in 19th Century Ireland'. *Dis(Placing) Empire*. Eds. L. J. Proudfoot and M. M. Roche. Aldershot: Ashgate, 2005, 15–40.

Durey, Michael. 'Abduction and Rape in Ireland in the Era of the 1798 Rebellion'. *Eighteenth-Century Ireland* 21 (2006): 27–47.

Eckerle, Julie A., and Naomi McAreavey. *Women's Life Writing & Early Modern Ireland*. Lincoln: University of Nebraska Press, 2019.

Egenolf, Susan B. '"Our fellow creatures": Women Narrating Political Violence in the 1798 Irish Rebellion'. *Eighteenth-Century Studies* 42.2 (2009): 217–34.

Eger, Elizabeth. *Bluestockings: Women of Reason from Enlightenment to Romanticism*. Basingstoke: Palgrave, 2010.

Eger, Elizabeth, Charlotte Grant, Clíona Ó Gallchoir, and Penny Warburton, eds., *Women, Writing and the Public Sphere, 1700–1830*. New York: Cambridge UP, 2001.

Fabricant, Carole. 'Colonial Sublimities and Sublimations: Swift, Burke, and Ireland'. *ELH* 72.2 (2005): 309–37.

Fasick, Laura. *Vessels of Meaning: Women's Bodies, Gender Norms, and Class Bias from Richardson to Lawrence*. Dekalb: Northern Illinois UP, 1997.

Feeny, Nollaig. 'King House, Boyle, Co. Roscommon' *History Ireland* 5.21 (Sept/Oct 2013).

Fitzpatrick, David. 'Divorce and Separation in Modern Irish History'. *Past & Present* 114 (1987): 172–97.

Fleming, David. *Politics and Provincial People: Sligo and Limerick, 1691–1761*. Manchester: MUP, 2010.

Fleming, N. C. *Ireland and Anglo-Irish Relations since 1800: Critical Essays, Volume 1*. Aldershot: Ashgate, 2008.

Forsythe, Wes. 'The Measures and Materiality of Improvement in Ireland'. *Journal of Historical Archaeology* 17.1 (2013): 72–93.

Garrard, Greg. *Ecocriticism*. London: Routledge, 2012.

Genette, Gérard. *Paratexts: Thresholds of Interpretation*. Trans. Jane E. Lewin. Cambridge: CUP, 1997.

Gibbons, Luke. *Edmund Burke and Ireland: Aesthetics, Politics and the Colonial Sublime*. Cambridge: CUP, 2003.

Gifford, Terry. *Pastoral*. London: Routledge, 1999.

Gifford, Terry. 'Pastoral, Anti-Pastoral and Post-Pastoral as Reading Strategies'. *Critical Insights Series: Nature and the Environment*. Ed. Scott Slovic. Ipswich: Salam Press, 2012, 42–61.

Gillespie, Niall. 'Irish Political Literature, c. 1788–1832'. PhD Thesis, TCD, 2013.

Glotfelty, Cheryll. *The Ecocriticism Reader.* Athens: University of Georgia Press, 1996.

Gómez, Miguel Casas. 'The Expressive Creativity of Euphemism and Dysphemism'. *Lexis* 7 (2012): 43–64.

Goodbody, Olive C. 'Irish Quaker Diaries'. *Guide to Irish Quaker Records, 1654–1860.* Dublin: IMC, 1967, 1–14.

Goodman, Dena. *Becoming a Woman in the Age of Letters.* Ithaca: Cornell UP, 2009.

Gores, Steven. *Psychosocial Spaces: Verbal and Visual Readings of British Culture, 1750–1820.* Detroit: Wayne State UP, 2000.

Gray, David. 'An Ecocritical Reading of Ulster-Scots Poetry c. 1790–1850'. PhD Thesis, Ulster University, 2014.

Gray, David. '"Stemmed from the Scots"? The Ulster-Scots Literary Braird and the Pastoral Tradition'. *Eighteenth-Century Ireland* 32 (2017): 28–43.

Gribben, Crawford. *The Rise and Fall of Christian Ireland.* Oxford: OUP, 2021.

Gribben, Crawford, and Graeme Murdock, eds. *Cultures of Calvinism in Early Modern Europe.* Oxford: OUP, 2019.

Gurrin, Brian, Kerby A. Miller, and Liam Kennedy. *The Irish Religious Censuses of the 1760s: Catholics and Protestants in Eighteenth-Century Ireland.* Dublin: IMC, 2022.

Ingram, Allan, Stuart Sim, Clark Lawlor, Richard Terry, John Baker, and Leigh Wetherall-Dickson. *Literature of the Long Eighteenth Century: Before Depression, 1660–1800.* Basingstoke: Palgrave, 2011.

Hall, Catherine, and Sonya O. Rose, eds. *At Home with the Empire*: *Metropolitan Culture and the Imperial World.* Cambridge: CUP, 2006.

Hannan, Leonie. *Women of Letters: Gender, Writing and the Life of the Mind in Early Modern England.* Manchester: MUP, 2016.

Harol, Corrinne. *Enlightened Virginity in Eighteenth-Century Literature.* Basingstoke: Palgrave, 2006.

Harris, Alexa. *Weatherland, Writers and Artists under English Skies.* London: Thames and Hudson, 2015.

Harte, Liam, ed. *A History of Irish Autobiography.* Cambridge: CUP, 2018.

Haslett, Moyra. "All pent up together": Representations of Friendship in Fictions of Girls' Boarding Schools, 1680–1800'. *Journal for Eighteenth-Century Studies* 41.1 (2018): 81–99.

Haslett, Moyra. 'Experimentalism in the Irish Novel, 1750–1770'. *Irish University Review* 41.1 (2011): 63–79.

Haslett, Moyra. 'Fictions of Sisterhood in Eighteenth-Century Irish Writing'. *Irish Literature in Transition, 1700–1780.* Ed. Moyra Haslett. Cambridge: CUP, 2020, 284–304.

Haslett, Moyra. '"For the Improvement and Amusement of Young Ladies": Elizabeth Carter and the Bluestockings in Ireland'. *Eighteenth-Century Ireland* 33 (2018): 33–60.

Haslett, Moyra. 'Introduction'. *Irish Literature in Transition, 1700–1780*. Ed. Moyra Haslett. Cambridge: CUP, 2020, 1–27.

Hatton, Helen Elizabeth. *Largest Amount of Good: Quaker Relief in Ireland, 1654-1921*. Montreal: McGill-Queen's Press, 1993.

Henderson, Desirée. 'Reading Digitized Diaries: Privacy and the Digital Life-Writing Archive'. *Auto/Biography Studies* 33.1 (2018): 157–74.

Herman, Joel. 'Imagined Nations: Newspapers, Identity, and the Free Trade Crisis of 1779'. *Eighteenth-Century Ireland* 35 (2020): 51–69.

Hershinow, Stephanie Insley. *Born Yesterday: Inexperience and the Early Realist Novel*. Baltimore: Johns Hopkins UP, 2019.

Higgins, Padhraig. 'Consumption, Gender, and the Politics of "Free Trade" in Eighteenth-Century Ireland'. *Eighteenth-Century Studies* 41 (2007): 87–105.

Higgins, Padhraig. *A Nation of Politicians: Gender, Patriotism, and Political Culture in Late Eighteenth-Century Ireland*. Wisconsin: University of Wisconsin Press, 2010.

Holmes, Andrew. *The Shaping of Ulster Presbyterian Belief and Practice, 1770–1840*. Oxford: OUP, 2006.

Holmes, Andrew, and Crawford Gribben, eds. *Protestant Millennialism, Evangelicalism and Irish Society, 1790–2005*. Basingstoke: Palgrave, 2006.

Howard, Martin R. 'Red Jackets and Red Noses: Alcohol and the British Napoleonic Soldier'. *Journal of the Royal Society of Medicine* 93 (2000): 38–41.

Hoyle, Richard W., ed. *Custom, Improvement and the Landscape in Early Modern Britain*. London: Routledge, 2017.

Hughes, Barbara. *Between Literature and History: The Diaries and Memoirs of Dorothea Herbert and Mary Leadbeater*. Bern: Peter Lang, 2010.

Hussain, Mobeen, Ciaran O'Neill, and Patrick Walsh, 'Working Paper on George Berkeley's Legacies at Trinity,' TARA, 2023. http://hdl.handle.net/2262/104216.

Huth, Kimberly. 'Come Live with Me and Feed My Sheep: Invitation, Ownership, and Belonging in Early Modern Pastoral Literature'. *Studies in Philology* 108.1 (2011): 44–69.

Jackson, Stanley. *Melancholia and Depression: From Hippocratic Times to Modern Times*. New Haven: Yale UP, 1986.

James, Felicity, and Julian North. 'Writing Lives Together: Romantic and Victorian Auto/biography'. *Life Writing* 14.2 (2017): 133–38.

Jansson, Åsa. *From Melancholia to Depression*. Basingstoke: Palgrave, 2021.

Jenkins, Brian. *Irish Nationalism and the British State: From Repeal to Revolutionary Nationalism*. Montreal: McGill-Queen's UP, 2006.

Jones, Catherine. 'Irish Romanticism'. *A History of Irish Women's Poetry*. Eds. Ailbhe Darcy and David Wheatley. Cambridge: CUP, 2021, 106–09.

Kelly, James. 'The Abduction of Women of Fortune in Eighteenth-Century Ireland'. *Eighteenth-Century Ireland* 9 (1994): 7–43.

Kelly, James, ed. *The Cambridge History of Ireland, Volume 3, 1730–1880*. Cambridge: CUP, 2018.

Kelly, James. 'The Consumption and Sociable Use of Alcohol in Eighteenth-Century Ireland'. *Proceedings of the Royal Irish Academy* 115 (2015): 219–55.

Kelly, James. '"A most inhuman and barbarous piece of villainy": An Exploration of the Crime of Rape in Eighteenth-Century Ireland'. *Eighteenth-Century Ireland* 10 (1995): 78–107.

Kelly, James, and Ciarán Mac Murchaidh, eds. *Essays on the Irish Linguistic Cultural Frontier, 1600–1900*. Dublin: Four Courts, 2012.

Kelly, Jim, ed. *Ireland and Romanticism: Publics, Nations and Scenes of Cultural Production*. Basingstoke: Palgrave, 2011.

Kelly, Matthew. *Nature and the Environment in Nineteenth-Century Ireland*. Liverpool: LUP, 2019.

Kelsall, M. 'Edgeworthstown "Rebuilding"'. *Literary Representations of the Irish Country House*. Basingstoke: Palgrave, 2003, 29–78.

Kennedy, Catriona. *Narratives of the Revolutionary and Napoleonic Wars: Military and Civilian Experience in Britain and Ireland*. Basingstoke: Palgrave, 2013.

Kennedy, Catriona, and Mathew McCormack, eds. *Soldiering in Britain and Ireland, 1750–1850*. Basingstoke: Palgrave, 2013.

Keogh, Dáire, and Nicholas Furlong. *The Women of 1798*. Dublin: Four Courts Press, 1998.

Kirsch, Hiltrud Susanna. 'The Body in Adolescent Diaries, The Case of Karen Horney'. *The Psychoanalytic Study of the Child* 57.1 (2002): 400–10.

Kittredge, Katharine. '"I delight in the success of your literary labours": Friendship as Platform for Reinvention'. *The Circuit of Apollo: Eighteenth-Century Women's Tributes to Women*. Eds. Laura L. Runge and Jessica Cook. Newark: University of Delaware Press, 2019, 155–75.

Kittredge, Katharine. '"It spoke directly to the heart": Discovering the Mourning Journal of Melesina Trench'. *Tulsa Studies in Women's Literature* 25.2 (2006): 335–45.

Kittredge, Katharine. 'A Long-Forgotten Sorrow: The Mourning Journal of Melesina Trench'. *Eighteenth-Century Fiction* 21.1 (2008): 153–77.

Kittredge, Katharine. 'The Poetry of Melesina Trench: A Growing Skill at Sorrow'. *British Journal for Eighteenth-Century Studies* 28 (2005): 201–13.

Knott, Sarah, and Barbara Taylor, eds. *Women, Gender and Enlightenment*. Basingstoke: Palgrave, 2007.

Kouffman, Avra. '"Why feignest thou thyselfe to be another woman?": Constraints on the Construction of Subjectivity in Mary Rich's Diary'. *Women's Life-Writing: Finding Voice/Building Community*. Ed. Linda S. Coleman. Bowling Green: Bowling Green State University Popular Press, 1997, 11–22.

Lakūs, Jelena, and Anita Bajić. 'Interpreting Diaries: History of Reading and the Diary of the Nineteenth-Century Croatian Female Writer Dragojla Jarnević'. *Information & Culture* 52.2 (2017): 163–85.

Lamata, Juan Pedro. "'[A]ltered that a little which before I had written": How Margaret Hoby Wrote and Rewrote Her Manuscript'. *Renaissance Studies* (2023): 1–20.

Langford, Rachael, and Russell West. 'Introduction: Diaries and Margins'. *Marginal Voices, Marginal Forms: Diaries in European Literature and History.* Eds. Rachael Langford and Russell West. Amsterdam: Rodopi, 1999, 6–21.

Lawlor, Clark. *From Melancholia to Prozac: A History of Depression.* Oxford: OUP, 2012.

Lawrence, Donna M., and Mary Jane Schank, 'Health Care Diaries of Young Women'. *Journal of Community Health Nursing* 12.3 (1995): 171–82.

Leerssen, Joep. *Mere Irish and Fíor-Ghael: Studies in the Idea of Irish Nationality, Its Development, and Literary Expression Prior to the Nineteenth Century.* Amsterdam: John Benjamins, 1986.

Lejeune, Philippe. *Aux Origines du Journal Personnel: France, 1750–1815.* Paris: Honoré Champion, 2016.

Lejeune, Philippe. *On Diary.* Eds. Jermey D. Popkin and Julie Rak. Honolulu: University of Hawaii, 2009.

Lenox-Conyngham, Melosina. *Diaries of Ireland.* Dublin: Lilliput Press, 1998.

Lett, Barbara Newton. 'A '98 Diary by Mrs. Barbara Newton Lett, Killaligan, Enniscorthy'. *The Past: The Organ of the Uí Cinsealaigh Historical Society* 5 (1949): 117–78.

Levy, Michelle, and Betty A. Schellenberg. *How and Why to Do Things with Eighteenth-Century Manuscripts.* Cambridge: CUP, 2021.

Liira, Aino, and Sirkku Ruokkeinen. 'Material Approaches to Exploring the Borders of Paratext'. *Textual Cultures* 11.1–2 (2019): 106–29.

Linder, Lynn M., ed. 'Co-Constructed Selves: Nineteenth-Century Collaborative Life Writing'. Special Issue of *Forum for Modern Language Studies* 52.2 (2016): 121–29.

Linkin, Harriet Kramer. 'Mary Tighe's Newly Discovered Letters and Journals to Caroline Hamilton'. *Romanticism* (2015): 207–27.

Livesey, James. *Civil Society and Empire.* New Haven: Yale UP, 2009.

Longley, Paul Arthur. 'Eighteenth-Century Imaginary Voyages to the Antipodes'. *The Eighteenth Century* 49.3 (2008): 197–210.

Looser, Devoney. *British Women Writers and the Writing of History, 1670–1820.* Baltimore: Johns Hopkins UP, 2005.

Lucas, Kristen, and Jeremy P. Fyke, 'Euphemisms and Ethics: A Language-Centered Analysis of Penn State's Sexual Abuse Scandal'. *Journal of Business Ethics* 122.4 (2014): 551–69.

Luddy, Maria. 'Irish Women's Spiritual and Religious Life Writing in the Late Eighteenth and Nineteenth Centuries'. *A History of Irish Autobiography.* Ed. Liam Harte. Cambridge: CUP, 2018, 69–83.

Mac Iomhair, Diarmuid. 'The Murder of Richard Dawson'. *Journal of the County Louth Archaeological Society* 15.3 (1963): 249–54.

Mac Suibhne, Breandán. 'Spirit, Spectre, Shade'. *Field Day Review* 9 (2013): 178.

MacCurtain, Margaret and Mary O'Dowd, eds. *Women in Early Modern Ireland*. Dublin: Wolfhound Press, 1991.

Magennis, Eoin. "'A land of milk and honey": The Physico-Historical Society, Improvement and the Surveys of Mid-Eighteenth Century Ireland'. *Proceedings of the Royal Irish Academy* 102C.6 (2002): 199–217.

Manly, Susan, and Joanna Wharton, eds. Special Issue: 'Worlds of Maria Edgeworth'. *European Romantic Review* 31.6 (2020): 655–786.

Markey, Anne. 'Honora Sneyd Edgeworth's "Harry and Lucy": A Case Study of Familial Literary Collaboration'. *Eighteenth-Century Ireland* 34 (2019): 50–65.

Maufort, Jessica. 'Multiple Convergences: Ecocriticism and Comparative Literary Studies'. *Recherche littéraire/Literary Research* (2019): 101–25.

Maxwell, Jane. 'The Personal Letter as a Source for the History of Women in Ireland, 1750–1830'. PhD Thesis, TCD, 2016.

McBride, Ian. *Eighteenth-Century Ireland*. Dublin: Gill & McMillan, 2009.

McBride, Ian. 'Reclaiming the Rebellion: 1798 in 1998'. *Irish Historical Studies* 31.123 (1999): 395–410.

McDonagh, Briony. *Elite Women and the Agricultural Landscape, 1700–1830*. London: Routledge, 2018.

McElroy, James. 'Ecocriticism & Irish Poetry: A Preliminary Outline'. *Estudios Irlandeses* 6 (2011): 54–69.

McGrath, Ivar, Suzanne Forbes, Imelda Haran, William Sheehan, Jennifer Shepherd. *Army Barracks of Ireland*. https://barracksireland.wordpress.com/.

Meaney, Gerardine, Mary O'Dowd, and Bernadette Whelan. *Reading the Irish Woman: Studies in Cultural Encounters and Exchange, 1714–1960*. Liverpool: LUP, 2013.

Mee, Jon. 'Introduction'. *Journal for Eighteenth-Century Studies* 38.4 (2015): 1–8.

Mendelson, Sara Heller. 'Stuart Women's Diaries and Occasional Memoirs'. *Women in English Society, 1500–1800*. Ed. Mary Prior. London: Routledge, 1985, 136–57.

Montgomery-Massingberd, Hugh, ed. *Burke's Irish Family Records*. London: Burke's Peerage, 1976.

Morin, Christina. *The Gothic Novel in Ireland c.1760–1829*. Manchester: MUP, 2018.

Morley, Vincent. 'Cíona lae na Gaeilge agus an stair,' *Cúnraí Staire* https://cstair.blogspot.com/search?q=dialann.

Morley, Vincent. 'The Irish Language'. *The Princeton History of Modern Ireland*. Eds. Richard Bourke and Ian McBride. Princeton and Oxford: Princeton UP, 2016, 320–42.

Morley, Vincent. *The Popular Mind in Eighteenth-Century Ireland*. Cork: Cork UP, 2017.

Morris, Marilyn. 'Negotiating Domesticity in the Journals of Anna Larpent'. *Journal of Women's History* 22.1 (2010): 85–106.

Mortimer, Anthony. 'Castle Rackrent and Its Historical Context'. *Études Irlandaises* (1984): 107–23.

Muir, Angela Joy. 'Midwifery and Maternity Care for Single Mothers in Eighteenth Century Wales'. *Social History of Medicine* 33.2 (2020): 394–416.

Müller, Anja, ed. *Fashioning Childhood in the Eighteenth Century: Age and Identity*. Aldershot: Ashgate, 2006.

Murtagh, Timothy. *Irish Artisans and Radical Politics, 1776–1820*. Liverpool: LUP, 2022.

Myers, Mitzi. '"Anecdotes from the Nursery" in Maria Edgeworth's *Practical Education* (1798): Learning from Children "Abroad and At Home"'. *The Princeton University Library Chronicle* 60.2 (Winter 1999): 220–50.

Ní Ghríofa, Doireann. *A Ghost in the Throat*. Dublin: Tramp Press, 2020.

Ní Mhunghaile, Lesa. 'Gaelic Literature in Transition, 1780–1830'. *Irish Literature in Transition, 1780–1830*. Ed. Claire Connolly. Cambridge: CUP, 2020, 37–51.

Ní Shíocháin, Tríona. 'The Oral Tradition'. *A History of Irish Women's Poetry*. Eds. Ailbhe Darcy and David Wheatley. Cambridge: CUP, 2021, 74–88.

Nussbaum, Felicity. *The Autobiographical Subject: Gender and Ideology in Eighteenth-Century England*. Baltimore: Johns Hopkins UP, 1989.

Nussbaum, Felicity. 'Eighteenth-Century Women's Autobiographical Commonplaces'. *The Private Self: Theory and Practice of Women's Autobiographical Writings*. Ed. Shari Benstock. Chapel Hill: University of North Carolina Press, 1988, 147–72.

Ó Ciosáin, Niall. *Print and Popular Culture in Ireland, 1750–1850*. Basingtsoke: Palgrave, 1997.

O'Connell, Helen. *Ireland and the Fiction of Improvement*. Oxford: OUP, 2006.

O'Connell, Helen. 'The Nature of Improvement in Ireland'. *Nature and the Environment in Nineteenth-Century Ireland*. Ed. Matthew Kelly. Liverpool: LUP, 2019, 16–34.

O'Connor, Catherine. 'The Experience of Women in the Rebellion of 1798 in Wexford'. *The Past: The Organ of the Uí Cinsealaigh Historical Society* 24 (2003): 95–106.

O'Connor, Thomas. 'The Catholic Church and Catholics in an Era of Sanctions'. *The Cambridge History of Ireland, Volume 3, 1730–1880*. Ed. James Kelly. Cambridge: CUP, 2018, 257–79.

O'Dowd, Mary. 'Adolescent Girlhood in Eighteenth-Century Ireland'. *A History of the Girl: Formation, Education, and Identity*. Eds. Mary O'Dowd and June Purvis. Basingstoke: Palgrave, 2018, 53–73.

O'Dowd, Mary. 'Deborah, Margaret, Mary and Sarah Shackleton'. *Sisters: Nine Families of Sisters Who Made a Difference*. Ed. Siobhán Fitzpatrick and Mary O'Dowd. Dublin: Royal Irish Academy, 2022.

O'Dowd, Mary. *A History of Women in Ireland, 1500–1800*. Harlow: Longman, 2005.

O'Dowd, Mary, and Maria Luddy. *Marriage in Ireland, 1660–1925*. Cambridge: CUP, 2020.

Ó Drisceoil, Proinsias. 'Cín Lae Amhlaoibh: Modernization and the Irish Language'. *Ireland and Romanticism: Publics, Nations and Scenes of Cultural Production*. Ed. Jim Kelly. Basingstoke: Palgrave, 2011, 13–25.

Ó Gallchoir, Clíona. *Maria Edgeworth: Women, Enlightenment and Nation*. Dublin: UCD Press, 2005.

O'Halloran, Clare. *Golden Ages and Barbarous Nations: Antiquarian Debate and Cultural Politics in Ireland, c.1750–1800*. Cork: Cork UP, 2004.

O'Kane, Finola. 'Design and Rule: Women in the Irish Countryside 1715–1831'. *Eighteenth-Century Ireland* 19 (2004): 56–74.

O'Kane, Finola. *Ireland and the Picturesque: Design, Landscape Painting and Tourism in Ireland, 1700–1840*. New Haven: Yale UP, 2013.

O'Kane, Finola. *Landscape Design in Eighteenth-Century Ireland*. Cork: Cork UP, 2004.

O'Loughlin, Katrina. *Women, Writing, and Travel in the Eighteenth Century*. Cambridge: CUP, 2018.

Ó Murchu, Liam P. *Cinnlae Amhlaoibh Uí Shúileabháin: Reassessments*. London: Irish Texts Society, 2004.

O'Neill, Ciaran. 'The Public History of Slavery in Dublin'. *The 24th Annual Sir John T. Gilbert Commemorative Lecture Delivered on 26th January, 2021*. Dublin City Libraries, 2022, 3–25.

O'Neill, Ciaran, and Juliana Adelman. 'Love, Consent, and the Sexual Script of a Victorian Affair in Dublin'. *Journal of the History of Sexuality* 29.3 (2020): 388–417.

O'Neill, Ciaran, and Finola O'Kane. *Ireland, Slavery and the Caribbean; Interdisciplinary Perspectives*. Manchester: MUP, 2022.

Ożarska, Magdalena, *Lacework or Mirror? Diary Poetics of Frances Burney, Dorothy Wordsworth and Mary Shelley*. Cambridge: Cambridge Scholars Publishing, 2014.

Paperno, Irina. 'What Can Be Done with Diaries?' *The Russian Review* 63: 4 (October 2004): 561–73.

Peikola, Matti. '2 Manuscript Paratexts in the Making: British Library MS Harley 6333 as a Liturgical Compilation'. *Discovering the Riches of the World*. Eds. Sabrina Corbellini, Margriet Hoogvliet, and Bart Ramakers. Leiden: Brill, 2015, 44–67.

Peri, Alexis. *The War Within: Diaries from the Siege of Leningrad*. Cambridge, MA: Harvard UP, 2017.

Prendergast. Amy. 'Elizabeth Griffith, Translation, Transmission, and Cultural Transfer'. *Women's Writing* 27.2 (2020): 184–202.

Prendergast, Amy. *Literary Salons Across Britain and Ireland in the Long Eighteenth Century*. Basingstoke: Palgrave, 2015.

Prendergast, Amy. '"Members of the Republic of Letters": Maria Edgeworth, Literary Sociability, and Intellectual Pursuits in the Irish Midlands, c.1780–1820'. *Eighteenth-Century Ireland* 31 (2016): 27–44.

Raughter, Rosemary. '"A time of trial being near at hand": Pregnancy, Childbirth and Parenting in the Spiritual Journal of Elizabeth Bennis, 1749–79'. *'She said she was in the family way': Pregnancy and Infancy in Modern Ireland*. Ed. Elaine Farrell. London: Institute of Historical Research/University of London Press, 2012, 75–90.

Raughter, Rosemary. '"My dear Lady C": Letters of Lady Arabella Denny to Lady Caldwell, 1754–1777'. *Analecta Hibernica* 41 (2009): 133–200.

Roddy, Sarah. *Population, Providence and Empire*. Manchester: MUP, 2014.

Rodgers, Nini. *Ireland, Slavery, and Anti-Slavery 1612–1865*. Basingstoke: Palgrave, 2007.

Ross, Ian Campbell. *Laurence Sterne: A Life*. Oxford: OUP, 2001.

Ross, Ian Campbell. 'Maria Edgeworth and the Culture of Improvement'. *Still Blundering into Sense: Maria Edgeworth, Her Context, Her Legacy*. Eds. Fiorenzo Fantaccini and Rafaella Leproni. Florence: Firenze UP, 2019, 29–48.

Ross, Ian Campbell. '"We Irish": Writing and National Identity from Berkeley to Burke'. *Irish Literature in Transition, 1700–1780*. Ed. Moyra Haslett. Cambridge: CUP, 2020, 49–67.

Ryrie, Alec. 'Writing'. *Being Protestant in Reformation Britain*. Oxford: OUP, 2013, 298–314.

Schutte, Kimberly. 'The Marriage Market'. *Women, Rank, and Marriage in the British Aristocracy, 1485–2000*. Basingstoke: Palgrave, 2014, 87–105.

Scobie, Ian H. M. *An Old Highland Fencible Corps: The History of the Reay Fencible Highland Regiment*. Edinburgh: Blackwood and Sons, 1914.

Shaw, Katy, and Kate Aughterson, *Jim Crace: Into the Wilderness*. Basingstoke: Palgrave, 2018.

Sherman, Stuart. *Telling Time: Clocks, Diaries, and English Diurnal Form, 1660–1785*. Chicago: University of Chicago Press, 1996.

Simonet-Tenant, Francoise. 'À la recherche des prémices d'une culture de l'intime'. *Itinéraires* (2009): 39–62.

Simons, Judy. *Diaries and Journals of Literary Women from Fanny Burney to Virginia Woolf*. Basingstoke: Palgrave, 1990.

Simonton, Deborah. 'Earning and Learning: Girlhood in Pre-Industrial Europe'. *Women's History Review* 13.1 (2004): 363–86.

Simpson, Mathew. '"Hame Content": Globalization and a Scottish Poet of the Eighteenth Century'. *Eighteenth-Century Life* 27.1 (2003): 107–29.

Sjöblad, Christina. 'From Family Notes to Diary: The Development of a Genre'. *Eighteenth-Century Studies*, 31.4 (1998): 517–21.

Slack, Paul. 'Improvement and Enlightenment', *Voltaire Foundation*. https://voltairefoundation.wordpress.com/2018/03/14/improvement-and-enlightenment/.

Slack, Paul. *The Invention of Improvement: Information and Material Progress in Seventeenth-Century England*. Oxford: OUP, 2015.

Smith, Sidonie, and Julia Watson. *Reading Autobiography: A Guide for Interpreting Life Narratives*. Minneapolis: University of Minnesota Press, 2001. 2nd ed. 2010.

Smyth, Alan J. 'Studying the Seasons: Weather Recording in Ireland in the Mid-Eighteenth Century'. MPhil Thesis, TCD, 2008.

Smyth, William J. 'The Greening of Ireland: Tenant Tree-Planting in the Eighteenth and Nineteenth Centuries'. *Irish Forestry* 54.1 (1997): 55–72.

Stachniewski, John. *The Persecutory Imagination: English Puritanism and the Literature of Religious Despair*. Oxford: Clarendon Press, 1991.

Starhawk, 'Power, Authority, and Mystery: Ecofeminism and Earth-Based Spirituality'. *Reweaving the World: The Emergence of Ecofeminism*. Eds. Irene Diamond and Gloria Feman Orenstein. San Francisco: Sierra Club Books, 1990.

Staves, Susan. 'British Seduced Maidens'. *Eighteenth-Century Studies* 14/2 (1980–1981): 109–34.

Tarlow, Sarah. *The Archaeology of Improvement in Britain*, 1750–1850. Cambridge: CUP, 2007.

TeBrake, Janet K. 'Personal Narratives as Historical Sources: The Journal of Elizabeth Smith 1840–1850'. *History Ireland* 3.1 (1995): 51–55.

Thorpe, Ruth. 'Elite Women and Material Culture in Ireland, 1760–1830'. PhD Thesis, QUB, 2017.

Torcson, Annalise. 'Ecocriticism and Ecofeminism in the Works of Contemporary Irish Poets Vona Groarke and Sinéad Morrissey'. MPhil Thesis, TCD, 2018.

Urquhart, Diane. *Irish Divorce: A History*. Cambridge: CUP, 2020.

Valladares, Susan. 'An Introduction to the "literary person[s]" of Anne Lister and the Ladies of Llangollen'. *Literature Compass* (2013): 353–68.

Vickery, Amanda. *Behind Closed Doors in Georgian England*. New Haven: Yale UP, 2009.

Wagner, Tamara S. *Longing: Narratives of Nostalgia in the British Novel, 1740–1890*. Lewisburg: Bucknell UP, 2004.

Walsh, Ann-Maria. *The Daughters of the First Earl of Cork: Writing Family, Faith, Politics and Place*. Dublin: Four Courts Press, 2020.

Wharton, Joanna. *Material Enlightenment: Women Writers and the Science of Mind, 1770–1830*. Woodbridge: Boydell Press, 2018.

Whelan, Ruth. 'Marsh's Library and the French Calvinist Tradition: The Manuscript Diary of Élie Bouhéreau (1643–1719)'. *The Making of Marsh's Library: Learning, Politics and Religion in Ireland, 1650–1750.* Eds. Muriel McCarthy and Ann Simmons. Dublin: Four Courts Press, 2004.

Williams, William H. A. *Creating Irish Tourism: The First Century, 1750–1850.* London: Anthem Press, 2010.

Wilson, Deborah. *Women, Marriage and Property in Wealthy Landed Families in Ireland, 1750–1850.* Manchester: MUP, 2008.

Wilson, Rachel. *Elite Women in Ascendancy Ireland, 1690–1745: Imitation and Innovation.* Woodbridge: Boydell & Brewer, 2015.

Winder, Alex. 'Nakba Diaries: Unsettling the Scale and Temporality of Historical Writing'. *AlMuntaqa* 2.2 (2019): 24–39.

Wray, Ramona. 'Recovering the Reading of Renaissance Englishwomen: Deployments of Autobiography'. *Critical Survey* 12.2 (2000): 33–48.

Yáñez-Bouza, Nuria. '"Have you ever written a diary or a journal?" Diurnal Prose and Register Variation'. *Neuphilologische Mitteilungen* 116.2 (2015): 449–74.

Ylivuori, Soile. *Women and Politeness in Eighteenth-Century England: Bodies, Politeness, Identities, and Power.* New York: Routledge, 2019.

Index

For specific titles see individual entries under author name